Media Praise for Energetic Literacy

In more than 900 media interviews, Rose Rosetree has introduced America to skill sets for energetic literacy. Here are some of the highlights.

"I decided to send her a picture of myself... with the caveat that my wife would 'check' her report for accuracy. 'She's got your number,' was my wife's simple response." — *The Catholic Standard*

"It's like she's known you forever...but that's crazy, because you just met. Still, she has described you perfectly, and not just your surface traits." — *The Washington Post*

"This, we figured, was but the next in a long line of hocus-pocus that includes astrology, palm reading and tarot cards.

"Boy, were we wrong. Our first assessment, you see, was before we sent her some photographs for analysis, picking such high-profile individuals from the Fort Worth-Dallas area as former Speaker of the House Jim Wright, Texas Rangers Manager Bobby Valentine and Fort Worth Mayor Kay Granger."
— *Fort Worth Star-Telegram*

Students "sat in rapt attention — despite white molded plastic chairs — for almost two hours, listening to her describe her craft and watching her read the faces and auras of audience members."
— *The Los Angeles Times*

"Rose Rosetree can spot a potential fibber a mile away. Or, in this case, 2,400 miles away." — *Las Vegas Sun*

"Rosetree is a renowned aura and face reader...even skeptics will enjoy it if they are open-minded." — *NAPRA Review*

"When giving a reading, she doesn't immediately seek feedback on her accuracy. She sits back, confident that she's at least partly on target.

"When she does ask, it's with a flat sense of curiosity, like someone peering out of a rain-splattered window to check on a storm's progress.... a recent slate of sessions held in Northern Virginia yielded a small stack of glowing reports from her students."
— *The Washington Times*

"Your readings for the *Kalamazoo Gazette* were the most amazing thing I've ever seen in a newspaper. I'm in politics myself. I know these people." — Michigan politician

"You haven't been reading my face, you've been checking with my Mum."
— John Maytham, "Capetalk Radio," South Africa

"As Rose Rosetree says, 'The truth of what we are shows in our faces and each face, in its distinctive way, is perfectly beautiful.'"
—*Style* , Hong Kong

Usually I debunk anything spiritual but... you really didn't know me before seing my photo? Your reading was like listening to my mother."
— Brendan O'Connor, "Tony and Julie," BBC Radio, England

"Wouldn't your life change if you had the uncanny bull's eye accuracy in judging people's character? 'What is needed is a deeper perception which has more than one layer,' says [Rose Rosetree].

"For more satisfaction in a relationship, for example, more happiness in social life, more success at work, we need to read deeper. "
— *Observer,* India, The largest circulation daily newspaper in Hindi

"[Michigan Governor John Engler and Mayor Terry McKane] were highly skeptical... [but] both men said they found Rosetree's readings uncannily true"
— *Lansing State Journal*

At The Heart Institute, Dr. Keon preferred not to comment himself [on Rosetree's profile of him], though his secretary was happy to offer her view of the analysis. She found it surprisingly accurate.

Said Sue Slater: "I've worked for him for 16 years, and I'd have to say this lady either knows someone in Ottawa or she's awfully good."
— *The Ottawa Citizen,* Canada

"Personally, I practiced and trained others on cutting cords for over 20 years. Because of my background and experiences I had with my clients, I feel Rosetree's book is precise and accurate. *Cut Cords of Attachment* would certainly have been part of the curriculum if it was available while I was teaching classes." — *Reader Views,* Irene Watson

Feedback from all six newsmakers profiled by Rosetree in *The Orange County Register* (each profile included both gift and STUFF):
- Frank Phillips, District Attorney: "This profile is so accurate, it's almost scary."
- Amy Christ, Philanthropist: "Amazingly accurate."
- Benjamin Gilman, Representative, "Very interesting. It sounds very plausible."
- Gilman's long-time friend, "If I had been asked to describe Ben Gilman, those are the words I would use. The woman is something — how on earth does she see all this?"
- Dennis Greenwald, Middletown Pharmacist: "Only two people could have written this assessment, my wife and my mother… I tell you, I don't know who this lady is, but she must be living in my house."
- Mary McPhillips, Orange County Executive: "Come on. This woman had to know who I am."
- Maurice Hinchey, Jr., Assemblyman: "I'm quite amazed by this. In fact, it's remarkable. I didn't think anyone knew me that well."

"[County Supervisor] Moore said [Rosetree's] assessment— especially the part about saving money — was accurate…. 'I shop at Frugal Fannie's. Does that tell you anything?'"
— *The Fairfax Journal*

"You have more credibility with me as an aura reader than any others I've interviewed." — Rob McConnell, Host of "X-Zone Radio" (The legendary Canadian broadcaster's show was syndicated internationally for 15 years prior to this interview.)

"So far, response from co-workers at the paper has been incredible — even our publisher, who's not one for handing out compliments, sent me a message saying he found it fascinating."
— Letter from Tim Lucas, Reporter for *The Indianapolis Star*

During a hotly contested election, Rosetree used energetic literacy on mayoral candidates, with her detailed profiles appearing on the editorial page of the *San Francisco Chronicle*. Afterwards she received over 100 letters from readers praising her accuracy.

"Well, I have to tell you, most of the stories I write don't generate this much interest. Clearly the nation is hungry to find out more about face reading."
— Email from Cathy Hainer, Reporter for *USA Today*

"Thanks again for the interview, it's been one of my favorites ever!"
— Email from Corinna Underwood, Feature Writer for *After Dark Magazine*

"All over America, singles are finding that face reading is far more reliable than computer dating. Rose Rosetree is the acknowledged expert and has evolved her own system from the ancient Chinese system of physiognomy."
—*Daily Mail*, England

"HOW we communicate is just as important as WHAT we communicate. We need to fine tune what we say according to how the listener hears."
—*The Topeka Capital-Journal*

"A startlingly cheerful and unusual figure in spiritual development…"
— *Los Angeles Valley Beat*

MAGNETIZE MONEY
ITH ENERGETIC LITERACY

10 Secrets
for Success and Prosperity
in the
Third Millennium

ROSE ROSETREE

Magnetize Money with Energetic Literacy:
10 Secrets for Success and Prosperity in the Third Millennium

Copyright© 2010 by Rose Rosetree
Cover design by Melanie Matheson, www.rollingrhino.com
Illustrated by Melanie Matheson. Editor: Dana Wheeler

This book was manufactured in the U.S.A. 10 9 8 7 6 5 4 3 2 1

Publisher's Cataloging-In-Publication Data
(Prepared by The Donohue Group, Inc.)

Rosetree, Rose.
  Magnetize money with energetic literacy : 10 secrets for success and pr
perity in the third millenium / Rose Rosetree.

  p. : ill. ; cm.

  Index included in online supplement.
  ISBN: 978-1-935214-06-9

  1. Finance, Personal. 2. Wealth. 3. Self-help techniques. 4. Aura.
5. Mind and body. 6. Success. I. Title.

HG179 .R674 2010
332.024/01

For **workshops, personal consultations, quantity discounts, o**
foreign rights sales, email rights@rose-rosetree.com, call
703-404-4357, or write to Women's Intuition Worldwide, LLC
116 Hillsdale Drive, Sterling, VA 20164.
Interact at www.rose-rosetree.com/blog.

Dedication

While fine-tuning this Magnetize Money Program, I got a call from my good friend "Hannah." Through all the years of knowing her, never had I heard her cry like this. She never had cried at all. Now her words were punctuated by sobs and tears.

> *Yesterday I got a letter. About $5,000 in back taxes. I didn't know this was coming. My accountant made some kind of mistake. As if I have money like that! You know I've been on the verge of bankruptcy. I can't keep the business. I've got to close down. This is it.*

Hannah's business was music. She happened to be a superb singer-songwriter. I didn't stop to tell Hannah what I had often told her before, that she was among the best I'd ever heard. Far as I was concerned, Hannah's work was genius.

No, during that conversation I simply listened.

And I certainly wasn't going to tell Hannah *my* news. Days before, my husband and I crunched the numbers about our financial standing. Over the past decade our business had gathered momentum. The very same economy, the one now walloping Hannah, had moved us significantly closer toward our financial goals.

You see, principles in this book have been working well for us. Certainly, bigger fortunes have been made and bragged about. Yet here's how far I have come. Decades ago, everything I owned fit into two cardboard boxes. Things are very different now. Today when there's something I really want, I buy it without a care in the world.

Later that night I called to check back with Hannah. If ever a friend of mine needed support, it was this brave woman. A single mother, she had raised three stand-up children. These days, she

struggled with more than money. She suffered from a weight problem, plus a serious lack of romance.

Hannah's business was pretty much her whole life.

For two years, Hannah had been a regular client. Her energy
field had been healed in many significant ways. She was emerging from
personality imbalances that resulted from her hard life... problems
that, left undetected, would continue to magnetize similar problems.

Given Hannah's progress, I didn't expect anything to stop her.
Sure, she still had some problems left. But she wouldn't quit on her
dream of being a big-time singer-songwriter.

Recently Hannah had hired a new marketing coach, her second.
She had improved her website. Again.

Far as I could tell, she had done everything right. Except the
economy stank. And she had maybe a tiny bit of competition in her
chosen field. Last night I called her to follow up. Hannah surprised
me with what she said:

> You know what is the worst part, the very worst part? All that New Age prosper-
> ity nonsense. "Do what you want and the money will follow." Right! It's such a lie.
> This work is the one thing in life I'm talented at.
> How dare those success experts tell you to dream and pretend that if you work
> hard and stay positive, you'll succeed? It's a great big lie! I really did believe. I did
> all the right things. To fail like this has broken my heart.

I believe that Hannah will heal this heartbreak. She will find an hon-
orable way to earn money again. This friend whom I love and respect
so much — she is a proven survivor. I dedicate this book to her, and to
other friends of mine who have gone through similar anguish.

If you (or somebody close to you) have staked all your best,
brightest hopes on prosperity teachings that failed you, I dedicate this
book to you as well.

Energetic literacy secrets in our Magnetize Money Program are
for prosperity seekers, success seekers, and every ambitious person with
a brain and a heart.

Contents

Dedication vii

Introduction 1

PART ONE:
WHAT DOES, AND DOESN'T, MAGNETIZE MONEY

1. Third Millennium Street Smarts 7
2. STUFF Attracts, Too 23
3. Basics of Energy Literacy 29
4. Researching the Rich 47
5. Oops, Your Aura Is Showing 61
6. Could You Have a Spiritual Addiction? 75
7. Auras of Mega-Rich Prosperity Teachers 83
8. LOA's Energetic Consequences 93
9. Spiritual Addiction Versus Enlightenment 101
10. Does Salvation Bring Enlightenment? 119
11. Which Auras Magnetize Money 127
12. How Auric Modeling Can Help You Grow Rich 139
13. Help from Your Highest Power 149

PART TWO:
MAGNETIZE MONEY AS ONLY YOU CAN

14. Why You Are the Best 167
15. No More Frozen Lettuce 175
16. Network Smarter with Energetic Literacy 191
17. Money Magnets in a Toxic Work Environment 205
18. Balance Give-and-Take… Or Else 215
19. The Financial Flow Quiz 227
20. Energy Secrets of the Seriously Rich 239

PART THREE:
THE BEST WEALTH WORKSHOP IN ALL THE WORLD

21. How Big Does Your Ego Have to Be? 253
22. Money Brings Power.
    Or Is It The Other Way Around? 271
23. Goals That Magnetize Money 283
24. Plans That Work Your Magnet 295
25. The Simplest Technique 307
26. Spirituality Made Accountable 319
Index and You Saw It Here First 331

ONLINE SUPPLEMENT

Photo Supplement
Index (Full)
Worksheet Samples

About Energetic Literacy:
*   Introducing Energetic Literacy
*   The Ethics of Profiling the Rich and Famous
*   Units of Measurement

Profiling the Rich and Famous:
*   Believe Carnegie's Aura, Not His Gospel of Wealth
*   Martin Buber's Brilliant Workaround
*   Links to Additional Energetic Literacy Profiles

Access the Online Supplement here:
www.rose-rosetree.com.
Interact at Rose Rosetree's blog,
"Deeper Perception Made Practical":
www.rose-rosetree.com/blog

Introduction

I would like to help you fall *in like* with yourself. And make more money in the process.

Liking yourself is way different from loving yourself, which you probably do already.

Here's an example. Look at your face in a mirror. Your eyes are great. You've got to admit that. There's something about the light, the expression, the color, the shape, or simply the who-you-be, shining out through those eyes.

That's the love part.

Next, how do you feel about the rest of your face? Might there be something about your nose, your teeth, the bags under your eyes… something you don't quite adore?

I'm a professional face reader, which means having a certain amount of experience with reading faces for character. Based on that, I assure you that every bit of your face data means something magnificent.

To like your entire face, you don't have to become a face reader. But if you did, you would appreciate in detail how every quirky thing about your face corresponds to a personal talent.

Also, if you're over 30 years of age, a face reader could compare your current face to an old mug shot and probably notice way more than you have, seeing how much on your face has changed physically. Every change tells a story.

That story would inspire you, and it would probably be a pretty long story. About 90% of face data can change over time, including your eyebrows, ears, nose, lips, and cheeks. Even the most subtle shift reveals how you have grown on the inside. Personally, I call all of this facial evolution "God's makeup."

When will you dare to like that? Could you ever like that as much as you now love your eyes?

Studying all these reasons to like your physical face, a.k.a. face reading… is another book. Frankly, this book is the one to read first, as your financial standing affects your free time for learning anything new.

More wealth can improve your enjoyment of hobbies, plus enjoying sex, plus feeling free to spend time and energy and, yes, disposable income, however you please.

In the past, what if you have sometimes acted in ways that weren't especially nice to yourself? Sure, you're used to assuming that you like yourself pretty well. But could you have, due to lack of knowledge, pursued wealth in ways that were really quite disrespectful to yourself as a person? (Unintentional actions of self-disrespect still count, you know.)

To Magnetize Money more than you have so far, you don't need to be perfect. Not by a long shot — as you'll read in our profiles of the very, very, extremely rich.

It will help, however, if you live and work as though you really do like yourself. No, I don't mean adding a thick Vaseline-like gloss of pretending to like yourself. Nor will it help to favor just one or two cherished portions of self, shoving the rest of the self-knowledge mess into denial.

Instead, making good money requires that energetically you show up fully, and unapologetically, as yourself. In ways that you may never have thought of before, but will read about soon, other people can tell how well you are doing this. They respond accordingly.

So you might as well fully like that who-you-be. If a bit of tweaking is needed, I'll help you find out which tweak is needed where, then supply workaround techniques that you can do quite painlessly.

Many hard-working wealth seekers have been living as though success were a tricky substitution game. Substitution: Where you take one part of yourself that you do like and use it to cover up all the rest.

That's like favoring just one shelf of your refrigerator, cramming all the food there, and then congratulating yourself on superior use of a lousy appliance.

Okay, that's an analogy. Here are some practical examples.

- Could you be overemphasizing spirituality? If this has been happening, I'll help you stop working so hard in an unproductive fashion. (Instead, you can grow spiritually in a way that is more balanced.)
- Have your power circuits been scrambled? Maybe you have paid attention to others in ways that weren't terribly kind to yourself. (You know, "yourself" is the person you most need to like in all the world. "Yourself" is not optional in your workplace, not if you wish to Magnetize Money.)
- Might you be slightly scared of your ego, that indispensable wealth generator? (How I would love to help you to like that part of who-you-be.)

This book aims to bring you useful, inspiring, wealth-generating discoveries about yourself. My perspective has been formed by helping thousands of people one-on-one, helping them to get unstuck, enjoy relationships more, relax deeper, and make money more easily.

Fact is, ways that you have been trying really, really hard to grow rich could be counter-productive. If you have been struggling to gain wealth, you might need just a slight shift of emphasis. Then you can work less hard, yet make more money.

Now is the time for life's wisest people to become truly effective. For that to happen in the real world, liking your full who-you-be is not optional.

PART ONE
What Does, And Doesn't, Magnetize Money

Money isn't magnetically pulled toward you just because you do the right things and affirm prosperous beliefs.

Something else must be right... especially in this third millennium. Which ingredient can't be supplied by old-school success and prosperity teachings? Learn what it is, plus how to get it.

1. Third Millennium Street Smarts

Vision without action is a daydream. Action without vision is a nightmare.
— Japanese Proverb

A suitcase full of money — that's what Hugo Rosenbaum would pack in the morning. Then he would carry it downtown. Could he manage to buy his family a loaf of bread and some milk?

Oy vey! That was my grandpa, living during Germany's crazy inflation of 1923. One thing hasn't changed since. Money remains unpredictable.

Even the best financial advice won't protect you from market hiccups. Nor can high-yield interest guarantee that you will make money long-term. Sadly, the opposite of earning big interest isn't earning small interest. Financial surprises can mean, "No interest, high inflation, and not enough money at all."

Only one form of interest can be absolutely guaranteed. That's your own personal interest in growing rich. Your drive to succeed can bring dividends, compounded daily.

Unfortunately, these dividends aren't called "money" but "wisdom." As in "Learning from your experience and not giving up until you really do grow rich."

Certainly, this wisdom is nice. Wisdom plus big success is nicer. I believe that people like you and me have the right to attract all the wealth we can, and that we can do it honorably, as part of our religious and/or spiritual striving.

If that's your plan, too, it's vital to understand how the process of gaining wealth is changing in the third millennium. With the evolution of human consciousness, certain kinds of make-or-break knowledge are required for your dreams to come true.

The basis of this knowledge is **energetic literacy.** That means using techniques to look beneath the surface of life. Call it "inside information" if you like. Anyone can access it, provided you have learned how to read in this particular way.

TODAY'S VERSION OF A GUTENBERG SHIFT

Since ancient times, a deeper form of perception has been available to a fortunate few, whether they were called prophets or oracles, shamans, gypsies, or healers. Many were publicly ridiculed. But when upstanding citizens needed help badly enough, they would sneak out of town to consult that counter-culture expert.

Regarding perception, what once seemed like a weird super-power has become normal. (And isn't that as good a way as any to view evolution?) Human consciousness today is going through a kind of literacy shift comparable to what happened during the Gutenberg era.

Now could be the first time in recorded history when energetic literacy is being used in everyday life by perfectly respectable, sane, everyday people... millions of them, maybe hundreds of millions.

Did you ever wonder how, once upon a time, book-smart literacy developed? In the first millennium, only the privileged few could read words. Then came the Gutenberg era, halfway through the second millennium. Movable type meant that printed books and pamphlets became easily available. Just about everybody learned how to read.

Fast forward to today's more intuitive kinds of reading. I have learned ways to do it. Maybe you have, too.

Or maybe you have had a close encounter — of a very practical kind — with somebody proficient in energetic literacy, perhaps a specialist in alternative medicine or psychological profiling.

So many people today have become seekers and finders of energetic literacy. Reading what makes people tick at the quantum level: That is becoming basic literacy in the third millennium. Now it can revolutionize how you build wealth.

SHOW ME THE MONEY

"But enough about literacy," you may be thinking. "This Magnetize Money Program is supposed to be about money. My money. How to have more of it."

Coming right up. Energetic literacy offers us very practical ways to increase success. Get ready for something radically new. This is third millennium knowledge. Maybe you're familiar with get-rich-quicker books from the late second millennium. We're going to take them to the next level, the deeper level where more power becomes available.

Why All Energy Is Not Created Equal

Taking action at the surface level of life, a certain amount of energy is available. For instance, we could take a sheet of paper and make a change at that level by ripping up that paper. (Not this page, please!)

The ripping sound could be quite satisfying. In terms of physics, that sound would come from energy released by making a structural change at the surface level.

Making change deeper, at the chemical level, a larger amount of energy would become available. If, for example, we were to burn the page of paper, what then?

Heat would be given off, sparks and flames. It wouldn't be enough to keep you warm all winter. Still, this chemically-based change would release more energy than changes made at the surface level.

Now, if we could go still deeper within and make a change at the atomic level — if, for instance, we could split just one atom within that sheet of paper — woo-hoo! Again, I'm not suggesting you do that with any page here. But wouldn't that be a rather memorable explosion, if you could manage it?

Energetic literacy isn't surface. And since deeper levels of life always contain more potential energy, our Magnetize Money secrets for the third millennium can bring bigger results than the more superficial techniques (even really great techniques) from earlier eras.

SUCCESS PRINCIPLES + PROSPERITY PRINCIPLES = \$\$\$

For historical perspective, consider. Second millennium books and workshops stayed at a surface level compared to now. They fell into two major categories:

- **Success writings** emphasized what to do in order to become rich, taking *objective* action steps to gain wealth.
- **Prosperity writings** emphasized how to think and be, offering *subjective* ways to attract wealth.

Success writings were especially likely to emphasize the surface of life. "Depth" came from thinking hard about what you should DO. These methods tended to be intellect-centric. If desired outcomes were slow in coming, you needed to think harder, work extra hours, make even more elaborate plans, network more cleverly, etc.

If ideas from Blanchard and Johnson's *One Minute Manager* couldn't get the job done, an ambitious reader might upgrade to Steven Covey's *Seven Habits of Highly Successful People* or Brian Tracy's *100 Absolutely Unbreakable Laws of Business Success.* (Brilliant men all, with Mr. Tracy a special favorite of mine.)

More tips and habits, larger numbers in the title — did they really add up to more money?

Second millennium success teachers were great at devising success strategies, except they ignored the inner resources required to make them really work. Energetic literacy is, among other things, a powerful tool for diagnosing inner blockages. Energetic literacy can also bring solutions at the deepest level, the level of the human energy field or aura. Only then can thought and actions gain their full potential.

Meanwhile, *prosperity* teachings from the second millennium had problems of their own. "Depth" came from feeling and thinking about spirituality. But the rest of a person's life was not approached with depth. Instead, spiritual beliefs were superimposed upon it.

Ideas like the Law of Attraction (LOA) or Seed Money might sound great in theory. But few people knew how to research, "What does this particular belief system do to my whole self — all of me, not only the part that seeks spiritual perfection or religious salvation?"

That matters. Every choice in life can set in motion significant long-term consequences. And these are real-life, complex consequences, not just, "After I wish upon a star, all of my dreams will come true."

Beautiful beliefs do not necessarily produce equally beautiful consequences for a person's entire energetic system. What if results are semi-ugly? Results could even limit a person's energetic effectiveness.

By analogy, behold a sumptuous chocolate layer cake, glistening to the eye, tempting to the tongue, and beautiful in every surface way. If you, or your doctor, had a way to go deeper into your physical system and test your blood sugar, the consequences of eating that cake might not be all sweetness (of crumb) and light (frosting).

Similarly, how can we tell what any success system or prosperity practice truly delivers at the level of energy?

Enter energetic literacy. Toward the end of the second millennium, millions of people began using energetic literacy and related healing methods to access that deepest level of insight. Pioneers of energetic literacy made life-changing discoveries such as these:

- Holistic healing methods could improve *physical health.* Techniques like Donna Eden's Energy Medicine, Reiki, acupuncture, homeopathy, Quantum Touch, etc., worked because they could improve functioning at the level of the human aura.
- Afterwards the aura-level improvement would work its way out to the surface level of life and bring physical healing.
- Other energy-based techniques became popular for improving *mental health.* For instance, Emotional Freedom Technique opened up the new field of Energy Psychology.
- For releasing cords of attachment and other astral-level debris, Energy Spirituality was developed. Here the goal was to improve *spiritual health* by permanently removing stuck energies.

But nobody, and I mean nobody, had figured out how to apply full-scale energetic literacy to the areas of success and prosperity.

THE HISTORY OF IDEAS... AND YOUR WALLET

Let's take the perspective known as "History of Ideas," where literacy can be seen in the context of human development. From this perspective, consider late second millennium terms like *holistic health, New Age,* and *mind-body-spirit.*

Although they seemed like huge breakthroughs at the time, these terms really played just a transitional role.

Sure, it was great when holistic healers prompted us to notice the whole person, including the component of energy. Can you remember the effect on you when you first encountered those concepts? Didn't it change your life?

"What, my doctor isn't the one responsible for my health? What, the responsible person is me?"

Millions of us began to take personal responsibility for our lives, thanks to a courageous doctor, a massage therapist or yoga teacher, someone who introduced us to alternative medicine.

Nevertheless, in the late 20th century, we practitioners and clients were just getting started. We needed something way deeper, even if we didn't know it yet.

Including all three parts of self, rather than one, didn't guarantee powerful results. Mind, body, and spirit can be approached in very superficial ways. And often were. But back in the day, how could a practical person distinguish what really was deep from what just attempted to be?

Fortunately, in this third millennium, leading-edge techniques for healing have begun to include an energetically literate approach.

It has become possible to evaluate energies with precision, to tell if spirit is being used as a substitute for human emotions or vice versa. We can distinguish what brings real change to objective reality versus feel-good fantasies.

Healing approaches to mind-body-spirit are changing with this new literacy. Old MBS methods like Relaxation Response and Stress Management moved people like propeller planes. Energy Medicine, Energy Psychology, and Energy Spirituality can fly us like jets. Evolving so much faster now, we can ask smarter questions about our financial health.

For instance, when it comes to success and prosperity teachings, finally, we can ask…

WHAT'S THE CATCH?

Energetic literacy can tell us precisely which energy consequences flow from any set of get-rich teachings.

Common sense tells us, "Don't put all your eggs in one basket." Yet consider the plight of prosperity seeker Carla before the days of energetic literacy. To her, trying something new might mean, "Paste an extra image onto your dream board."

And even a veteran success seeker like Chris might be fooled by good-sounding advice. For instance, say that Chris is a big fan of Brian Tracy. Chris reads a brilliant success technique in *The 100 Absolutely Unbreakable Laws of Business Success* and tries to apply it.

All of us think and act based on how we, personally, are using our energy systems. Let's suppose that Mr. Tracy's techniques were developed based on using the full moneymaking power of his energy field. (According to my research on him, this is true. You can read the details later, since Brian is one of the success experts I'll be profiling.)

By contrast, suppose that Chris is energetically limited right now. It's due to problems with old patterns of dysfunction —problems that can be changed, but haven't been changed yet — patterns that Chris is now clueless about.

Say that, technically, the part of Chris' energy field that works well for him now is his Solar Plexus Chakra. As for the rest, it's pretty shut down. (According to my research with clients who emphasize success teachings, hidden patterns like this are common.)

Taking Brian Tracy's advice, Chris tries his hardest. But, remember, Chris is still using just a fraction of his full energetic resources. Consequently, he is doomed to be ineffective, no matter how hard he tries… so long as, energetically, he positions himself in his typical "one basket" way.

How obvious would Chris' problem be, especially before energetic literacy became widely available? Not at all. Yet, once we *can* read patterns of energy use, anyone who chooses can locate a problem like this one. And solve it.

Sometimes an "all in one basket" problem can even be *caused* by enthusiastically applying a success or prosperity teaching. The expert doesn't intend this, of course. Nevertheless, it happens.

And how would you or Chris know if such a thing were to happen? Using only on surface literacy, you wouldn't. For months or years, you could be working diligently, succeeding in terms of that new program.

Eventually, you might do a reality check. And then you'd feel very depressed, because you were doing everything right without getting the promised results. (This, of course, is exactly what happened to Hannah, whom you met in our Dedication.)

By adding the perspective of energetic literacy, I'm going to teach you how to spot hidden problems, then solve them. Energetic literacy can reveal the "Sounds great but" part, i.e., The catch.

I'm going to help you tell if hidden problems at the level of energy could be sabotaging *your* success. Then I'm going to provide you with energetic workarounds. Nothing could be more individual and personal (and rewarding) than this kind of do-it-yourself.

Some common problems, or catches, are worth considering right from the start. Here are three big ones.

SUCCESS STRATEGIES — THE CATCH

Success teachings often appeal to your sense of can-do. Authors like Steven R. Covey are brilliant, and they speak from experience. Only consider the possibility of a missing ingredient.

If you investigate what success experts take for granted, you'll see what I mean about success being sabotaged at the level of the human energy field. (And in future chapters you will learn specifics, because I'll be using energetic literacy to read some of those auras for you.)

Success teachings are great at systematic, step-by-step self-improvement. Well, that can apply to your energy field, too. Our Magnetize Money Program can help you identify places in your energy field where you have been stuck or imbalanced. Then I'll provide workarounds, based on work with my clients.

PROSPERITY STRATEGIES — THE CATCH

Inspiring prosperity theories may bring near-disastrous consequences in objective reality.

If you want material success here on earth, pure inspiration won't deliver. Energetically, the long-term consequences of a prosperity teaching could be downright destructive (and as you'll soon read, many of them are).

THE UNIVERSAL CATCH

In the past, were you drawn more to prosperity teachings or success strategies? Either way, one catch has been the same. Lacking energetic literacy, you had to settle for a surface-level technique I know you're very familiar with. It's called "Trial and Error."

In this Magnetize Money Program, I'm going to expose problems that couldn't be revealed without energetic literacy. Yes, there are definite reasons why a Resourceful Reader like you can do all the "right things" as advocated by experts yet, sadly, remain financially stuck, stuck, stuck.

OUR MAGNETIZE MONEY PROGRAM

Problems are found with energetic literacy, but so are solutions. And that's why the underlying tone of this program is joyful rather than sobbing.

Regarding examples used in this print book and also the Online Supplement, what about names? Full names are accurate but when first names only are used, they're fictitious. My stories come from very real clients and workshop participants. I have promised them confidentiality. Of course, I have changed their names and revealing details.

Ethically, I do feel it is appropriate to share these stories, also to profile famous people who have chosen to be in the limelight. Not only will I name some of them. I will use energetic literacy techniques to explore who they really are... sometimes in marked contrast to how they describe themselves.

When a success expert teaches seminars or creates a fabulous website, this is no blushing, aw-shucks, ignore-me kind of person. Same goes for the mega-tycoons who supplied their color photos for Forbes Magazine's famous annual lists of the wealthiest people in the world.

For those who deliberately hold themselves out as experts on success or prosperity, what could be fairer than researching their who-you-be?

Read more on this topic on the Online Supplement, "The Ethics of Profiling the Rich and Famous."

Incidentally, every one of my books on energetic literacy contains a photo of me suitable for profiling, often accompanied by an invitation to go ahead and read me. With the rise of energetic literacy, why would a writer do otherwise? On the level of auras, there are no secrets.

How to Gain the Most from this Program

Resourceful Reader, to benefit from my discoveries you don't need full energetic literacy. Sure, I'd love to teach you the skills, having already helped over a quarter million people in that particular way. However, that kind of how-to would be… a different book.

For *this* book, you need no energetic literacy at all, simply your regular everyday common sense. You have your own sniff test. Well, use it.

Personally, I've had it with people I care about — smart and ambitious people who are trying with all their might to Magnetize Money — being sold prosperity ideals that make them *less* effective in life, not more effective at all.

Of course, you're invited to bring along whatever energetic literacy you do possess. Use that to supplement my research, especially the more controversial profiles. You can refer to the very same photos I've used, convenient to access with our "Photo Supplement" online.

When you come to the practical techniques (mostly in Parts Two and Three of this program), you can research yourself, too. Check out the immediate and long-term benefits of every single energetic workaround.

All that is optional, though. I will be using energetic literacy on your behalf. It's high time to clear up confusion and, in some cases, expose teachers who practice the opposite of what they preach. Let's tweak prosperity practices to make them more effective.

Here are seven practical ways to do this.

1. Regular Reading, Paced to Match Your Needs

You might prefer to start with a quick skim through all the chapters, enjoying the juicy parts. (Yes, there will be juicy parts.) Later, you can read start-to-end more methodically.

Whatever your pace of reading, I hope you'll soon appreciate why I often refer to a "Magnetize Money Program" rather than a "book." The difference, to me, is that a program implies personal involvement and discoveries. Your desire to Magnetize Money isn't merely a theory, is it?

Consider This

Please, if you do skim through these pages, skip all the exercises and workarounds.

Don't browse them. Instead, save that first reading for a time when you can sit down and spend a few minutes, reading purposefully. This will bring you a fresh, direct experience.

To make these chunks easy to find — or to avoid, if you're doing a quick browse — all are put in boxes like this one.

2. COMMON SENSE

This will help you to check all my ideas against what you already know, including objective reality. My goal is to help you to Magnetize Money in practical ways, so definitely bring along your common sense. No amount of energetic literacy can substitute for that.

3. YOUR INNER WISDOM

Of course, you already have a form of inner wisdom, whether formally trained or not.

Inner wisdom doesn't require that you become a renowned Christian preacher like Joel Osteen or a world-class trance channeler, like Esther Hicks. Your inner smarts count.

All along you have had powerful wisdom mojo. Maybe you're used to calling it a *truth signal* or a *gut reaction* or *hunch*. Maybe you simply call it your *B.S. Detector*.

At my publishing company, we call it *Women's Intuition*, and know that men are allowed to have it, too. Whatever you call that, bring it along for the ride.

4. YOUR SENSE OF HUMOR

Laughter is just a sense of proportion in disguise.

5. SEARCHING FOR SECRETS

Secrets that you can use for more success and prosperity — let's team up to find them.

In Napoleon Hill's *Think and Grow Rich,* readers were invited to treasure hunt in this way. Other influential prosperity writings do it, too. Is this just a gimmick popular for prosperity literature, like putting pink covers on chick lit novels? Hardly.

Your subconscious mind contains a treasure trove of wisdom. Any success you have ever had in business, every event, in every lifetime, is stored within you like data within a computer.

What happens when you pose an open-ended question like, "What secret knowledge will make me rich?"

That gives your subconscious mind a command to search through all that data, as though googling all your accumulated wisdom.

However long you're exploring this Magnetize Money Program (whether hours or years), until you get to the very last page, you will be in a success-boosting zone. Your subconscious mind can support you to discover 10 really powerful secrets of success, most or all of which you haven't consciously considered yet.

To access this inner wisdom, just open to the possibility that you will find 10 great secrets on your own. Maybe they will match the ones in the last chapter of this book, maybe they won't.

Who knows?

Who cares?

My goal in this program is to bring you really effective Aha!s about how to Magnetize Money. Whenever you have one of those "light bulb goes on inside, woo-hoo" experiences, do yourself a favor. Take a few seconds to write down the related *secret* that can bring you more success and prosperity.

Jot down any idea that comes to you. Incidentally, one great place to do that is...

6. A Magnetize Money Journal

Journaling is an excellent, though totally optional, way to gain maximum results from this program.

Your Magnetize Money Journal

Your Magnetize Money Journal can make this program especially powerful for you. Here's all you need do.

Schedule just 5-10 minutes into your daily routine. At the appointed time, write about your latest Aha!

Add whatever secrets you figure out, plus your results from experimenting with the new concepts and workarounds in our Magnetize Money Program.

That journal can become your personal coach, helping you think through the concepts that are most relevant to your life now. Add thoughts related to your current money making strategy, dialoging away.

After you finish this Magnetize Money Program, go back over your journal. Highlight the insights that have helped you most. Choose your favorite 10 Secrets for Success and Prosperity. And then consider yourself a graduate of our interactive seminar.

The book I wrote for you plus the journal you gave yourself — now that's a great team.

7. Blog about Your Aha!s

For years I have hosted a blog called "Deeper Perception Made Practical." Find it at www.rose-rosetree.com/blog. Search for posts and comments by me and Magnetize Money Program participants.

And if you have a blog of your own with posts that relate to the Magnetize Money Program, comment about THAT. Blogroll may await.

8. MUSE ON THIS

While exploring the Magnetize Money Program, feel free to add inspiration from your favorite prosperity hero. It could be somebody living or dead. For instance:

- Dale Carnegie, whom you always wanted to have in your life, winning your friendship and influencing you — but only in the nicest possible ways.
- Bill Gates, adding the bonus of nerd power.
- Oprah, inspiring you as only she can.
- Your fascinating Uncle Joe, a self-made billionaire who left no money to you. Regardless of whether he was a nice man, he might serve as inspiration for the getting rich part.
- Renee Fleming, since you're constantly playing her opera singing in the background. Whatever your soul music, whoever your personal muse might be, you're invited to bring him or her along.
- George Clooney. Sure, you could invite him just because you like him. He's also rather wealthy by human standards, which won't hurt.

We won't be conducting a séance, which would be… another book… and not one by me.

Instead, you can simply add a particular person's consciousness to your team. Either tape a photo to an index card or write that person's name on a new index card in nice big letters.

Bill Gates

Your muse can become such a fine bookmark! Another option: When using your Magnetize Money Journal, place the card/photo version of your inspiring person on a chair next to you It's that simple.

Once upon a time you played with dolls or action figures, right? As a grownup, you're still allowed to imagine you're hanging out with somebody interesting. In this case, choose somebody really smart and very, very successful.

Resourceful Reader, I don't know how much trouble and expense it would take before you or I could hire Bill Gates, in person, to sit with us on the bus and whisper sweet somethings into our ears. At a minimum, I'm guessing, I would have to buy myself a much fancier computer, because if he saw what I have now he might not really want to become my muse.

Our index card version of muse, luckily, can be totally low-tech. Or before bringing in Swooney Clooney, you won't have to dress up one bit. You get the idea.

As we Magnetize Money, we're going to do more than imagine things. I promise. Still, you can do all those practical things and still bring along your choice of imaginary friend. Me, I'm considering Gates.

2. STUFF Attracts, Too

If there are areas where you don't fully accept yourself, it can show up as stress, anxiety, depression, or insomnia; as guilt, anger, or resentment; or as being often upset by the actions of other people or by the way the world is.
— Richard Brodie, *Getting Past OK*

For 40 years, I have been able to help people solve problems — financial problems, sexual problems, all sorts of horrible problems — by moving out STUFF.

STUFF is my technical term for emotional and/or spiritual imbalances at the level of auras. This astral debris is a real substance, only don't try weighing it on a scale. Although STUFF is physical, it exists only at the metaphysical level of the human energy field.

The first 17 years of my career, I helped people move out STUFF through meditation. Then, starting in 1986, I began to teach dedicated techniques for energetic literacy. Shortly before writing this book, I checked with the U.S. Patent and Trademark Office. Surprisingly, my four methods related to energetic literacy are the only trademarks in their respective fields:

- Aura Reading Through All Your Senses®
- 12 Steps to Cut Cords of Attachment®
- Face Reading Secrets®
- Empath Empowerment™

All these systems make it easier to perceive and/or release stuck STUFF. Your clients, co-workers, the people you manage, any boss lucky enough to employ you — all of them would become easier to satisfy if they had less STUFF.

To improve your financial standing, however, the most important STUFF to release will always be your own. Doing this will help you think more clearly, act more decisively, and improve the overall quality of your chosen career. Let's examine why.

ATTRACTING SUCCESS MORE EASILY

Have you heard about the Law of Attraction (LOA) and found it inspiring? Excellent!

The perspective in LOA teachings is *energy-aware* but not yet *energetically literate*, a vital difference that I'll explain more in our next chapter. For now, here's the bottom line. (You could call it "The secret about The Secret.") *Everything about us attracts,* including the degree to which we are willing to like ourselves and be fully human.

Let's put this in the language of energetic literacy: To Magnetize Money, what you do is important. What you think is important. And **who-you-be** is the most important of all.

"Who-you-be." Not a grammatical phrase, but at least it got your attention.

"Who-you-be" means the totality of who you are as a person. This is more than all the roles you play socially, e.g., "I'm a fun-loving, Lexus-owning, single, attractive salesperson with big career aspirations."

"Who-you-be" is bigger than, and often different from, how you think of yourself on a good day.

In *The Secret,* Rhonda Byrne wrote, "The only reason any person does not have enough money is because they are *blocking* money from coming to them with their thoughts."

Thoughts only? I don't think so. Full energetic literacy helps us to understand more about a person's specific causes of prosperity blockage. Also what to do about them.

MAGNETIZE MONEY AS WHO?

Who-you-be is the only person you have available for magnetizing money. And who-you-be means the totality of you. Just as the real you on the job isn't only the perky dressed-up version, complete with job interview manners.

The who-you-be striving to Magnetize Money is more than the part of you reading this page. Our Magnetize Money Program aims to transform the totality of who-you-be and align it better, making it more internally balanced and also more effective externally, when your who-you-be goes forth into the world to bring back big bucks.

Sometimes we success-driven folk try so hard, striving for the ideal. (Which is great.) However, as a side effect, we may fool ourselves into mistaking that hard-working, idealized version of self for who we really are. (Which is sometimes called "denial.")

Like it or not, who-you-be attracts wealth for you, not who-you-*want*-to-be or who-you-would-*prefer*-to-be.

Psychologists sometimes talk about a "shadow side" to people. One example is Martin Buber, the great theologian.

Talk about who-you-be! Buber wrote movingly about "I and Thou," the depth choices we make when connecting to others. This sacred adventurousness and striving was Buber's passion.

On the surface of life, yes, Martin Buber was a great theologian. But what about his who-you-be at the level of energetic literacy?

Adam Gopnik divulged some shocking hearsay about this in his memoir, *Through The Children's Gate*. According to Gopnik, when Martin Buber would lecture, he would hide sexy photos of women among his notes, peeking as needed.

Given energetic literacy, that makes perfect sense. Lecturing about *I and Thou*, let's say that Buber moved into a high state of awareness. Doing spiritual work set off delight in Martin's higher chakras (part of his energy system). Meanwhile his lower chakras struggled to keep up: "Mayday! Mayday! All this intense connection to God is making me crazy!"

How could Martin Buber keep himself from flying so high that he went out of control? He needed a strong, grounding influence. And one thing you can say for erotic images. They sure can help a guy or gal remember that who-you-be includes a physical body.

I hasten to add that there are better ways to integrate huge spiritual inspiration. Only maybe Buber didn't know what they were. (See the article "Martin Buber's Brilliant Workaround" in our Online Supplement, where I applied energetic literacy to the great theologian.)

Before reading Adam Gopnik's book, I had no inkling of Buber's secret. Mr. Gopnik only learned of the alleged pictures during psychoanalysis with a highly quirky Freudian.

Even without lying on an analyst's couch, surely you too have heard your share of embarrassing gossip concerning the rich and famous. Outrageously inspired, doing amazing work, such people create workarounds to keep themselves sane.

Reading *My Life and Other Unfinished Business* by mega-successful Dolly Parton, I was struck by her version of this.

Two topics always interested her most, Dolly explained: God and sex. That simple.

Given those interests, hasn't Dolly found the perfect way to balance out her aura? She sings with the voice of an angel while dressing up as a hooker. Working as an entertainer, that's acceptable. Had Dolly tried to Magnetize Money as a dentist or accountant, her strategy might not have been so successful.

Resourceful Reader, you have been improvising energetically too, just like Dolly and Martin, only perhaps less outrageously.

Coping isn't "A Secret." But to Magnetize Money, you might do better than resort to outrageous coping methods like Parton's surgically enhanced and glammed up appearance or Buber's alleged visual aids. With the Magnetize Money Program, you need not compartmentalize yourself in ways that might shock your admirers.

Nor need you force a perpetual smile on your face while an embarrassing shadow side of your personality remains in denial.

Instead, you can use energetic literacy to balance your life at the deepest level, find where you're stuck, and fix it. At a minimum, you can use techniques designed to effectively work around problems that limit financial success.

Then the version of you that goes forth in the world to make money — wow! It really will be the best it can be. So money can follow.

BENEFIT FROM ENERGETIC LITERACY

Reading life deeper, you gain access to very detailed information about what is happening inside a person. This is the new form of literacy needed for the third millennium. Just as math is the language of science, aura reading is the language of energy.

Even if you haven't yet studied aura reading specifically, you're aware of energy — good vibrations and bad. Beginners sometimes start by feeling flows of energy between people; they may see subtle light or colors. Quirky little things happen that may not be placed in the category of "aura reading" but deserve to be, something as natural as noticing the magnetic field around a purring kitten.

Many equally talented beginners notice nothing at all. They simply sign up for alternative forms of healing, like acupuncture or Reiki. Energy is what has made so-called "alternative medicine" into the *primary* form of medicine for millions of us. When I googled "energy" this morning, how many hits came up? Exactly 431 million.

Consider for a moment how much more aware of energy you (and your friends) have become over the years. Compare your energetic awareness today to a decade ago.

This book's 10 Secrets for Success and Prosperity have resulted from my very focused exploration of energetic literacy, facilitating healing for clients who have gone on to become more successful. These dynamic interactions have prepared me to share strategies that are powerfully effective in this third millennium.

Back in the 20th century, Napoleon Hill conducted face-to-face interviews with over 500 outstanding business leaders. Today, I can "interview" hundreds of successful money makers simply by reading their photos off the Internet. And I have.

Some of what I found may shock you. More important, it can help you, provided that you're serious about living your dreams. (And for some of you Resourceful Readers, provided that you're also willing to stop dreaming harder than you have been living.)

Regarding the accuracy of my profiles of the rich and striving, you have two very good choices. The better one would be to become an aura reader yourself, which is… another book entirely. If you're skilled at energetic literacy, you can do your own readings of all the photos provided in the "Photo Supplement" online.

Your second, very workable, choice is sit back, relax, and let me use the expertise developed over decades. Use your common sense to evaluate what I present.

With energetic literacy, my resume includes an international bestseller, plus teaching aura reading to students on four continents. Many have turned professional; others simply enjoy using energetic literacy in their own lives.

Although nowhere as rich as Oprah, I do make a very good living as an aura reader, a healer at the level of auras, and a teacher of related skills. Because some people like testimonials, I have made some of them viewable at my main website, www.rose-rosetree.com.

For the sake of what follows, it's also worth mentioning that I have developed easy-to-learn techniques for reading auras from *regular photos.*

Internet pictures and cell phone shots — sure, I read them professionally on a regular basis and, clients say, accurately.

Well, Resourceful Reader, that skill will be useful for this program as well. I'll be reading many important role models to help you learn how to Magnetize Money. Bill Gates, Rhonda Byrne, and Andrew Carnegie don't happen to live next door.

Thanks to the "Photo Supplement" online, you can easily locate the photos for everyone named in a profile. You'll find some bonus articles as well. By all means, check out these celebrities for yourself.

But first, let's use deeper perception on the most important person of them all, you.

3. Basics of Energetic Literacy

He is not the most energetic speaker. When Bill Gates speaks, however, people listen with bated breath... he doesn't rally a room, he inspires it. Those who hear him take what he says and carry his words with them for weeks, months or years.
— Simon Sinek, *Start with Why:*
How Great Leaders Inspire Everyone to Take Action

Like Bill Gates or, for that matter, Simon Sinek, you have a physical body. Around that, you have other layers of body. They're just as real as the physical one, except made of electro-magnetic energy. Your full set of energy bodies, together, make up your **aura.**

Sometimes it's called "The human energy field."

What matters isn't the name but the huge amount of information included. Quality matters too. At the level of auras, nothing can be faked.

Some of that information is permanent or very long term, like gifts of your soul.

Much of the information changes moment-by-moment, depending on factors like the choices you're making, the people you're with, your current life priorities, your physical health.

Having an aura comes naturally for any human. *Reading* an aura is natural, too, only this requires developing skills of **aura reading.** This has two steps.

1. You use a technique for direct *perception* of a person's aura.
2. You find a way to *interpret* your perceptions meaningfully and accurately.

Then, lo and behold! You can start exploring the financially-linked inside information within chakras.

CHAKRAS, A PRACTICAL INTRODUCTION

Maybe you already know that information in your aura is especially concentrated in places that correspond to parts of the physical body. These are known as **major chakras.**

Illustration #1 pictures their locations as shown on our volunteer model, Money Magnetizer Billy.

As I go through the list, you might want to find these locations on your own body. All are standard-issue human, whether you're a guy or a gal.

1.   The Root Chakra is where your legs come together.
2.   The Belly Chakra is a couple of inches below your navel.
3.   The Solar Plexus Chakra is in the ribcage area, the soft part in the center. (Notice, you have "floating ribs" on either side.)
4.   The Heart Chakra is in the center of your chest, near the tender spot on your breastbone. (Prod there with a fingertip and you'll find the spot I mean.)
5.   The Throat Chakra equals the front of your neck.
6.   The Third Eye Chakra is on your forehead, between the eyebrows and above them.
7.   The Crown Chakra is at the top of your head. So consider the star in our illustration to be our substitution for an aerial view.

     To get a sense of where exactly you would find this chakra when looking down at the top of your head, think of that soft spot babies have. You have that location still, even if that soft spot has become quite solid by now.

Six of these seven major chakra locations can be seen easily in a full-length mirror. To make this assortment of chakras more useful for research in our Magnetize Money Program, I subtract one and substitute another.

The problem with including the Crown Chakra in our research isn't just the fancy combo of ladders and mirrors, etc., that might be required in order to get a good look at your own Crown Chakra. Its databanks are pretty abstract, mostly related to subtleties about how you pull in spiritual energy.

FIGURE 1. MAJOR CHAKRAS, TRADITIONAL VIEW

FIGURE 2. MAJOR SUCCESS AND PROSPERITY CHAKRAS

Frankly, this topic isn't terribly useful for our quest to Magnetize Money. Far more relevant is your High Heart Chakra.

Often, that's considered a sub-chakra, not so terribly important. Well, this chakra contains loads of information about expressing your **soul,** that most human part of you. To Magnetize Money, that part of you needs to be working well.

So the chakra diagram WE will use to research what helps to Magnetize Money will include "Major Success and Prosperity Chakras." See the illustration on the facing page.

How can you locate your own High Heart Chakra? It's at the upper chest, halfway between the Heart Chakra and Throat Chakra. Tarzan might have given it thumps in the movies; you can do that in real life. Hey, that sound isn't bad!

Now comes chakra info. that is very third millennium... and indispensible for our goal of increasing wealth.

CHAKRA DATABANKS

During the first and second millennia, most aura reading systems were heavily invested in the concept that "auras are colors." Because I developed a more nuanced system, appropriate to the third millennium, I have been able to make some advances in basic energetic literacy.

My system of Aura Reading Through All Your Senses® includes over 100 tested techniques for accessing information from auras. This system emphasizes finding practical information, which led to a discovery that is essential for our Magnetize Money Program.

Every major chakra contains 50 databanks of information.

That's right. Reading any chakra or sub-chakra as one unit is quite a simplification.

Each **chakra databank** matters. It concerns a particular aspect of your life, such as:

- Your ability to accumulate wealth
- Your ability to save money
- Your ability to shrewdly invest money
- Believing that you deserve to be rich

Here's a way to picture your chakra databanks. Think of a magnificent pipe organ in an old church. Looking around, you can see pipes that are short, medium, large. Each pipe is a different size, actually. It must be, in order to sound different notes.

Try out the concept like this. Choose a body part corresponding to a major chakra, like your forehead or ribcage. Now imagine that you have 50 church organ pipes, all random sizes, sticking out from that body part. (Think "Porcupine." Or "Wacky church organ pipes.")

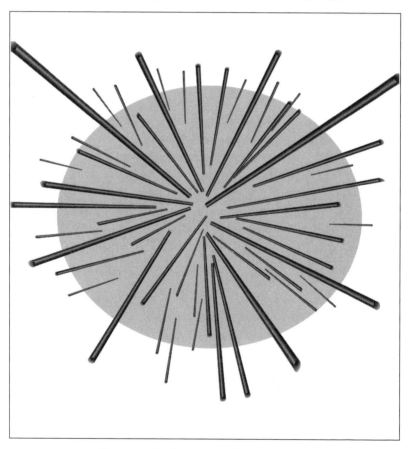

FIGURE 3. CHAKRA DATABANKS

Our next illustration shows a symbolic close-up of Billy's Third Eye Chakra, where all 50 of his Third Eye Chakra databanks can be seen at once. Does Billy physically look this way? No, this is a more like an anatomy illustration, conceptually useful if not visually true.

FIGURE 4. CHAKRA DATABANKS ON ONE MAJOR CHAKRA

That's a hint of the variety *you* have in each of your own chakra databanks. Every major chakra contains 50.

Depending on how you're doing at any given time, these chakra databanks can vary in size even more than organ pipes do. Size relates to the amount and quality of STUFF in any particular chakra databank. Size matters enormously, as you'll learn in later chapters.

Will the size of your chakra databanks show to complete strangers? No, it isn't as though any aura reader will clairvoyantly see you walking down the street looking just like our pipe organ image. Instead, every skilled aura reader can choose to access any one bit of information at a time. (That's how a mere mortal can do detailed energetic literacy without going nuts.)

With full energetic literacy, you choose where to aim, use a technique, and then access the appropriate data.

Ever use a personal computer? This literacy process is a lot like opening up a document in your electronic files. If you're really into storing documents, you might organize each document within electronic folders.

Sure, any major folder could contain 50 different documents. And you might pull up any one of them with a simple keystroke, right? Instantly, that particular document would display on your computer screen.

This choose-and-read sequence is similar to what happens with energetic literacy. Auras contain their information, stored like folders for every major chakra.

Incidentally, you also have **minor chakras** or **sub-chakras** in places like elbows, knees, and the soles of your feet. And each minor chakra contains many chakra databanks, as well.

How much detail can you read right now, choosing any chakra databank you like? That will depend on your development so far in the emerging field of energetic literacy.

STAGE 1 ENERGETIC LITERACY

Beginners at energetic literacy are (rightly) thrilled to notice anything at all about auras. This is akin to a child's first book with great big pictures. One special day, the blobs on the page start to shift. Suddenly you can make out people and objects within a picture. Aha! The first connection has been made.

Noticing the human energy field is different from touching a toaster or seeing a kitchen sink. The perception is real but subtle.

In terms of energetic literacy, you'll start making discoveries like "Billy has great vibrations."

STAGE 2 ENERGETIC LITERACY

More developed energetic literacy is akin to reading picture books that tell a story. At this stage, you'll find it a breakthrough to receive information from one major chakra at a time.

There will be generalizations like, "Billy's Root Chakra is open today" or "I get good energy from Billy's Root Chakra."

STAGE 3 ENERGETIC LITERACY

Energetic literacy becomes far more useful once you own the concept of chakra databanks and, then, start reading them.

This opening into greater detail is comparable to reading *Green Eggs and Ham* or, with a bit more practice, *War and Peace.* You can access a more complex story.

With full energetic literacy you can compare and contrast Billy's Root Chakra databanks, or databanks anywhere else in his auric field.

- For instance, you could compare his **Earning Money** Databank at the Root Chakra to the one for **Spending Money.**
- Or you could contrast Billy's **Connection to Spiritual Source** Databank at the Third Eye Chakra with his one about **Awareness of His Human Life.**

What if there's a problem with one of these chakra databanks? Billy can either seek healing or use an energetic workaround. (Part One of our program provides the underlying concepts needed for doing this, followed by Parts Two and Three which supply specifics.)

Success in the marketplace often depends on finding a competitive advantage. This Magnetize Money Program, being based on Stage 3 Energetic Literacy, gives you the advantage of inside information that anyone *can* access but everyone *isn't* accessing, not yet.

My quest has been to make deeper perception practical. What's the point of reading auras if you can't use it to make life better?

Insights that I have been testing for years are specifically geared toward helping people like you to become more successful and happy.

How to Read Chakra Databanks

Here's an overview that will be meaningful if you're already at Stage 2 or 3 Energetic Literacy.
Keep in mind that this book won't supply more details about

developing skills at aura reading, as other books exist for that purpose. In this book, I'll be doing the readings for you, so you won't need to use energetic literacy at all. Instead, you can concentrate on improving your success and prosperity.

Still, you may find our concept of chakra databanks really exciting. Just in case you want to start reading them on your own right now, here is a summary of how to proceed.

1. You focus on one chakra databank at a time, e.g., Heart Chakra Databank: **Emotional Giving.**
2. Use whatever technique you find reliable for *perceiving* auras. Given your intention to read one particular databank, the appropriate information will pop out.
3. After you experience that initial perception, you're not done yet. Use whatever technique you find reliable for *interpreting* information from auras.

PERCEPTION + INTERPRETATION = AURA READING

GIFTS AND STUFF

In the past, energy workers would read chakras in very simple ways, using words like "open" or "closed." An entire major chakra was viewed as one unit. I did that too, while at Stage 2 Energetic Literacy.

With more experience, however, I found that way more information became available. For example, Billy might have both these patterns right now in his Third Eye Chakra:

- Third Eye Chakra Databank: **Connecting to Spiritual Source** could be huge.
- Third Eye Chakra Databank: **Awareness of His Human Life** could be teensy.

To help you appreciate the contrast, our next illustration shows both of these chakra databanks appearing at once.

This is a conceptual illustration, of course, not what you would see in real life. In reality, you would read just one chakra databank at a time, then draw your own comparison.

FIGURE 5. TWO CONTRASTING CHAKRA DATABANKS

You see, various databanks within the same chakra can be extremely different in terms of size and everything else. Another way-important pair of chakra databanks (which we'll investigate in Chapter 18) can be found at the Heart Chakra. With Billy right now:

- Heart Chakra Databank: **Emotional Giving** could be huge.
- Heart Chakra Databank: **Emotional Receiving** could be teensy.
- Or just the opposite could be true. And either version might be a habit that could be corrected with an energetic workaround.

Ideally, both databanks would become relatively balanced. In real life, however, any combination is possible.

What matters most, in reality, if you are to Magnetize Money? You'd better have patterns favorable to receiving wealth in *your* money-related chakra databanks.

Do you give far more than you receive emotionally? Do you pay far more attention to spirituality than to your own human life? Either choice would drastically limit your financial success.

In later chapters, you'll be able to consider what it would mean to have problems like these. Also, fortunately, how to solve them. (Hint: The energetic workarounds that I provide might be related to the *reasons* why some of your chakra databanks are extra big or small.)

Meanwhile, let's continue exploring these exciting new concepts of energetic literacy. Sure, you can skip ahead to Chapter 4, bypass this theory base, and still benefit from the practical ways that this program is designed to help you Magnetize Money. But you're now *very close* to completing the full set of concepts.

Remember, these next concepts aren't mere abstractions, useful for fictional Billy and maybe a handful of real-life people. Each of these concepts most definitely applies to *you* and your current financial portfolio.

Each of your chakra databanks can contain two different types of information.

- There's always a **gift of your soul**, something you do well. This is hardwired into you, a particular knack for success at a particular aspect of life. Every gift of your soul is permanent. Think "Fingerprint."
- A second type of information is often found in chakra databanks: Stored-up emotional and spiritual pain. Or fear. Or sadness. As you already know, I call that **"STUFF."**

This STUFF can be lodged within you as a blob of stuck energy, a chemical imbalance, or a structural imbalance such as an energetic subroutine (to be discussed later). Any of this counts as astral-level debris.

STUFF could result from short-term problems or long-term ones. You might find STUFF a wee bit annoying, pretty darned awful, or nightmarishly horrible.

Just don't be intimidated by STUFF. In my experience, STUFF can always be healed. With my clients, most sessions involve using various skill sets to facilitate healing STUFF. Based on thousands of these sessions, guess what I've learned?

- The more STUFF you have, the less money you'll make. However, certain kinds of STUFF hurt a career more than others — a vital point if you aim to Magnetize Money.
- Some STUFF causes a chakra databank to over-function.
- Most STUFF causes a chakra databank to under-function.
- Either way, STUFF can always, always, always be healed.

By now, some of you Resourceful Readers are beginning to appreciate that energetic literacy could be extremely useful for diagnosing and solving problems that block your flow of wealth. Well, you'd be right.

Even if you're still getting used to concepts like chakra databanks, gifts of your soul, and STUFF, no worries. This program is meant to make the concept relevant to all you have done so far — and whatever you will do in the future — to Magnetize Money.

What, STUFF Can Limit My Money?

The more STUFF you have, the less money you'll make. Sounds simple. So how come nobody told you before? These otherwise well educated people didn't yet have Stage 3 Energetic Literacy.

Now things can change for you. When the millionaire is ready, the success coach comes. I'm going to help you to learn which kinds of hidden STUFF could limit your money, and what to do about it.

Must your aura be perfect in every way before you can Magnetize Money? Of course not! Some of the world's top billionaires function very effectively despite rather nasty forms of STUFF. Only *none* of them carries STUFF in certain money-related chakra databanks; *none* has STUFF that actively repels wealth.

Surely you know many sweet people who deserve way more success than they have. I have known plenty too, including Hannah, who was introduced in our Dedication. Hundreds of my clients. And, once upon a time, me.

Granted, I still don't know as much about energetic literacy as a five-year-old will in the year 2500. At least I know enough to tell that the problem isn't just "Life stinks." Nor is the solution to money problems "Stay positive" or "Try harder."

It's time for life's wisest people to become truly effective! You can make it your business to clean up this part of your act.

Resourceful Reader, that's exactly how I'm going to help you, as we move through this program. STUFF has way more to do with prosperity than most people realize… yet. Being able to sniff out that kind of problem makes certain old-fashioned success skills obsolete.

OBSOLETE SKILLS FOR SUCCESS AND PROSPERITY FROM THE SECOND MILLENNIUM

Energetic literacy in this millennium means deep exploration of reality, like working in nanotechnology or genetic engineering. Today's discoveries are improvements over some of yesterday's big thrills and skills.

Of course, you're living at the historical time when energetic literacy is emerging, not yet universal. Do you realize what a competitive advantage that can bring you in the workplace?

If you really wish to Magnetize Money, understand this: Moving out anti-prosperity STUFF will demand something different from solving problems with those familiar strategies from the 1990's or earlier.

To mobilize our full potential for wealth, we need to move out the STUFF that blocks prosperity. None of the following methods brings true results for healing STUFF.

AFFIRMATIONS AND POSITIVE THINKING

They can persuade you into believing you don't have STUFF. But you'll still have the STUFF regardless, stuck deep inside at the level of auras.

DENIAL

Pretending that you don't have STUFF, or the problems that come from STUFF — oh, how tempting! Denial can be a useful makeshift method, only it will keep you stuck at your present earning level… or worse.

Worrying

Not many books have been written in praise of worry as a technique for those who want to grow rich. Yet somehow most of us have discovered this technique on our own.

Maybe worrying isn't the most effective way to get ahead in life. Worry definitely won't move out STUFF.

Blaming

How sweet it can be, holding others responsible for consequences that result from our own STUFF. You probably know people who blame their financial woes on a boss, an economy, energy vampires, or different something-or-others.

Blaming may be a fine consolation prize. At the level of auras, however, it won't heal a thing.

Analyzing Your Stuff

Close but no cigar! Analyzing problems related to STUFF or simply analyzing the STUFF itself, fascinating though such insights can be, they won't move out STUFF.

Note: The most elegant form of STUFF analysis could be "talk therapy." Psychotherapy is great for insight. Working on issues can bring important healing to the surface of life and uncover some interesting concepts.

Unfortunately, that level of healing doesn't fix STUFF. With each passing year, I do more referrals back and forth with therapists. After I help a client to move major STUFF, the therapist's talent and training can help a client to heal way faster.

Prayer and Meditation

Sure, they are magnificent. Sure, they can help to improve your quality of life overall. But apart from the rare miracle, neither prayer nor meditation will move out STUFF that blocks prosperity.

Prayer won't wash and wax your car either, will it? Heaven helps those who help themselves… to effective forms of STUFF removal.

Why Settle for Kindergarten Literacy?

I love the quote at the start of this chapter, where Simon Sinek admits that Bill Gates doesn't seem like an "energetic" speaker. Yet Gates inspires people with his leadership.

How can that be? The answer involves the very understanding you have gained in this chapter. You're starting to appreciate the difference between Energetic Literacy Stage 1 versus Stage 3.

Let's explore that difference just a bit further. Can you remember what it felt like when you first started noticing energy?

Stage 1 Energetic Literacy is quite amazing. And you may have had exciting moments discovering other forms of energy as well.

There's sexual energy, the big giggle-inducing discovery from puberty. And let's not forget other types of energy that are part of your life now, whether or not you're aware of them consciously: Earth-based energy, emotional energy, interpersonal energy, Kundalini energy, and spiritual energy.

Resourceful Reader, you may have called these energies flowing through you by altogether different names than "energy." You could have used one of these:

- The Field (thanks to the brilliant Lynne McTaggart)
- Orgone (as with controversial psychoanalyst Wilhelm Reich)
- Kundalini (as in Kundalini Yoga)
- Chi (as in Tai chi)
- Qi (as in Qigong)
- Ki (as in Reiki)
- The Force (as used by Obi-Wan Kenobi in "Star Wars")

Whatever you have called That, you may have noticed it within you or as a flow between people, animals, all living things.

Healers often start by paying attention to energy exchanges *between* people. (Sometimes beginners find it helpful to use negative terms like "energy vampire" and "psychic attack" but most energy interactions between people are positive, even inspiring.)

What does it mean to direct energetic literacy toward emphasizing energy exchange between people? Depending on your gift set, you might feel vibes, hear information, or see the movement of light. One way or another, you start to recognize that energy underlies all human interactions.

For you to Magnetize Money in a big way, energy flow between you and otheres matters enormously. However, our approach emphasizes the flow *within* you, helping you to take responsibility for that and improving it.

If you enjoy following the energetic flow between people, you're going to love observing the improvement in your own interactions. Even for the sake of helping others, you need strong chakra databanks in a good balance with each other.

I believe that everyone alive will be more successful and healthier with true energetic literacy. So many illusions and problems lose their hold over us when we can read what is happening at the level of energy.

And, of course, we can use this skill to investigate what attracts money, what doesn't, and how to do a better job at making money.

Full energetic literacy takes some time to develop (just like the Gutenberg version). What matters isn't how long it takes learning to read, or how many teachers you need. What matters is that, once you do become literate, you own that skill for the rest of your life.

Here are some tip-offs about being stuck at Stage 2 Energetic Literacy :

- Quentin feels good or bad energy. Or sometimes he "gets things" from a photo.
- Queenie insists on "figuring it out for myself" rather going to a qualified teacher to learn good quality skills.
- Quashawn equates "talent" with "seeing the colours." Once he tried to see them and didn't. Therefore he is convinced that any future aura reading would be a waste of time since he doesn't have "the gift."
- Quadira has had some success at "seeing the colours." She uses the "color-by-number" approach to energetic literacy, where every color is supposed to have one universal meaning and success means that she can see exactly the same things as her favorite psychic.

Nice tries! Approaches like these are the energetic literacy equivalent of a kindergartener who "reads" books by scanning the pictures and making up a story.

In terms of regular literacy, that's the stage where all these letters look alike:

b, p, q, d

Why? Each letter is circle + handle. They're lollipops.

Differences between letters matter only when a reader progresses beyond kindergarten level. Full Gutenberg literacy opens up the ability to read words, pages, and paragraphs.

Only full literacy is detailed and practical enough to improve a person's financial bottom line.

If you want to grow rich, you need information from adult-level Stage 3 Energetic Literacy. You'll need that, for instance, to understand what's the deal with Bill Gates.

Does he really lack energy as a speaker? (Check out his profile in our next chapter.)

As for you, what is really happening with your own energy at the level of chakra databanks? What will help you to mobilize that energy so that you can Magnetize Money?

Bring on secrets for success and prosperity based on that emerging skill of the third millennium, full energetic literacy.

4. Researching the Rich

The key to success — at least for me — is relentless optimism, determination, and not taking things personally. I've always taken things seriously. Insecure people take things personally.
—Cathleen Black, President, Hearst Magazines

As a pioneering prosperity writer, Napoleon Hill interviewed the most successful people of his day in order to learn their secrets. In this book, my approach is more direct. I have researched today's rich and successful by interviewing their auras.

Energetic literacy is a more direct way to learn true secrets of success because auras are not the realm of public relations or wishful thinking. They can't be faked.

Cathleen Black's wise words, quoted above, are from a book of interviews by Michael J. Berland and Douglas E. Schoen, *What Makes You Tick? How Successful People Do It — and What You Can Learn from Them.* Research on Black's aura is coming up in a later chapter. For now, suffice it to say that Cathie Black's aura practices what she preaches.

By contrast, consider Andrew Carnegie. The second richest man on earth during his lifetime, Carnegie wrote an influential article called "The Gospel of Wealth."

As a captain of industry, back in the day, Carnegie's aura had the perfect ciruits for business success. But as a teacher of success principles? Ouch!

With all respect to the man's best intentions, his words bore only a passing relationship to the who-you-be factor.

Here's a hint. When I profiled him for our Online Supplement, I titled the article "Believe Carnegie's Aura, Not His Gospel of Wealth."

How do I use skills of energetic literacy to "interview" experts on success and prosperity? Here are the basics.

RESEARCHING AWAY

The methods I use are simple, straightforward techniques to read people energetically via their photographs. Any photo includes more than an image at the surface level. There will be a complete record of that person's energy field. Therefore, every single chakra databank is available to anyone who can read with Stage 3 Energetic Literacy.

Sometimes newbies wonder about the time factor. Is there such a thing as using one photo to read a person for all time?

Maybe for a psychic reading, but this is simple literacy. People are profiled at the time of the photograph, that simple.

And speaking of simple, I'll be the first to admit that my profiles are simply the best I can do, not the work of some Almighty Omniscient Authority. You're definitely invited to supplement my findings with your own. Like Gutenberg literacy, energetic literacy is an art, not a hard science.

Here are some technical points about my methodology doing the profiles in our Magnetize Money Program.

LAYERS

If you are very skilled at energetic literacy, you know that all the first seven layers of aura are related to chakras. The first layer corresponds to the Root Chakra; the second layer links to the Belly Chakra, etc.

For practical purposes, it's fine to specialize in reading just one layer. This brings consistency. Generally I prefer reading auras at the third layer out, unless there is a compelling reason to do otherwise.

When researching any photo that shows the subject's full torso and head, I read that third layer.

Head shots present one of those compelling reasons to do things differently. Researching such pictures, I access different chakras through reading layers. Usually my base of operations will be the Throat Chakra. From that location, I'll research chakra databanks by moving through one layer at a time.

Size

One fascinating aspect of chakra databanks is their size. Researching this, I enjoy using the term coined in 2009 by a European client named Chloe Irving: **Inch-age.**

Of course, you could substitute a metric-style term, such as **centimeter-icity.**

Researching the Magnetize Money Profiles and Snapshots, I will supply approximate size for each chakra databank. This could be inches, miles, or a symbolic distance such as "out to the sky," "out to the moon," or "out into deep space."

One reason inch-age can be so useful is that it provides a way to appreciate how different aspects of a person may be strong, weak, or anything in-between. Also, the proportion between chakra databanks is extremely relevant to a person's likely success at pursuing wealth.

More about Inch-Age

Using energetic literacy skills to research chakra databanks related to financial prosperity, I have developed specialized units of measurement. Each term is used as a spatial analogy about inner experience.

Whether reading auras from photos or profiling a client in the room with me, I use the method of Aura Reading Through All Your Senses®. This form of energetic literacy isn't old-fashioned "seeing the colours." Instead, I'm using my full combination of subtle senses. Given my personal gift set, that means depending mostly on subtle touch, hearing, knowing and emotional experiencing.

How does one quantify such abstract information? The measurement terms I've developed combine physical information about a particular chakra projection with a dimensional component.

Consistent use of these terms makes it possible to compare apples and oranges, Cathie Black versus Andrew Carnegie.

Inches, Feet, and Miles

The measurement terms I use most often are **inches, feet,** and **miles.** Gauging inch-age makes it easy to compare the size of different chakra databanks. If you're more familiar with the metric system, use an online conversion link like www.onlineconversion.com to translate the data in my profiles.

Most people, doing reasonably well in mind-body-spirit, have chakra databanks out to five feet or more.

FILLS THE ROOM

Certain executives possess such charisma, even the energetically illiterate feel something is going on. It's like an actor having **"chemistry."**

Sitting in an audience on Broadway, you might say, "Angela Lansbury fills the whole theater with her presence." Those with Stage 1 Energetic Literacy might simply say, "I love her energy. She fills the room."

Even when using Stage 3 Energetic Literacy, "fills the room" can be a convenient way to describe what some people do aurically.

Bill Gates may never perform like Angela, singing and dancing his way into your heart. To perceptive Simon Sinek, Gates appears to not have "energy" yet simultaneously possess a unique kind of charisma. What's with that?

Energetic literacy is a way to understand better who has "It," who doesn't. Who has how much? Of what kind? Even more fascinating, how does the special excellence of one person's "It" compare to somebody else's?

Doing the profiles I share with you in this Magnetize Money Program, I always will include quality characteristics along with inchage terminology like **"Fills the room."**

With this expression, I literally mean that when someone like Bill Gates speaks in a venue of any size, he energetically fills up the place. More precisely, certain chakra databanks expand to affect everyone present. That could mean filling a small conference room or reaching someone sitting in the last row of the Albert Hall. Consciously, a spectator might register a presence like that as a "Wow!"

Sometimes I'll use a term like "Fills the room plus two inches." That means the lucky owner of that particular chakra databank sends out such charisma that it not only fills but overflows the venue, be it a small conference room or the Albert Hall.

Consciously, a spectator might register that as a "BIG WOW!"

OUT TO THE SKY

Okay, scientists will be the first to tell you that, technically, there is no such thing as "the sky." Yet most of us do have a sense of sky, right? So I consider it a workable concept… especially because this is my best way so far to describe a very important quality of aura presence.

Even if, technically, "sky" doesn't exist, clouds can be measured. Atmospheric scientists sort clouds into three categories:

- Low clouds extend from the ground up to 6,500 feet, or a bit over 1 mile.
- Middle clouds range from 6,500 to 20,000 feet.
- High clouds are over 20,000 feet.

How high into the clouds must we look before we can call that place "sky"? To me, the height of a low cloud is plenty. Technically I consider **"Sky distance"** to be approximately 1 mile or 2 kilometers.

What distinguishes this from a simple horizontal distance measurement like 1 mile or 2 km.? The direction is upward, not outward.

You see, when I perceive that a chakra databank extends toward the sky, to me that means a vibrational shift in the direction of Higher Power. Or Highest Power. In other words:

- The person cares passionately about that aspect of life
- And that drive is combined with a spiritual intent to overcome all human limitations.
- When that person means business, all the way down to the level of chakras, a chakra databank can reach all the way "out to the sky." Or farther still….

OUT TO THE MOON

Measuring **"From here to the moon"** must take into account that the moon moves, relative to the earth.

For our purposes, let's keep things simple and use the closest elliptical distance. That would be 2, 214, 815 miles or 3,564,400 kilometers. If it helps you to round off numbers, go ahead and think 2 million miles or 3 1/2 million kilometers.

Subjectively, the meaning is that the person enlists astral-level help. This could come from one's personal spirit guide, an angel who is helping out for a while as part of a person's energetic entourage, or a channeled being like Abraham.

The astral-level info. might be consciously received as such, or be completely unknown to the person, or even be consciously misunderstood, e.g., "This is the voice of God" whereas really this is the voice of a low-frequency astral-level being. (Sometimes a human listener can be confused about the nature of beings from "The Other Side.")

Regardless of a person's conscious knowledge about teaming up, it is always done by agreement, even if this agreement is transacted at the level of aura that corresponds to a person's subconscious mind.

What is the nature of such a partnership? In fiction, you're familiar with the plot where an ambitious character sells his soul to the Devil. You find it in "Damn Yankees" or Goethe's "Faust."

In real life, energy partnerships occur often, although not necessarily with a "Devil." Also, these arrangements can be flexible, much like one-night stands or dating.

Partnerships that register to me as "Out to the moon" mean that, for the purposes of helping out with one chakra databank or another, the person teams up on a regular basis with one or more beings from the astral plane.

OUT TO THE STARS

Using numbers to compare distances, let's settle for nearby stars. That's a very manageable 1,500 light years — "manageable" because the speed of consciousness goes way faster than the speed of light or the speed of sound. To my perception, it's very possible for a person's chakra databanks to move out this far.

Bringing our units of measurement down to earth, a light year is the distance that light can travel in a year, about 6 trillion miles or 10 trillion kilometers.

Thus, a nearby star is "only" 9.5 trillion kilometers, which translates into 13,537.5 trillion kilometers or 8412 trillion miles.

How much is a trillion? Using inches, or miles, or stacks of $100 bills, even one trillion boggles the mind. It is a 1 followed by 12 zeroes.

Understanding numbers in terms of money is fun, isn't it? So here's a way to visualize "one trillion," courtesy of technology writer Amit Agarwal. At www.labnol.org, he gives this analogy:

> A bundle of $100 notes is equivalent to $10,000 and that can easily fit in your pocket. One million dollars will probably fit inside a standard shopping bag while a billion dollars would occupy a small room of your house.
> With this background in mind, 1 trillion (1,000,000,000,000) is 1000 times bigger than 1 billion and would therefore take up an entire football field.

Whatever analogy helps you to make the number concrete, "Out to the stars" is an extremely far distance. The reason I choose it for our profiles is that it symbolizes a different dimensional shift: When a human being co-creates with the Divine.

This is Spiritual-Level consciousness, neither astral nor human. When a chakra databank goes out this far, it never fails to inspire me. (Although, as we will see later, having this kind of emphasis in chakra databanks can be a mixed blessing.)

Ironically, at the surface of life it's pretty hard to distinguish a huge "I give my life for Spiritual Source" type of connection versus "I have a very satisfying belief about Spiritual Source but (truth be told) I have no authentic spiritual experience."

Two people could share identical religious beliefs, and both be absolutely sincere, while one has a half-inch connection and the other's connection extends for trillions of miles.

DO THE MATH

As you use energetic literacy, try out my units of measurements. Or create your own. So long as you stay consistent, you can make meaningful comparisons like these:

- Between one chakra databank and another.
- Between one person and another, reading the same chakra databank.
- Taking a good sample of chakra databanks and using them as a baseline for doing a profile related to our Magnetize Money Program.

- Detecting an addiction, where one or more chakra databanks are way, way bigger than all the rest. (More on that later.)
- Evaluating if a person is spiritually Enlightened (which we will also discuss in more detail later).

THE TOP 10 MAGNETIZE MONEY DATABANKS

Using energetic literacy to profile the rich and successful, I have found that 10 chakra databanks matter most. All but one must be in good shape for someone to Magnetize Money successfully.

Can you guess which of the following databanks is *not* especially relevant to worldly success?

Meet the Magnetize Money Profile

When you're using energetic literacy to investigate anyone's prospects for major wealth creation, start here.

1. Root Chakra Databank: **Earning Money**
Yes, you have a talent for earning money, a way that is most effortless and natural for you. STUFF in this chakra databank can act as a deterrent to receiving the fruits of your actions.

2. Root Chakra Databank: **Saving Money**
A gift for accumulating wealth — of course you have that deep down. Therefore, you have no need to force yourself to manufacture talent for doing this. Your particular knack has been part of you since the day you were born.
Unfortunately, if you are carrying STUFF like guilt over having "too much money," that won't be good for your bottom line. The consequence of money-repelling STUFF, especially in these Top 10 Databanks, can attract patterns of self-sabotage until the problem has been cleaned up.

3. Root Chakra Databank: **Personality at Work**
First impressions do count. Where in the aura would you look

first to discover the first impression that you give to others? Here, at this chakra databank!

In later chapters, we will add the concept of "auric modeling," which does a lot to modify this first impression. Still, no matter how sophisticated and detailed your aura reading, this chakra databank remains your best quick way to read first impressions that you automatically give to any potential customer, boss, etc.

4. Root Chakra Databank: **Personality PROJECTED at Work**

Some people, like Rhonda Byrne, have talent for appearing charming, forceful, etc. This can be useful for selling yourself. Others, like Bill Gates, don't do especially well at this form of selling, so they won't project anything special. Consequently, people will feel the lack of oomph but mostly respond to what the person is really like, whatever shows in the previous chakra databank.

Profiling business superstars, I often find major talent for projecting something special, making this chakra databank an especially amusing one to research.

5. Solar Plexus Chakra Databank: **Self-Confidence at Work**

Yes, it's true. Confidence begets confidence, a positive spiral that will benefit anyone... unless STUFF is distorting your natural gift at this chakra databank.

Later in this Magnetize Money Program, I'll be helping you to upgrade your true self-confidence. So please don't worry if confidence isn't that strong for you yet.

I have helped other people to gain an authentic and strong self-confidence. We can definitely team up through this Magnetize Money Program to help you build confidence.

6. Solar Plexus Chakra Databank: **Handling Conflict at Work**

When you were a kid, did you ever play the board game called *Candy Land?* Even in that sugar-coated world, you can draw a bad card and, consequently, suffer a setback.

When playing Candy Land, there's not much you can do, except to turn sore loser, pick up the game board, and hurl it at your opponent. (Sadly, this isn't in the official rules. But who cares? Hurling could help you for a good two seconds.)

In real-life business transactions, when bad things happen, you can fight back *effectively.* In fact you had better. This part of your aura reveals you at your best, using your personal power to get what you want.

Except often, alas, this databank reveals crippling amounts of STUFF.

7. Heart Chakra Databank: **Emotional Intelligence at Work**

Thanks to Daniel Goleman's bestselling book, *Emotional Intelligence: Why It Can Matter More Than IQ,* most of us have heard that business success will increase if we can educate ourselves about human emotions.

Actually, energetic literacy suggests that everyone possesses at least one gift for emotional intelligence. But will the STUFF outweigh the gift? That's what we can investigate, one Magnetize Money Profile at a time.

8. Throat Chakra Databank: **Communication at Work**

Speak up for yourself, won't you? For greatest success, you'll use your talent for communication.

What is that talent, anyway? And could it be a wee bit stuck?

9. Third Eye Chakra Databank: **Awareness of Your Human Life**

No amount of career success or money can satisfy all human needs. Most of us, at least, need community, creativity, intimacy, sex, a keen sense of self in the world.

Getting a life is not optional, not for this chakra databank, anyway. Sometimes, sadly, a person is bedazzled by an ideal, ambition, or belief system. Consequently the quirky, very individual, human part is forgotten. How can you tell if such a thing has been happening to you? Perspective won't come from within that belief system. Energetic literacy to the rescue!

10. Third Eye Chakra Databank: **Connection to Spiritual Source**

Of course, you have a direct pipeline to That. And it's *your* personal pipeline, your gift of the soul.

When STUFF clogs this chakra databank, life is diminished. No lamenting, though. STUFF can be removed. Beyond that, contact with the Divine can become as simple or complicated as you wish it to be.

PROFILING THE RICH AND FAMOUS

Let's do our first energetic literacy profile on the richest man in the world today, Bill Gates. Mega-rich, self-made, builder of a techno-empire — if you could look deep inside the Microsoft founder to learn how he Magnetized Money, wouldn't you be curious?

Meanwhile, remembering that 1 out of 10 databanks in our Magnetize Money Profile isn't required to grow rich, any theories yet?

Find the photo used for this profile at the "Photo Supplement" online.

Bill Gates: Magnetize Money Profile

1. Root Chakra Databank: Earning Money
50 miles. A super-fluid intelligence dominates.

Immediately this informs us that Gates inhabits a different kind of inner world than traditional captains of industry who are more socially oriented and down to earth.

Without trying, Gates has resources of flexible thinking, comfort with ultra-high-level abstractions, and other intellectual gifts associated with computer technology.

And here's what really moblizes gifts like these: Bill's extreme determination to win at the game of making money.

2. Root Chakra Databank: *Saving Money*

50 miles. Gates isn't content to save. He aims to grow wealth.

Again, the man shows a fascinating mixture of playfulness, abstract thinking, and extreme determination to be rich.

3. Root Chakra Databank: *Personality at Work*

Fills any room he is in, minus one inch. Bill's intellect expands to hold the conversation. He doesn't merely follow points of view. He understands them at depth, then stores all interesting details in a computer-like manner.

Gates doesn't bring a *personality* to work so much as a unique *intellect* paired with a quick-moving consciousness. But his genius at doing this can be felt by any perceptive person in that room.

4. Root Chakra Databank: *Personality PROJECTED at Work*

14 inches. Pleasantly nerdy and playful, Gates is no performer. He's more an accomplisher.

5. Solar Plexus Chakra Databank: *Self-Confidence at Work*

50 miles. Bill displays immense confidence, to the point of serenity —unless angry about something that affects business, in which case expect him to display ruthlessness.

Moreover, this man receives high-vibrational input to supplement his personal striving for success. As an experienced co-creator with his Spiritual Source, Bill Gates receives input on demand in terms of his own creative ideas.

This keeps him in a constant state of resourcefulness. And this, in turn, brings feedback to augment his confidence.

6. Solar Plexus Chakra Databank: *Handling Conflict at Work*

50 miles. Although this chakra databank mostly shows the quality of serenity I've just described, the man does have a hot temper.

Under certain conditions, anger burns. Then Bill will project intense rage within the first three feet past his physical body. If you stand anywhere within that distance, you won't have to be skilled at aura reading to feel the scorch.

7. Heart Chakra Databank: *Emotional Intelligence at Work*

30 miles. The probing, curious intelligence is quite relentless.

Standing before this man, you cannot hide how you feel. What's really fascinating, however, is something you might **not** notice when being in Gates' presence.

How does he pay attention? This is no mushy gushy "I know how you feel" kind of probe. Bill Gates computes the bits and bytes of human emotion, analyzing the information as needed, storing it all. For Gates, this is a gift of the soul.

8. Throat Chakra Databank: ***Communication at Work***
50 miles of simple clarity. Don't expect Bill Gates to steal Bill Cosby's job any time soon. Instead, the Microsoft Bill has a specialized gift for work communication: He speaks to geeks.

It's as though he can transmit a special subtext that makes techies feel understood. (Actually, it's more as though Bill can speak Techie Talk up a dimension or two; meanwhile the English language serves as his very bland subtext.)

9. Third Eye Chakra Databank: ***Awareness of His Human Life***
50 miles. Bill Gates isn't human so much as a person who appears human.

Okay, part of Bill Gates is human. Only, I'd have to say that, from my perspective, it's a very small part. The rest of him has circuits that probably will be considered average, and human, 500 years from now.

In his own futuristic way, is this man self-aware about his own "human" life? Yes, very.

10. Third Eye Chakra Databank: ***Connection to Spiritual Source***
50 miles. What's really lovely about Bill's experience, at the time of this photo, is his automatic and effortless connection to God.

To conclude, Bill Gates doesn't merely have a megawatt, powerful aura. He's balanced to a degree that I call spiritually Enlightened.

Not every chakra databank from our survey is huge. Did you notice the one puny one? It's at the Root Chakra: **Personality PROJECTED at Work.** I called Gates, "Pleasantly nerdy and playful," and " no performer."

This lack of fancy facade may be a choice. Or a habit. Or maybe that's just how the man is inwardly designed to function, a gift.

One of the fascinating discoveries you'll make with Stage 3 Energetic Literacy concerns a person's degree of talent for impressing others. Who projects a personality with an extra-strong facade?

Some have a great deal of talent this way, sending out a powerful add-on kind of oomph at this chakra databank. Rhonda Byrne would be an example.

Ginormous energetic facades are created purposely by some people. Other people send them out consciously without trying, as a reflexive kind of soul-level gift for popularity.

Still other people have zero talent for sending out a big energetic facade. Even if they try. Even if they're Enlightened and try, they simply cannot do it. In my opinion, Bill Gates is one of those people.

And one of the ironies of using Stage 1 Energetic Literacy is that an observer will perceive just enough to be strongly influenced by an add-on facade (or lack of facade). Yet this level of literacy isn't enough to discern when a projected thin slice of self is highly misleading. Hence Simon Sinek's observation in our last chapter.

One more important point from our reading of Bill Gates in this chapter: Does Enlightenment or talent make the richest man in the world a "nice person"? Hardly.

With such acquisitiveness and determination at databanks like the first two on our list: Ouch! I sure wouldn't want to stand in Bill Gates' way.

His company, Microsoft, has lost at least one rather serious lawsuit over its software monopoly. Not everything about the man or his company can be considered "perfect," like an old-fashioned ideal of a Philosopher-King.

But that brings up an important point as we introduce the concept of spiritual Enlightenment from the perspective of energetic literacy. You'll read more on this topic in a later chapter. For now, consider this.

Enlightenment isn't about being nice in every way, according to your taste or mine. Instead, Enlightenment means playing one's role in life perfectly (suiting God's standards if you will) but not being all things to all bystanders.

Is Enlightenment required to Magnetize Money? Let's keep exploring before we decide that one, okay?

5. Oops,
Your Aura Is Showing

What the mind of man can conceive and believe, it can achieve.
— Napoleon Hill, *Think and Grow Rich*

Napoleon Hill famously wrote these words and changed the minds of millions. But did those minds — and auras — change in a direction that was profitable?

"I'm desperate to find my life work," Barry told me. Quickly he filled in the background: Schoolteacher for 16 years, but last year he had so many problems, he quit his job. Three long months followed, where this caring man struggled to find purpose in life.

Deep in his heart, Barry found that purpose.

"I must become a full-time Reiki healer," Barry told me. "Read me, Rose. Tell me what you think of my prospects."

Although I don't make predictions during sessions, I can use energetic literacy to read the present in depth and detail. It's called **Thrill Your Soul Research.** Over the years, I have used this skill set to give clients accurate feedback about their life choices; I've also advised business executives, reading auras of their job candidates.

One of my regular clients, Ben, runs a large company in a third world country where government officials must routinely be bribed. Because of this fact of life, for certain positions Ben must hire personnel who are sleazy enough to bribe officials effectively... yet not be so crooked as to also steal from Ben's company.

Energetic literacy to the rescue! Compared to distinguishing degrees of dishonesty for Ben's job candidates, it's a snap to evaluate choices like Barry's.

It's a matter of doing baseline research on 10 relevant chakra databanks. Then, together, we research one choice at a time. Every life choice affects every databank. So I go in, researching the impact of any proposed choice on the 10 selected baseline databanks. Every one of them tells a story related to success. Or lack of success.

Alas, full-time Reiki was awful for Barry. It worsened an ongoing problem, a syndrome that I have come to call "**spiritual addiction.**" This pattern (which shows clearly with energetic literacy) results from over-emphasizing spiritual life. Common causes include:

- Interpreting everything in life spiritually.
- Crushing on angels.
- Falling in love… with a cult.
- Perpetually using a pendulum, testing energy, or dowsing.
- Constantly seeking guidance from angels and guides.
- Smoking marijuana.
- Going crazy over mediumship or channeling.
- Not trusting "ordinary life" or "ordinary people."
- Paying attention only to what lies deep in your heart, ignoring the surface of life (objective reality).

With a spiritual addiction, people tend to make choices in the direction of their addiction. Only spiritual interests have strong appeal. Well, how much do you think that would help anyone to grow rich?

Too much reliance on The Secret or LOA teachings will almost guarantee poor financial prospects. Ironic, isn't it? Any belief that over-emphasizes subjective life can bring on a spiritual addiction.

The good news? Imbalances in auras can always, always, always be healed.

The bad news? When someone is very far gone into this syndrome, she/he may have to hit bottom before making a change.

Sadly, Barry might be one of those people. Being with him in session was tough because he literally couldn't hear most of our conversation. It was too different from what he expected me to say.

Trying to be tactful yet clear, I described in detail the implications of his going full-time as a Reiki healer. Meanwhile, Barry kept giving me a strange, blank stare. It was as though he was doing a simultaneous translation, urgently re-interpreting every word to match his belief system.

Repeatedly Barry protested that he must, must, must be brilliant at Reiki and have great career prospects. And why? Because he felt so very sure. Besides, "everyone knows" that when you really want something, you will attract loads of money.

WHICH SHOUTS LOUDER?

Which shouts louder to your boss, employees, and customers, the who-you-be that shows in your aura or your beliefs?

Like it or not, who-you-be has the last word.

We could consider Barry a poster child for too much Law of Attraction and not enough "Get a life." Principles of positive thinking can work wonders. Except the person who does that thinking must be relatively balanced to begin with.

Having "interviewed" Napoleon Hill's aura, I'm convinced that he didn't suffer from a spiritual addiction. Nor, I suspect, did the many millionaires he interviewed when preparing his masterpiece, *Think and Grow Rich.*

Hill could ask, "What's the secret of your success?" He could receive an answer. And did. But all that conversation on the surface level of life cannot close the heartbreaking kind of gap that Barry experienced.

Until the energetic version of a person functions effectively, beliefs may sound perfect, but so what? Actions in pursuit of wealth aren't likely to be particularly effective.

Real-life success depends on the who-you-be factor supplemented by our words and actions. Wealth isn't won simply because a person really, truly believes in success teachings, as did Barry. Nor were his financial prospects likely to improve without an upgrade to his who-you-be.

In the future, after he tidies up some of his hidden STUFF, Barry's behavior can improve and so can his status at work. Even a person's long-held beliefs about permanent limitations in life can change, and circumstances evolve from the inside all the way out.

Another example is Beth. When we first met, she wasn't going to be voted "Most likely to succeed" any time soon. Here's how she introduced herself one Friday night at the start of a workshop:

"Hi. I'm Beth. I don't know how much I'm going to get out of your workshop, but don't take it personally. I have ADD."

Attention Deficit Disorder isn't a fun diagnosis, nor is it linked to great wealth. Have you ever heard a business wunderkind proudly say during an interview, "What is the secret of my success? I guess I would have to thank my ADD."

First thing the next morning, Beth announced, "Sorry I'm late. But you know, for me, 20 minutes late isn't too bad. With my ADD, I'm usually much later."

Now, I liked Beth. She wasn't just honest but endearing, with a very big heart. Would I have hired her for a job, however? No way, which was sad.

Beth spoke well. She dressed well. She had skills. Unfortunately, even without those announcements about "my ADD," Beth portrayed herself energetically as a loveable loser.

During the lunch break, I had an opening for a healing session. Beth took that appointment.

In little more time than it would take to say "Attention Deficit Disorder," I found a problem that was moving Beth's aura way out of balance. Neither a life sentence nor a gloomy long-term diagnosis, this was merely a habit that distorted how Beth paid attention to herself and others.

Deeply religious, Beth prayed a lot. Whenever she found herself in difficult situations, rather than taking effective action, Beth would pray extra hard. In theory a beautiful habit, energetically this was a problem. As part of her healing session, I gave Beth a show-and-tell demonstration about how this well meant approach threw her chakra databanks out of proportion.

Next, we discussed the refrigerator analogy you will read in Chapter 14. Finally, Beth received some practical suggestions to re-balance her energy field long term.

A few hours later, Beth astounded the group (and me) by making this announcement:

"Hey, everyone. Remember how I used to have ADD? Maybe it wasn't ADD after all.

"Whatever it was, I don't seem to have it any more. I really feel like I'm here. You know, in the present. Paying attention."

The improvement was obvious to all.

Another client, Betty, had such a hard time at work, she wondered if maybe she was "meant to do something different."

When work is going badly, and a person feels well and truly stuck, it's not unusual to seek refuge in belief about "meant to be." The longing to find purpose can become an obsession. Because "obviously" there must be one missing piece of information that would magically end the chronic frustration.

After trying every which way to succeed at work, yet consistently failing to impress her demanding boss; after hating her job every day for years, it was understandable that Betty began to suspect that she was "supposed to" be doing something different.

Actually, there was no "supposed to." Betty had a good job and she was well prepared to excel at her place of employment. The problem was that all-important hidden factor of who-you-be.

During her first session with me, Betty received feedback about some easy-to-change things she could do immediately to improve the quality of some vital success-related chakra databanks.

No, Betty's chronic problems weren't the same as Beth's intense problems (or any other client's extreme problems). Betty needed direct feedback about how to change the ways that her aura was screaming to all the world — including her boss — "I hate having to work at this lousy job."

Even though Betty's problems were sabotaging her career, it wasn't too late to turn things around. Which she did. By making changes at the powerful level of who-you-be, results came quickly. A few weeks later, Betty sent an email to report on her progress:

- I have had *significantly noticeable* improvement in my ability to consistently focus and be productive at work.
- This is in contrast to the really painful malaise and lack of focus I've had for, dare I say, well over a year now at my job.
- I would be able to concentrate and get things done one day and then, the next two, back to malaise, depression, and inability to concentrate.
- Of course, I tried various strategies to get over this, including counseling, but nothing worked until your healing.

- And I have to admit that I wasn't expecting such big results from the healing; in other words, wasn't programming myself to expect this change.

FOR BETTER WHO-YOU-BE AT WORK

So consider that any work problems you have might be related to the fact that, oops, your aura is showing. Don't let that discourage you. Whatever amount of success you have achieved so far, it can only increase when you upgrade the balance within your auric field.

Even if this very third millennium concept is new to you, rest assured that I have spent decades researching it.

Not only have I helped clients with concepts, healings, and workarounds to improve that who-you-be factor. At my blog, and even longer for my personal edification, I have been profiling the rich and famous at the level of their energy fields.

Expressly for this book, I did hundreds of additional readings, focusing on secrets of making money.

Often I used the profiling protocol done on Bill Gates in our last chapter, The Top 10 Magnetize Money Databanks. Other times I used the following super-quick way to assess a person's three most important money making databanks.

The Magnetize Money Snapshot

Who has the chops to make really good money? Find out, with this Stage 3 Energetic Literacy version of a first impression.

Living today, we are offered way too many potential business providers, target customers, friends (on Facebook and off). So many resources and so little time! All of us have to become choosers, profilers, like farmers who sort wheat from chaff.

This snapshot is my favorite way to do that initial choosing for business relationships. If I need to know one thing right away, it isn't attitude or grooming, credentials or allies or a generalized hunch. I want to figure out which people have the standing, energetically, to deliver what they claim.

1. Root Chakra Databank: **Earning Money**
Our first chakra databank reveals a person's comfort with bringing in money, both personal level of interest, gifts of the soul
and, of course, the presence or absence of STUFF.

2. Solar Plexus Chakra Databank: **Handling Conflict at
Work**
Even in Disneyland, there can be conflicts. Any business en-
terprise has them. So it's vital to preview a person's default way
of dealing with conflict.

3. Third Eye Chakra Databank: **Connection to Spiritual
Source**
In my personal value system, more than anything, I care about
spiritual growth. If I have a choice to do business with somebody with a lovely spiritual connection versus someone who
lacks it, you just know which person I'll hire.
Merely talking the talk means nothing, however. Some people
who never mention religion or spirituality have Third Eye
Chakra databanks that are absolutely lovely. And vice versa.

In a famous commercial for Clairol, the tagline went, "Does she or
doesn't she? Only her hairdresser knows for sure."

During this exciting era of energetic literacy, we can always tell
about authentic spiritual connection, who has it for sure and what
luscious kind it might be. Does she or doesn't she, indeed!

AURIC MODELING

Why can energetic literacy help you so much to Magnetize Money?
Being able to learn the truth about business partners and customers —
anyone you choose, really — can give you quite a competitive advantage.

Being able to identify minor problems in yourself and fix them
before the small problems turn big... okay, that's not bad, either. But
for me, the single biggest advantage of energetic literacy for earning

money involves the concept I call **auric modeling.** Every time you make direct contact with another person, something important happens on the level of the human energy field. It's as though everybody gets naked and sits together in a bathtub, exchanging information.

- What does each person do at the level of chakra databanks?
- Which are the really distinctive gifts?
- Where is the STUFF? Whose is bigger?
- Who tells the truth? Who lies a lot? Whose business message is congruent?
- Evolution check: Attending "Earth School," each person has been engaged in a heroic spiritual journey. Which triumphs are been especially inspiring? (Because all of them show.)
- What messages do *you* send to your boss, colleagues, and customers?

Exchanging all that information and more, thanks to auric modeling, people share in amazing energetic conversations. We're receiving direct (and complete) downloads at depth about who-you-be.

How can this be, if you have never heard about it before?

Thank energetic literacy. With it, you can check out that auric modeling consciously whenever you choose. Otherwise, all the exchange of information happens between people just at the level of auras and subconsciously.

Meanwhile, apart from what you choose to do, the current truth about you always shows fully to others. Auric modeling is one of those aspects of life where, truly, there are no secrets. So doesn't it make sense to take your auric modeling into consideration from now on?

Maybe you are surprised to learn about this hidden energy exchange. Does it inspire you to evolve faster?

I hope so. It's a big deal, exploring the auric modeling of someone who has acted so courageously that heroic patterning shows all the way through to the level of that person's energy field.

That soul-stirring inspiration makes me think of a reverse domino effect, where one fallen- down domino rights itself, which reminds other dominoes in line how they can stand up straighter, too.

Auric modeling can accelerate the *rhythm* of change as well as the quality. As each of us evolves faster and faster, living at ever-higher vibrational frequencies, THIS faster pace becomes the norm for human evolution. Further, I believe that auric modeling has a special function at this time in human history. During an era where energetic literacy is becoming common, it's a big deal that "Oops, my aura is showing."

Maybe embarrassment is the prod that some of us need to stop making excuses and get our acts together. Millions of us have incarnated now, I believe, because we aim to make this a **wrap-up lifetime.** We aim to tie up loose ends from all our previous human incarnations. Yes, we may have come to earth this time as part of a large cohort of souls who are ready to become spiritually Enlightened at last.

When enough of us gain that freed-up consciousness, we may move the world as a whole into a higher state of evolution. Auric modeling can entrain us with a powerful momentum.

Whatever you believe about grand questions like these, let's focus on the aspect of auric modeling that relates to your growing rich. The business implications for you are extremely practical.

Energetically, you have the option of reading those with whom you do business. And it isn't about turning into a psychic but simply becoming fully literate in the third millennium.

Meanwhile, know that other people are busily reading you. That includes all your competitors and potential clients. They're checking out your auric modeling, whether subconsciously or consciously.

Of course, all of us can develop fabulous skills of energetic literacy. And once we have those skills, we can read as much as we want, whenever we want. What fascinating conversations go on beneath the texting, Twittering, shimmering surface of everyday life!

The research you will read in this Magnetize Money Program is definitely something you can duplicate on your own, using photos in our Photo Supplement online. Or you may prefer to just take a peek at each picture and form a quiet hunch any way you like.

Supplement my findings with yours. After all, you are the one who is on a treasure hunt for 10 Secrets for Success and Prosperity in the Third Millennium.

DARING TO RESEARCH LOA

Clients like Barry got me curious. So did friends like Hannah, introduced in our Dedication. What was going on with the auric modeling of people who practiced the Law of Attraction? To find out, I researched 50 grassroots LOA leaders.

First the good news. Everyone looked happy. And I mean really, really happy. Never have I seen happier-looking people, even Oscar winners who want to prolong their acceptance speeches for as long as possible. We're talking great smiles! Really attractive, confident-looking people, striving for success! People who could easily get second jobs selling toothpaste!

Seriously, I found much to admire in these prosperity leaders. Every single one showed a big, juicy Third Eye Chakra databank about Connection to Spiritual Source.

So if these prosperity experts gained nothing more from their involvement in New Thought than big spiritual development, they gained something magnificent.

Doesn't everyone alive have a fabulous spiritual connection? Everyone *could*. But that doesn't happen automatically.

In fact, it doesn't even happen to people who hold themselves out as spiritual authorities, as you can read in more detail in Chapter 9.

What, a firmly held belief won't necessarily perfect your aura?

THE LIMITATIONS OF MERE BELIEF

Beliefs, yum! You know as well as I do that beliefs can be lovely. They can be delicious. Beliefs can be so inspiring they make a person want to stand up and cheer.

Maybe at some point in your career you responded that way to beliefs about prosperity or success. You thought, fervently, "Yes, I believe." Ever since, you have felt greatly inspired whenever you remembered that particular message.

Lovely and beautiful, yes! However, life on earth doesn't move forward based on ideas alone. In the opinion of this energy healer, no single bit or byte of information will ever perfect someone's aura.

Information can change people when it serves as a springboard to action, initiative, or healing. Mere belief, however, creates only the illusion of perfection.

At best, we get a preview of how we might change, some day, maybe, at the level of our totally straight-talking auric modeling.

Energetic literacy separates illusion from reality. Here's one of the reasons why, an important ability you have that I call "**energetic hologram storage**."

How You Store Holograms of Energy

You have already read that each major chakra contains 50 databanks of information. Sub-chakras contain databanks as well. Also, you know that each chakra databank contains both gifts and, possibly, STUFF.

Around the time I made these discoveries — described in print for the first time in *Cut Cords of Attachment*, published in 2007 — I realized that information about gifts is stored in the portion of auras that corresponds to your Higher Self. By contrast, the information about STUFF is stored in the portion of auras that corresponds to your subconscious mind.

Once I made this connection, I began to expand the research I was doing with energetic literacy. I began telling clients (because it was true), "I can read any chakra databank you have had at any time in your life.

"Also, I can read any chakra databank in anyone you have ever known, however briefly, so long as you had a conversation face-to-face or voice-to-voice. This stored in your subconscious mind as an energetic hologram."

Because we store energetic holograms with full data about ourselves and others, very experienced aura readers can learn how to track the consequences of any major shift in your beliefs. That's a useful possibility to have available, isn't it? Anything that I can do reading chakra databanks, you can learn to do, too. So consider the implications.

For instance, what if you choose to research the time when you read your first success or prosperity book. Sure it had a huge impact. But what kind of impact? Working at success:

Did you become more capable, with stronger auric modeling? Or did you become more inspired but less effective? You might compare before and after that experience, reading databanks like your Root Chakra Databank about **Earning Money.**

> The version of "you" in that incident is encoded in a complete energetic hologram.
>
> With advanced energetic literacy, it is easy to research your Magnetize Money Databanks at any time in your life, present or past.

Let's say that, once upon a time, you were so inspired by prosperity teachings, it changed your life. Ever since, you have done your best to make your life "Everything LOA."

Whatever you believe strongly will cause you to say "Yes" to some choices in life, "No" to others. Over time, these actions create consequences aurically, as well as at every other level of reality. Consequences of any belief system can include your magnetizing wealth or having it slip through your chakras.

Yes, every belief that you live, day by day, will impact your aura. Beliefs make us more effective or less, one chakra databank at a time. Energetic literacy can reveal how your personal evolution has been affected, whether for good or ill. Just compare those databanks now to your previous version, stored as an energetic hologram.

A Big "Keep Out" Sign

What about you attracts money most strongly? It's the patterning at the level of your aura. Do you naturally project balance, strength, credibility? Authentic qualities like these do attract wealth.

Strength in your auric modeling switches on the Law of Attraction. Lack of presence, at any part of your aura, creates something akin to a "Keep Out" sign.

What have I learned about the consequences of emphasizing the Law of Attraction as taught by Abraham-Hicks or The Secret? Here's a preview.

The theory is beautiful. And LOA teachings can bring beautiful consequences at the level of auras. Except these consequences definitely don't bring wealth. In fact, they correlate rather strongly with the syndrome of spiritual addiction.

I know you have just read something blunt. Well, you're invited to be equally honest and direct with yourself, testing out what applies personally to you, in this chapter and what follows.

Consider the appeal of your favorite success and prosperity teachings. What effect have they had on you energetically?

Might you be carrying something to work that, consciously, you never meant to bring? Could your aura contain the equivalent of a "Keep Out" sign that limits your financial success?

As I go into detail about spiritual addiction and other energetic habits that sabotage success, am I just discussing other people who are interested in this Magnetize Money Program? Would you be an exception because other folks haven't been as clever as you at applying prosperity principles? Sure it's possible but, frankly, the odds aren't with you.

Shocked by the Truth

Once I gave a Magnetize Money Workshop in Tokyo, a one-evening bonsai version of the full Magnetize Money Program.

After explaining about auric modeling, I got to the concept of spiritual addiction. Every person in the crowd listened mega-politely, as only a Japanese audience can. Then I outlined what to do if spiritual addiction were present, encouraging audience members not to be dismayed if they had this syndrome.

The problem could be solved quite easily if they changed certain counter-productive habits (practical workarounds that later became expanded into Parts Two and Three of this Magnetize Money Program).

Usually Japanese students understand my material beautifully. Based on previous experience giving dozens of popular workshops in Japan, I figured that the audience was with me 100 percent. Except was I ever wrong!

At the end, I offered a brief aura-level check-up to each participant who wanted one. All my bright-eyed students lined up. Each received a Magnetize Money Snapshot, the quickest way to use energetic literacy to expose a possible spiritual addiction.

*We didn't have a representative sample of guy-and-gal-in-the-street here but, rather, a self-selected group of spiritual seekers. Not surprisingly, about 49 of the 55 people tested **did** show this type of imbalance. Some had it worse than others but nearly everyone's aura revealed a rather serious level of spiritual addiction.*

Because I had described the syndrome in lavish detail during my talk, I didn't expect that this news would come as a shock to anyone. Yet the audience turned nearly hysterical, one horrified student after another. For the rest of the evening, participants kept running over, mobbing me and the interpreter.

"What can I do about this?" they asked frantically.

I wondered, hadn't they listened to a thing I said? After all, I had literally spent hours describing what life was like with spiritual addiction, plus what to do if it happened to be a problem.

Apparently most of the audience members had ruled out the possibility that THEY, personally, could have such a problem. They considered themselves to be doing perfectly well. In fact, thanks to their diligent use of prosperity practices, they were attracting wealth beautifully and soon would grow rich.

Perhaps they had come to the workshop because they thought I would suggest one extra refinement of dream boarding that would clinch their deal with the Universe.

So very sure were they that "How could I, personally, have a problem?" that most of my audience members skipped over many practical solutions I had just offered them.

Meanwhile they listened with polite faces. Perhaps they were thinking how sad it was that a few weird people in the audience had this unusual problem of spiritual addiction, something that could never, ever happen to them.

Yes, to my knowledge, this is the first book to describe spiritual addiction related to auras. And, no, most sufferers have no clue.

Why should that be surprising? Do people in cults know their oh-so-special group is, technically, a cult? Do all problems here on earth carry obvious warning labels?

In our next chapter, I'm going to supply additional information about spiritual addiction; later chapters will show how to fix it, as well as plenty of success and prosperity secrets for *everyone,* whether you have this syndrome or not.

Before you turn to that next chapter, repeat after me, "STUFF can always, always, always be healed." If it turns out that you do have a spiritual addiction, it really is totally curable.

6. Could You Have a Spiritual Addiction?

Real and lasting change and success always emerge by first choosing your state and then setting a clear intention for what you want to achieve. They require something more, though, to actually yield results. That "something more" is inspired action.
— Deanna Davis, Ph.D., *The Law of Attraction in Action*

Jennifer kept trying to smile as she told me her story. She was a large woman, maybe 300 pounds. Her face looked sweet and vulnerable above all that weight, and often she would struggle to paste a pleasant smile on her face. As Jennifer spoke, however, her mouth gave her away, drooping down to reveal a sadness that she couldn't conceal.

"I just got back from a professional training. Imagine hundreds of people in a large ballroom. Sometimes we did exercises in breakout groups. I'd be talking in my small group and people would ignore everything I said.

"Hey, I'm used to that. Happens to anybody who is fat.

"But guess what else happened? And this was a new one, coming at me in this conference. People would walk over me.

"And I mean literally walk right over me, as though I wasn't in the room. These weren't drunks in some dark alley, mind you. We were all professionals, dressed like professionals, at a professional conference. Some of these people would start to physically walk right over me.

"I know it sounds crazy. But I don't know a better way to describe what they did. People wouldn't notice me until they literally bumped into me, and then they would look so surprised.

"Rose, how fat do I have to become before people stop treating me as if I'm invisible?"

The first step in Jennifer's healing was to explain the cause of her problem. She had an extreme case of spiritual addiction. At the level of auric modeling, what did Jennifer project? "Hey, folks, I'm not here, except for my Third Eye Chakra."

After removing a bit of STUFF from her aura, then introducing ideas like those you'll find in Parts Two and Three of this book, Jennifer's energy imbalance ended. She began to project a strong, authentic presence at all her chakra databanks.

- Energetically, somebody with a spiritual addiction looks like a lollipop: Long stick-like body topped by a great big colorful head.
- Somebody with a balanced aura is more like a wide cylinder: Big everywhere, and big in proportion.

You can be sure that strangers, at a business conference or elsewhere, will check out your aura. Because auric modeling happens to us all. It happens in the present whenever we meet someone face-to-face or voice-to-voice. Energetic hologram storage guarantees that we'll remember each person's auric modeling.

Yes, all this generally happens subconsciously. Nonetheless, that inner impression will strongly influence any kind of respect shown to you.

And, yes, there is something you can do about this. You can live in such a way that your aura shows power, the kind of power that attracts wealth.

In the third millennium, when more and more of us are developing energetic literacy, you can check at will to find out how well you are doing.

And here's something else you can do. We will do it right now. Staying right on the surface of perception, let's critique the energy implications of certain success and prosperity teachings.

Previously you read my observation that teachings like The Secret can cause spiritual addiction. Now let's find out why, exactly.

SECRET TEACHINGS + ENERGETIC LITERACY

To evaluate some of the main "Secret Teachings" about LOA, I'll use exact quotes from a Rhonda Byrne website (www.thesecret.tv). For convenience, I'll compare her perspective and mine as though we were having a dialogue, although obviously this is not a real-time conversation. I did NOT interview Rhonda Byrne directly.

RHONDA: Money is magnetic energy. You are a magnet attracting to you all things, via the signal you are emitting through your thoughts and feelings.

ROSE: You don't emit signals only with thoughts (at the Solar Plexus Chakra) and feelings (at the Heart Chakra). Here is a chakra-by-chakra summary of how every human being emits energy signals.

CHAKRA	TYPE OF ENERGY TRANSMISSION
1. Root	Projecting a first impression, interest in money, physical self-awareness, sense of objective reality.
2. Belly	Creativity, libido, sexual self-esteem.
3. Solar Plexus	Sharing power, handling conflict, self-confidence.
4. Heart	Emotional self-awareness, emotional intelligence, emotional giving and receiving.
5. Throat	Effectiveness at communication, verbal integrity, ability to ask for what you need and want.
6. Third Eye	Spiritual connection, psychic development, awareness of your human life.
* High Heart	Expressing your soul through your human personality, gusto for life, overall empowerment as a person.

RHONDA: Speak, act, and think from the mindset of being wealthy now. Eliminate thoughts and words of lack such as "I can't afford it," "It is too expensive."

ROSE: Part of this concept does relate to prosperity. It's a valid spiritual law that thoughts produce consequences. *Whatever you think about grows stronger in your life.*

So a case can be made for thinking and speaking in a way that accentuates the positive. But do you notice that Rhonda also advocates *acting* as if you are wealthy now? Would that mean spending on credit perhaps?

- Lying to oneself isn't good for any chakra databank.
- Living beyond one's means creates ugly new STUFF that gets deposited in all the major and minor chakras.
- Beyond that, Byrne's advice might encourage a person to stop using aura-level circuits about reality and substitute spiritual activity instead. This would be especially damaging to the first three major chakras.

Other chapters in Part One will explore the relationship between beliefs and a person's energetic relationship with reality. Even before then, doesn't common sense suggest that wealth would flow better for those who are relatively sane, people who do make good contact with objective reality?

RHONDA: Do not speak or think of the lack of money for a single second.

ROSE: Now there's another way to disconnect from reality. Financially, this one could be dangerous.

Let's make an analogy to feeling pain when your hand touches fire. That pain serves a purpose, right? Pain reminds you to take a very important physical action, moving your hand away.

Similarly, a realistic sense of financial limitation doesn't bring dire consequences for prosperity. It's smart to pay attention to life around you: Physical, touchable, external reality.

Knowing the limits of one's present budget, even having a budget in the first place, doesn't banish prosperity. Fiscal common sense is part of a Magnetize Money lifestyle.

Sadly, ignoring financial limitations is tantamount to ignoring physical pain. And, for those who ignore pain, life has a built-in safety mechanism at the level of auric energy.

When we blithely ignore feedback like sticker shock, chakra databanks about reality stop functioning well. Inadvertently, we increase the risk of attracting **major life shakeups.**

Jennifer's being walked over is actually a relatively mild example of major life shakeup related to being, energetically, out of synch with reality.

Major life shakeups can take the form of financial pain, physical pain, or relationship problems — problems so big they can't be ignored, despite a person's preference for a Rhonda-like form of denial.

"I won't think about that problem. I won't speak about that problem. If I just stay positive, my problem will go away."

In what world?

Eventually drama can escalate into a major life shakeup. A screaming landlord, an unfaithful lover, a car crash, a very real pain in the butt… problems like these demand attention. Now I don't want to sound as if pain from major life shakeups doesn't hurt. Nor do I mean to suggest that all drama in life comes from a single cause. It's just one cause of drama, when major energetic imbalance results from a distorted way of perceiving reality and then, due to LOA, major drama results.

In any case, dealing with major life shakeups can be therapeutic, snapping a person back into reality as nothing else can. When that happens, a person's aura often registers a far better balance than before.

Fortunate are those whose prosperity work has brought them major life shakeups… provided that they learned from the wake-up call.

RHONDA: Be grateful for the money you have. Appreciate it as you touch it.
ROSE: This concept, along with Byrne's other teachings, could be energetically dangerous if taken to extremes. Touching money, or anything else, is a physical action. It stimulates parts of your aura related to dealing with reality, especially all your chakra databanks from the ribcage down.

In effect, Rhonda is suggesting that people engage energetically from the chest up while handling money. At least, that's what it would mean to activate spiritual awareness as a substitute for making direct contact with the physical world.

Actually, money is made to feel like paper or coins, not to supply the spiritual equivalent of a full-body orgasm.

It's only common sense that Rhonda's strategy can divide attention, causing a person to become less present to reality. Adding the perspective of energetic literacy, I am tempted to scream, "Danger! Do you really want to weaken a person's root chakra functioning?"

Beyond that, like any professional consulting hypnotist, I can recognize Rhonda's advice as akin to a post-hypnotic suggestion. Money is a physical thing, yet Rhonda is encouraging people to play with it as though it is really a spiritual thing, and to make this inner substitution a matter of routine.

I'm tempted to stop typing this part of the chapter and shriek

RHONDA: Affirm to yourself every day that you have an abundance of money, and that it comes to you effortlessly.

ROSE: Walk around constantly affirming things? Oops, could that be another way to scramble your chakras?

Whenever people work really hard with affirmations, it certainly shows in their energy fields. Third-eye chakra databanks about belief system may grow bigger while all the other databanks — ones about making contact with reality — can shrink through lack of use.

Truth is, excessive dependence on affirmations may put a susceptible person at risk for disassociating from reality and developing a spiritual addiction.

RHONDA: Make lists of all the things you will buy with an abundance of money.

ROSE: Hey, I'm all for making lists. But how about making all the other lists, Rhonda?

Folks, unless you want spiritual addiction, you need to make other lists, such as:

- How I plan to earn all that money.
- The practical steps I will take in order to get a good job.
- My five-year plan for career development.
- My balanced budget.

RHONDA: Remind yourself everyday that you are a money magnet, and ask yourself often during the day, am I attracting money now or pushing it away with my thoughts?

ROSE: Now it's just getting silly. Say that Jeb is working as barista at Starbucks. (Not the most lucrative job, but at least he'll be paid more than staying home, practicing how he can push and pull things around with his thoughts.)

Picture it. Jeb is busily brewing that latte. Meanwhile a paying customer waits. Is it really going to improve Jeb's job performance, thinking about the push-pull of money on a spiritual level?

Sure, that spiritual exercise may add to the size of certain Third Eye Chakra databanks. Remember, "Whatever you think about grows stronger in your life."

If Jeb works really, really hard contemplating his push-pull, he just might spill some of that very hot liquid all over his hand. And get a wake-up call.

Starbucks doesn't pay baristas to do fancy tricks in their heads. It's all about the coffee. (Okay, the coffee, the excellent chocolate chip cookies, the cool mugs you can buy to give others, fascinating gifts, etc., etc.)

Life, itself, doesn't reward people for acting as if they were elsewhere, not at this lowly job but doing something oh-so-fabulously-glam.

And customers respond more favorably when coffee lands inside the cup.

RHONDA: Do whatever it takes to feel good. The emotions of joy and happiness are powerful money magnets. Be happy now!

ROSE: At this point, reading Rhonda Byrne's advice, I'm feeling emotions all right. "Happy" isn't one of them, though.

When I encounter a client like Jennifer, energetically so crippled that life feels like hell, that doesn't make me happy, either. What brings joy to my heart is helping people like her to wake up, stand up for herself, get back to normal, and make a good income.

Energetic literacy shows you naked truth. No brave smile, stuck on a lollipop face, is going to change that.

Now that we have considered the energy implications of Secret-type prosperity teachings, are you curious? If my analysis is correct, anyone who avidly follows these teachings as directed is likely to develop a spiritual addiction.

So what about the auras of the big household names in this field? Rhonda Byrne, Esther Hicks, and Jerry Hicks have amassed great wealth by teaching these principles. Did The Secret and Law of Attraction somehow work differently for them?

Because they really, truly believed, did something miraculous happen, a kind of quantum leap of consciousness?

Sure I became curious, motivating me to do detailed research with energetic literacy. Before I share the results with you, can you guess what I found?

7. Auras of Mega-Rich Prosperity Teachers

*If you're not running into major challenges, you're doing something easy, and prob-
ably not that valuable — and it's probably not going to make much money for you.
A big problem often signals a big opportunity. Be prepared to work long and hard
for it.*
— Donald Trump, *Never Give Up*

Donald Trump is the kind of rich guy people either love or love to hate.
Regardless, what's one great thing he has going for him? Energetically
the man is congruent.

When The Donald says outrageous things in his very public career, they match beautifully with his energy field.

So Trump doesn't merely advocate pushing through problems.
His track record backs it up. And that very same snowplow pushiness
appears unapologetically in his relevant chakra databanks.

Want more specifics? Below is my research on seven scintillating
chakra databanks, based on reading Trump's cover shot for Newsweek
magazine in 2004. In honor of Trump, I chose a selection of chakra
databanks for assessing personal ego.

By this time, Trump had become so famous for his role on the
reality TV show "The Apprentice," the magazine cover didn't even bother
to name him. Newsweek's caption simply read, "You're fired."

Donald Trump: Ego Assessment Profile

1. Root Chakra Databank: ***Presence in the Room***
90 miles. Strong sense of self, slightly detached and amused at
himself. Yet seriously committed to appearing larger than life.

2. Root Chakra Databank: *Earning Money*

90 miles. Feeling as though he possesses a version of the Midas Touch. Trump's power of command over people and money can practically hypnotize them. Because he comes on so strong, and never flinches, "weak people" usually go along with his demands.

3. Belly Chakra Databank: *Sexual Self-Confidence*

50 miles. Huge libido and a sense of showmanship about his sex life. Very confident that he is a lifelong thrill for any woman he favors. Sexual attention from Trump is almost like being kissed by a god, back in the days of Zeus. (He thinks.)

4. Solar Plexus Chakra Databank: *Personal Self-Confidence*

90 miles. "I am a law unto myself. By coming on strong and having complete faith in my ability to get what I want, usually I get it."

5. Solar Plexus Chakra Databank: *Handling Conflict at Work*

90 miles. Enjoys exerting his authority. Especially likes telling people how things are going to be, and that's that. Playing this role makes Donald Trump feel good about himself as a "real man."

6. Throat Chakra Databank: *Asking for What I Want (At Work)*

90 miles. "Absolutely sure that I will get what I request. My word is a law unto itself."

7. Third Eye Chakra Databank: *Connection to Spiritual Source*

10 feet. In his relationship with Spiritual Source, this executive feels like Mommy's loveable favorite. Donald takes his secure position for granted. Inspiration will always be there when he needs it.

Because this spiritual connection is so effortless, Donald Trump may find it hard to understand why anyone would worry about forging a relationship with the Divine. To him, life means automatically having a lovely, juicy spiritual connection.

That auric modeling is marvelously consistent with Trump's public persona, isn't it?

Energetic literacy makes it possible to investigate in depth the aura-level consequences of following any success system. Trump's books and public appearances advocate action, material focus, caring about results, and stubbornness. His aura matches up perfectly.

Only, hold on. Isn't *material prosperity* also supposed to be the goal of Abraham-Hicks and The Secret? Esther and Jerry Hicks, Rhonda Byrne — clearly, they have become rich encouraging people to do something completely different.

When LOA practitioners like my friend Hannah don't Magnetize Money, what's their problem? Are they just not doing a good enough job of following the examples set by their world-renowned teachers?

Let's research auras belonging to the biggest names in LOA, starting with Rhonda Byrne and Esther Hicks. From their teachings, you'd expect a passionate commitment to spiritual life, right?

If my discoveries shock you, I can only recommend that you apply your own skill at energetic literacy. Then you can read the truth directly and shock yourself.

RHONDA BYRNE

The Australian-born prosperity teacher has done more than all right. Her chakra databanks certainly help explain that huge success. (See the photo used for this profile at the "Photo Supplement" online.)

Rhonda Byrne: Magnetize Money Profile

1. Root Chakra Databank: **Earning Money**
50 miles. Intense determination and self-reliance abound.
This huge drive to succeed would be something that Byrne takes for granted.

2. Root Chakra Databank: **Saving Money**
50 miles. "Having money matters so much to me."
Clearly, Rhonda *does* have the passion for having wealth which features so strongly in The Secret.

3. Root Chakra Databank: **Personality at Work**
20 feet. Confidence is huge, tinged with a sense of destiny.

The quality in Rhonda's energy field is both demanding and focused, suggesting a strong sense of how things must be done.

4. Root Chakra Databank: *Personality PROJECTED at Work*
80 feet or more, enough charisma to fill any theater, expanding as needed. Loving. Compassionate. Sexually exciting. Having a super-wonderful life.

You can appreciate how effective a presence like this would be for inspiring Rhonda's audience.

5. Solar Plexus Chakra Databank: *Self-Confidence at Work*
5 miles. Extreme self-confidence is evident. "I know exactly what I want and how to get it."

6. Solar Plexus Chakra Databank: *Handling Conflict at Work*
40 feet. So many women shy away from using their power. But no problem for Ms. Byrne. She may even welcome conflict. Certainly, she expects to win; intimidation may often be used in her approach to solving problems in the workplace.

Concentrated, forceful energy in this chakra databank can be mobilized quickly to take decisive action.

7. Heart Chakra Databank: *Emotional Intelligence at Work*
7 inches. "I can always tell who's on my side and who isn't."

For most people, practical assessments about power dynamics with others come through databanks at the solar plexus chakra. But my research suggests that various types of solar plexus functioning have taken over many of Rhonda Byrne's heart chakra databanks.

A technical term for this is "energetic sub-routine." (In Chapter 14, we'll discuss this important topic more thoroughly.)

8. Throat Chakra Databank: *Communication at Work*
Ask any doctor. The organ positions studied in medical school are approximations, not precise diagrams for the position of each person's organs. Energetic literacy often reveals something similar, plenty of room for individual variation.

For Rhonda, two distinct patterns show within this throat chakra databank:

- *Communication with the Public*
50 feet or more, large enough to fill any theater.
Charm and apparent effortlessness are on offer. Rhonda conveys an endearing quality of intimacy, as if she is good friends with every single member of the audience. She also has an uncanny ability to sense a person's greatest need, or vulnerability, and speak to it.

- *Communication with Work Associates*
17 inches. Rhonda will be pleasant and gracious, provided that her instructions are followed. Otherwise, communication circuits can turn icy. And fast.

*9. Third Eye Chakra Databank: **Awareness of Her Human Life***
5 miles. Rhonda is exquisitely aware of the material goals that a person might visualize when using The Secret. For instance, this databank shows marvelous discernment about material life, like the feel of clothing on her body and how that relates to cost and prestige.
No wonder Byrne can be so convincing as an advocate of visualizing material success!

*10. Third Eye Chakra Databank: **Connection to Spiritual Source***
4 inches. "This aspect of life has been handled. Now it's time to do my part and go claim ever more success."

Rhonda Byrne certainly doesn't suffer from spiritual addiction. Instead she focuses, hard, on material success. No wonder she's so successful when she tries to Magnetize Money.

For me, this research into Byrne's aura turns The Secret inside out. Her words makes sense in a new way. They come from someone who is extremely focused on fulfilling material desires. Aurically, that's exactly what she has the habit of doing.

When Byrne advocates paying attention to attracting money, auric modeling shows that she does this based on an ultra-strong Root Chakra connection.

What doesn't Byrne do?

Certainly she doesn't use spiritual circuits at the Third Eye Chakra to visualize wealth.

Yet her followers wind up doing the opposite. Oops.

Byrne may not be the first spiritual expert to talk a great deal about something she doesn't exactly experience. Like any other human being, she can confuse over-using one part of her auric energies with something entirely different.

Without full energetic literacy, how could Byrne tell if "Spiritual Connection at the Third Eye Chakra" is dwarfed by personal ambition flavored by spiritual thoughts or that, really, spiritual connection energies might be more directly related to a very active Solar Plexus Chakra and even an energetic sub-routine?

Byrne has written, "Feeling happy now is the fastest way to bring money into your life."

Wouldn't you expect to find an aura that radiates happiness? Yet her Heart Chakra shows very little emotion… and, at the time of her publicity photo, even less happiness. Instead, Rhonda Byrne's success would appear to result from extreme, and extremely well focused, ambition.

Any set of prosperity or success teachings comes to life for one human being at a time. It seems clear that, for Rhonda Byrne, "feeling happy" relates more to her Root Chakra databanks about making and keeping money. She can't help it if people who follow her advice don't have her same energetic sub-routine. I'm guessing that the thought has never once crossed her mind.

Maybe Esther Hicks does something different aurically, when it comes to happiness.

What happens within her, inspired by a somewhat different version of LOA principles? Let's investigate.

ESTHER HICKS

Esther's warm, contagious smile helps to explain her huge popularity. Currently, she is America's most famous trance channeler, as well as the originator of teachings about Laws of Attraction in the very early third millennium.

From the perspective of energetic literacy, what does a **channeler** do? She or he allows an astral-level entity to take over the mind-body-spirit system, becoming a mouthpiece for an entity's message. Esther

Hicks is the real deal, someone whose aura changes drastically because she trusts the process so completely.

So it's a complex job to investigate this channeler's aura compared to what sometimes moves through it. Two separate readings are needed, really.

In this chapter, I'll investigate Ms. Hicks' chakra databanks while she is posing for a publicity photo along with her husband. Esther is being herself, "Esther Hicks not channeling." (See the photo used for this profile at the "Photo Supplement" online.)

In a future chapter, I will read Esther's aura while channeling Abraham. Really, that will mean doing a reading on Abraham, since he takes her over completely.

Usually energetic literacy explores one person at a time, where a physical body is part of that person's auric modeling. With channeling, however, the channeler's body becomes a temporary vehicle for one or more other beings to live, speak, teach, and otherwise enjoy human life.

In a way, researching this channeler is like the sessions I do with pregnant women:

- First I'll focus on one chakra databank, describing the mother-to-be.
- Then I have the option of shifting attention to the soul of the child and reading that very different individual's presence at that same chakra databank.

Pregnant women glow because of an extra soul housed within them, someone extra looking out through the mother's eyes. When you have Stage 3 Energetic Literacy, it's not rocket science, reading mother and child separately. Nor is it hard to distinguish the aura of a channeler like Esther from any entity, or entities, she channels.

Esther Hicks: Magnetize Money Profile

1. Root Chakra Databank: **Earning Money**
2 inches. Esther positively glows with faith and surrender to Abraham, her group of teachers from The Other Side. This channeler has totally given up trying to earn anything on her own. Instead, she serenely trusts that God, or Abraham, will provide for her every need.

2. Root Chakra Databank: **Saving Money**

½ inch. The quality emanating from Esther Hicks' aura is absolutely saintly. "Why would I ever worry about saving money?" She trusts Abraham to provide for her every need.

3. Root Chakra Databank: **Personality at Work**

1 inch. Extreme humility here is so inspiring — such beautiful auric modeling! Most human beings care a great deal about being respected by others, being right if there's an argument, etc.

Not Esther. She approaches an ego-less state, adoring her help from The Other Side in the way that one finds in certain monks and nuns. Her aura is more that of a renunciate than a householder.

4. Root Chakra Databank: **Personality PROJECTED at Work**

1 inch. Esther projects nothing. She lives serenely in her celestial connection.

Resourceful Reader, you may be starting to wonder, "What does this lovely aura have to do with *any* principles at all in the Law of Attraction?"

5. Solar Plexus Chakra Databank: **Self-Confidence at Work**

½ inch. How can Esther remain so serenely confident? You guessed it. She lets go and allows herself to be provided for, a state of surrender that many mystics have described.

6. Solar Plexus Chakra Databank: **Handling Conflict at Work**

1/8 inch. Clearly, Esther doesn't do conflict, period. She'll withdraw from any argument and trust in Abraham to take care of her. By surrendering so completely, the famous channeler doesn't need to waste energy on resisting a thing.

Esther prefers to simply attract her good. As this chakra databank suggests, if she were to lose an argument, the famous channeler wouldn't care anyway.

It's fascinating to read the enveloping sense of protection lodged here and elsewhere throughout her aura.

Of course, one reason serenity works so well for Esther is that, as other chakra databanks suggest, she doesn't care about anything but her celestial connection. Gone are cares about being respected by people, earning money, etc. Hers is the serenity of a renunciate.

*7. Heart Chakra Databank: **Emotional Intelligence at Work***
1 inch. Ms. Hicks doesn't bother with human emotions. Why should they interest her? Because of her ever-present connection to Abraham — even when not actively channeling — Esther feels a perpetual delight.

*8. Throat Chakra Databank: **Communication at Work***
1/8 inch. No special effort is needed for communication, not when Abraham can speak through her.

Imagine feeling no struggle, ever. Esther Hicks knows she will always say the right thing because the words come directly from Abraham.

*9. Third Eye Chakra Databank: **Awareness of Her Human Life***
1/8 inch. "Perfect spiritual surrender" is one name for this way to live. Of course, "Not paying attention" is another.

*10. Third Eye Chakra Databank: **Connection to Spiritual Source***
Out to the moon. Abraham fills Esther's consciousness. This is the one big, huge chakra databank in all of Esther Hicks' aura. (Okay, to be precise, she does have other huge Third Eye Chakra databanks, such as her databank about "Connection to the Psychic Realm.")

Note that the quality here has nothing to do with Esther Hicks as a human personality. It's like having a heart transplant, where the organ donor's vibration lives in that part of the patient's body.

Esther connects magnificently to her Higher Power. It's her whole life. However, it's not exactly HER life.

If you're looking for a saint, I would definitely nominate Esther Hicks. Her chakra databanks are exactly what you might expect to find in a nun or mystic of any faith. (And I write this as someone who has spent decades doing detailed research on the auras belonging to great renunciates like Mother Teresa, Sai Baba, and the Dalai Lama.)

Much as monks and nuns inspire us, however, they don't generally come to mind as role models for learning how to get rich. Nuns take a vow of poverty, not prosperity.

So I can't avoid mentioning the aurically obvious. Esther Hicks may often talk about money but personally she couldn't care less.

Frankly, she couldn't show a higher degree of spiritual addiction.

Does that explain her success, however? Does it *cause* her success? If not, what does?

Investigating further, it may help to consider the auras of her very significant others, the beings she channels, a.k.a. Abraham, and also her husband, Jerry.

But first, let's bring a similar level of detail to the who-you-be *caused* by LOA. Let's use energetic literacy to explore some of Esther and Rhonda's devoted followers.

Every prosperity or success teaching produces consequences that show at the level of auras. What will we find in grassroots LOA teachers who volunteer to help others grow rich?

8. LOA's
Energetic Consequences

When you are connected to healthy resources, and there are fewer disruptions in your system, then the energy flow can move effortlessly through you.
— Suzanne Scurlock-Durana, *Full Body Presence*

Every belief system produces consequences. Each person is a fluid system energetically, physically, mentally, emotionally, financially. So our beliefs and spiritual practices can move us in different directions, affecting the size and quality of every chakra databank.

Will those results necessarily match up with the goals of our cherished ideals? Alas, there are no guarantees. At least, we can do a full-scale reality check. What does a prosperity system like The Secret really accomplish at the level of personal energy flow?

I decided to "interview" 50 grassroots LOA teachers. Where did I find them? Each LOA practitioner ran a group at www.meetup.com. Some were also certified coaches or had published books on how to be successful with LOA. I call them all "grassroots teachers" because they were hosting free groups advertised on the Internet.

To help ensure the accuracy of my research, I read group leaders only. For many LOA meetup groups, extra photos of group members were available. However, I didn't consider it fair to read them; meetup members might have a relatively casual involvement. Naturally, I used Stage 3 Energetic Literacy for this research.

What if all I had done was to "feel the energy" of these 50 role models for prosperity? Happy people, adorned with large smiles, send off a fine vibe. So Energetic Literacy Stage 1 is a good beginning but not sophisticated enough to uncover problems.

There's more to anyone than a mood. A convincing smile could be totally sincere, yet it could cover a cesspool of conflicting emotions.

Reading with Stage 1 Energetic Literacy, **big conflict** could seem like **"big energy,"** indistinguishable from huge spiritual inspiration.

So let's bring out a truly third millennium resource to find out the who-you-be aspect of each LOA teacher. Bring on the Magnetize Money Snapshot. Here's why it matters for this particular research project.

Relating Magnetize Money Snapshots to LOA Teachings

1. Root Chakra Databank: Earning Money

Beliefs about Law of Attraction aren't just meant to inspire. They're meant to make a person rich.

Do those beliefs automatically translate into effectiveness in the part of an aura where effectiveness is needed? Root chakra databanks reveal best how a person makes contact with financial reality.

2. Solar Plexus Chakra Databank: Handling Conflict at Work

The Secret doesn't offer a lot of specifics for dealing with conflict. For instance, Rhonda Byrne advises readers that, "The Creative Process helps you create what you want in three simple steps: ask, believe, and receive."

No calls for Judge Judy there! But what if some problems develop along the path of receiving? This databank can reveal a vital requirement for real-life success.

3. Third Eye Chakra Databank: Connection to Spiritual Source

LOA is all about spiritual connection. You won't find a lot of atheists sitting around listening to channeled wisdom from Abraham. I was curious whether or not LOA volunteers merely read these teachings like a kind of study guide. Or, instead, were they striving for a personal connection? Either choice would show in this Third Eye Chakra databank.

What did I find with this research instrument? No two of my research profiles were alike... except that 50 out of 50 showed an interest in psychic or spiritual awareness so extreme, it threw the rest of that person's energy field completely off balance.

For instance, consider the LOA teacher I'll call "Dave."

Dave: Magnetize Money Snapshot

1. Root Chakra Databank: **Earning Money**
5 feet. Sure he's an expert. "I have this money thing handled."

2. Solar Plexus Chakra Databank: **Handling Conflict at Work**
4 feet. Defensive, pushy way of handling conflict.

3. Third Eye Chakra Databank: **Connection to Spiritual Source**
90 miles. Seeking the outer edge of spiritual experience, fascinated by exploring the limits of consciousness.

Some LOA teachers were truly capable people, although not balanced energetically. I was moved by this reading of Doris.

Doris: Magnetize Money Snapshot

1. Root Chakra Databank: **Earning Money**
7 feet. Very capable and experienced as a businesswoman.

2. Solar Plexus Chakra Databank: **Handling Conflict at Work**
7 feet. Proven strength for dealing with problems effectively.

3. Third Eye Chakra Databank: **Connection to Spiritual Source**
To the sky. Formerly a very religious Christian, she is branching out into the experience of direct, free contact with Spiritual Source.

Unfortunately, many other LOA teachers were severely unrealistic. Frankly I wouldn't have trusted them to organize a kid's birthday party.

Daisy, whose photo suggests that she is in her early 30s, has an expression that exudes complete confidence in her ability to grow rich. Reading her with Stage 1 Energetic Literacy, Daisy would seem like a wonderful success story for LOA. But check out the Stage 3 truth about her who-you-be.

Daisy: Magnetize Money Snapshot

1. Root Chakra Databank: **Earning Money**
6 inches. "I have things on earth all figured out. They're simple."

2. Solar Plexus Chakra Databank: **Handling Conflict at Work**
3 inches. "The trick is to disengage, then flow and concentrate on God. This will get you whatever you want."

3. Third Eye Chakra Databank: **Connection to Spiritual Source**
Out to the stars. "I long for heaven."

One big problem with The Secret and related systems is that they can cover up problems rather than solving them. With auric modeling, STUFF shows anyway, blockages at a deeper level of life than beliefs.

Even if STUFF is never discussed in LOA, STUFF will block results. Auras always reveal the truth about what is happening, whether or not the blocked person consciously knows that problems exist.

Unless someone comes to The Secret STUFF-free, that very STUFF will contradict the big, happy smile that supposedly fixes all problems.

In "The Secret," Rhonda Byrne advises readers, "Feeling happy now is the fastest way to bring money into your life."

Philosophically a person might find this concept believable, or at least mighty attractive. Unfortunately, here's a typical example of this belief in action, profiling devoted grassroots teacher Denise.

Denise: Magnetize Money Snapshot

1. Root Chakra Databank: **Earning Money**
4 inches. Escapes from problems with reality and money by focusing hard on her favorite beliefs.

2. Solar Plexus Chakra Databank: **Handling Conflict at Work**
5 inches. Blames others for her problems, sometimes people in her present and sometimes people in her past

*3. Third Eye Chakra Databank: **Connection to Spiritual Source***
Out to the moon. Denise would like to be a missionary for this kind of experience, it is so sweet.

Or consider the STUFF in Derek, who is puppy sweet and totally trusts LOA to fix his life.

Derek: Magnetize Money Snapshot

*1. Root Chakra Databank: **Earning Money***
12 inches. Although a hardworking guy, he feels inadequate. Derek tries so hard to "be a man."

*2. Solar Plexus Chakra Databank: **Handling Conflict at Work***
11 inches. Huge amounts of STUFF related to using power are clustered around "Never show weakness" and "Be a man."

*3. Third Eye Chakra Databank: **Connection to Spiritual Source***
Out to the stars. Deeply devotional, this is a loving man with an uncommonly pure heart. Whatever his sexual orientation, Derek is loaded with feminine energy. He finds living as a man, here on earth, really difficult.

Rhonda Byrne hammers away at the idea that "The only thing you need do is *feel good now*." Feeling good does generate positive energy. But it doesn't clean up STUFF in the auric field. If my research is correct, Derek and Denise have become way more stuck than they know.

SERIOUS BELIEF, REAL RESULTS

Sure, I found the occasional slight phony among LOA leaders, but only one scammer. To their credit, nearly all these leaders were extremely serious about practicing what they preached.

Okay, what do I mean by "scammer"? You've gotta laugh over the next guy I'm going to read, Donald. (At least you can afford to laugh if you're also able to protect yourself by using full energetic literacy.)

Donald: Magnetize Money Snapshot

1. Root Chakra Databank: **Earning Money**
9 inches. Positive he is destined for wealth

2. Solar Plexus Chakra Databank: **Handling Conflict at Work**
40 feet. Loves to use his power to control people and outcomes.

3. Third Eye Chakra Databank: **Connection to Spiritual Source**
Out to the stars. Seeks a spiritual connection so he can have extra power over people. Donald does have a large spiritual connection, only it is distorted by a personality overlay, a scammer's agenda:
Skilled at manipulating people, Donald seeks to show others that he goes extra-deep spiritually, wanting to be treated like a guru.

Before developing full literacy, it's easy to fall for liars and power freaks. At Stage 1 Energetic Literacy, you might be bowled over by Donald's strong energy presence, his confidence. Energetic literacy reveals the details that inquiring minds really want to know.

BENEFITS FROM LOA PRACTICES

Prosperity practices can help people to evolve spiritually and materially. To balance my research into LOA consequences, it's only fair to discuss four very appealing and potentially important benefits from Law of Attraction teachings.

1. TAKING PERSONAL RESPONSIBILITY

LOA provides an alternative to victimology, that warm-fuzzy "Let's feel sorry for all the poor victims" which infuses so much popular culture, such as TV network news in America.

The Law of Attraction encourages everyone to take personal responsibility for personal finances. Rhonda Byrne has written, "The only reason any person does not have enough money is because they are *blocking* money from coming to them with their thoughts."

Personally, I couldn't disagree more. How could any socially responsible person truly believe that bad thoughts are the "only" reason for poverty? Why vote, if you believe this? Why take any action in objective reality to help other human beings?

But, at least, Byrne does advocate taking personal responsibility. And she hasn't written, "The only reason you don't have enough money is that other people are blocking your money, so you ought to kill them."

2. Vigorous Striving

LOA advocates making a strong connection to Spiritual Source, rather than wishing or praying in a vague manner. Excellent! And speaking of being proactive...

3. Choosing Real-Life Goals

From 1980-2000, I noticed a strong trend of fatalism growing within the New Age Community. More and more people were asking for psychic guidance in a sweet, trusting way that was also quite passive.

"I'll have my heart's desire... if it is meant to be," was the attitude. Also popular: "Spirit knows what I should be doing with my life."

Big applause to all LOA teachings that have encouraged spiritual seekers to choose what they want and take action to get it! Specific goals are an important part of our Magnetize Money Program, too.

4. A Juicy, Big Connection at a Higher Vibration

Finally, let's not discount the spiritual growth that millions have gained through Law of Attraction.

Overall, I found much to admire in the auric modeling of grassroots prosperity leaders. Of the 50 I researched, every single one showed a big, juicy Third Eye Chakra databank about **Connection to Spiritual Source.**

Doesn't everyone on earth have a fabulous spiritual connection?

We could. Unlike Donald Trump, however, most of us aren't simply born that way, with a lifelong spiritual talent that requires no special maintenance. Energetic literacy can help us to distinguish:

- Those who are *born* spiritually connected.
- Those who *achieve* spiritual connection.
- Those who *wish* they could have spiritual connection thrust upon them.
- And plenty of people who really *don't care* whether or not they're connected spiritually — and aren't (regardless of whatever they may say in public).

Hey, there are worse things than the consequences of using The Secret or other LOA teachers. Only I think it's important to call the resulting syndrome by its appropriate name....

SPIRITUAL ADDICTION

Addiction, now that's pretty strong language! But you know what that term means by now. So consider what you already know about addictions in general.

Perhaps you, personally, have never attended a meeting of Alcoholics Anonymous. Nor have you ever known a crack addict. Surely, though, you have absorbed some 12-step concepts through popular culture. So think about it:

- People who go through an addiction find it irresistible.
- Often, an addict is the last one to know there is any problem at all because that addictive substance or activity "feels so good."
- Addictions tend to grow, causing the person to become more and more unbalanced.
- Addictions can keep a person from being fully effective at work.
- Also, addictions can ruin personal relationships.
- Sometimes an addict may have to hit bottom before recovery can start.
- However, any addict can choose to recover *before* hitting bottom.

What makes a spiritual addiction especially tricky? Using surface awareness, it can be easily confused with something very desirable, the kind of spiritual expansion called "Enlightenment."

9. Spiritual Addiction Versus Enlightenment

The practice of being with the way things are calls upon us to distinguish between our assumptions, our feelings, and the facts – that is, what has happened or what is happening. These are not easy distinctions to make considering the ongoing inventive power of perception.
— Rosamund Stone Zander & Benjamin Zander, *The Art of Possibility*

Prosperity principles have been taught long before Abraham-Hicks and The Secret. They have been taught in the name of religion.

Every major religion instructs its worshippers in how to deal with money. Prosperity teachings are even central to relatively new religions, like Unity and Science of Mind. Mystical teachings, meditation practices, and other self-actualization practices are part of every spiritually-oriented belief system.

Religions that depend more on commitment and ritual also provide prosperity teachings. Televangelists, starting with Oral Roberts, have explained how "Seed Money" given to a religious organization can jump-start your wealth.

Even those who belong to what I call "disorganized religion" often follow prosperity teachings.

So chances are that, as part of your search to Magnetize Money, you have been exposed to spiritual and religious ideals. What results do they produce, as evaluated with today's literacy skills?

SPIRITUAL IDEALS + ENERGETIC LITERACY

Can we use today's energetic literacy to evaluate the results of yesterday's spiritual ideals? Sure, and who wouldn't be curious! Investigating at the level of energetic who-you-be can help you to evaluate your own history with success and prosperity teachings. Or you might simply want to make more sense of an Esther Hicks.

Yes, in a previous chapter I have described her as having an extreme form of spiritual addiction. I have also called her "saintly." Does that combination make her spiritually Enlightened?

Throughout recorded history, spiritual writing has documented Enlightenment. Through different paths and religions, complete surrender to the Divine has been extolled as the ultimate goal of life. Without energetic literacy, one might hear descriptions of a life like Esther's and think, "Surely this must be Enlightenment."

But full energetic literacy adds a degree of precision not available with beginner perceptions of energy, where one simply feels "a lot of energy" and assumes all varieties to be interchangeable.

Delving into chakra databanks, the nature of Esther Hicks' serenity can be described with more discernment. She has been having a beautiful life on a path of willing surrender to an astral being.

Anyone could have such a life, if desired. But anyone could also aim for a life of Enlightenment… or completely different goals, as we'll discuss further in Chapter 10.

Being present to what *is,* in contrast to what a person *wishes to be* — how are we to tell the difference? Energetic literacy helps us explore that who-you-be aspect, which can distinguish true spiritual Enlightenment from states that might seem similar but really are significantly different.

This aura profiler's hobby is collecting inspiring people to read. Sometimes I blog about them at "Deeper Perception Made Practical," www.rose-rosetree.com/blog. There I even keep an "Enlightenment Life List," akin to a bird watcher's life list. So far, this includes just 63 people whose energy fields have convinced me they have attained full-blown spiritual Enlightenment.

- Some are very famous spiritual authorities (e.g., Eckhart Tolle and Sai Baba).
- Some are well known performers (e.g., Meryl Streep and, as of 2010, George Clooney).
- Some are not the least bit famous (like the American transplant in a Hindu ashram who sent me her photo for an aura profiling report).

FIGURE 6. OVER-EMPHASIZING ONE CHAKRA

- Some are among the wealthiest men in the world (as you'll read later).
- That Enlightenment Life List does not include me yet, unfortunately. In case you're wondering, energetic literacy doesn't create Enlightenment any more than regular word-type literacy does.

Perspective on Enlightenment

Every spiritual path and religion exists for a reason. People who "fit in" at a particular house of worship have similar levels of consciousness and auric patterns.

Let's bring back Chakra Guy Billy to illustrate. If he had a spiritual addiction, Billy might show a pattern like the one in Figure 6.

In other words, most of his Third Eye Chakra databanks are huge. The exceptions would be those Third Eye Chakra databanks about recognizing his human life. They would be like his other chakra databanks: Puny. Poor guy! (Including literally!) With a spiritual addiction, aurically Billy looks like a lollipop.

FIGURE 7. SPIRITUAL ADDICTION

By contrast, here is the equivalent drawing for someone who is spiritually Enlightened. Lucky Billy, I'll get him to illustrate again. Only fair since eventually Billy can move out all STUFF, get his aura nicely balanced, and live in bliss.

Not only is this possible. Becoming fully Enlightened — for Billy, for you, for me — some day we might magnetize That along with more money.

FIGURE 8. ENLIGHTENMENT

EXAMPLE OF A REAL-LIFE ENLIGHTENED GUY

I think it's important to view the gold standard. Each of us can potentially become vibrantly alive, STUFF-free.

Energetically, what would that look like? Meet a representative from your own future, an aura with full spiritual Enlightenment.

Jeffrey Chappell is a concert pianist and composer. Also, he is the author of *Answers from Silence,* with a blog and the website www.answersfromsilence.com. (Disclaimer: Jeffery has been a good friend of mine for the past 20 years.) See the photo used for this profile at the "Photo Supplement" online.

Jeffrey Chappell: Magnetize Money Profile

1. Root Chakra Databank: *Earning Money.*
Out to the stars, merging with spiritual light. Joyful non-attachment to material life makes money a stress-free aspect of life. Jeffrey delights in the process of giving out into the world and, in return, receiving money. It's a delightful game, with a feeling of winning available to him in each eternal moment.

2. Root Chakra Databank: *Saving Money.*
Out to the stars. It's enough to make you giggle. Jeffrey feels so absolutely secure in life. His every need is met instantly. Saving and having, at the level of enormous material abundance — none of this requires the least bit of effort.

3. Root Chakra Databank: *Personality at Work*
Out to the stars. The distinctively quirky, playful, smart, sexy presence of Jeffrey is fully alive. He's that way everywhere throughout his chakra databanks. Only one nuance is different for this particular databank: He would love to be of service to everybody he encounters through work.

4. Root Chakra Databank: *Personality PROJECTED at Work*
Out to the stars. The jazz composer projects to his audiences exactly the same personality as usual just being himself. He performs in a human kind of eternity.

5. Solar Plexus Chakra Databank: *Self-Confidence at Work*
Out to the stars. It's exciting, playing out a human lifetime while so connected with the Divine. Jeffrey loves the adventure. Every moment of his life happens during a moment of timeless joy.

Having his human ego is no more difficult than owning hands or feet. There's neither worry nor conflict, only delight.

6. Solar Plexus Chakra Databank: *Handling Conflict at Work*

Out to the stars. Listening to others, listening in the deepest way possible, is Jeffrey's instinctive reaction. No fear of conflict is present within this chakra databank, only a bit of excitement about the creative potential for conflict resolution.

7. Heart Chakra Databank: *Emotional Intelligence at Work*

Out to the stars. The power of love in this databank could knock you over... if you felt its full extent and didn't feel worthy.

Yet why would anyone not feel worthy to receive that signature combination of perceptiveness and caring?

8. Throat Chakra Databank: *Communication at Work.*

Out to the stars. Jeffrey's talent as a performer shows clearly here. Playing music, he transforms the audience, shaking everyone up with a childlike joy. All the music (and energy exchange) feels improvised, even if a particular piece has been practiced for hours.

9. Third Eye Chakra Databank: *Awareness of His Human Life*

Out to the stars. Does this Enlightened man care much about his human life? He sure does. Day-to-day living for Jeffrey means savoring the uniqueness of his personal way of living, the ever-changing variety of his relationships.

Picture a core of golden light, filled with a serene kind of bliss. Wrapped around that core are ornaments, like colored wires, with glorious patterns of decoration. That's how Chappell lives in the moment, gloriously, himself.

10. Third Eye Chakra Databank: *Connection to Spiritual Source*

Out to the stars. Also right in front of his nose, in his nose, in the air, etc. Everything, and I mean everything, shimmers with the presence of God. Top to toe, that presence expresses qualities of Jeffrey Chappell, consistent and joyful. No STUFF shows anywhere in that aura. It's all gifts, all the time.

Finally, a perfectly balanced aura in a really advanced state of Enlightenment! Pay close attention because that kind of balance just might be your destiny, too.

ENLIGHTENMENT VERSUS CHANNELING

Does this Enlightened musician manage to Magnetize Money? Sure. Chappell is extremely successful. In a profession where full-timers often struggle, this man makes an excellent living.

It helps that he can connect with people persuasively and authentically. At the level of auric modeling, he emanates an attractive, credible openness.

Here are more important points about the auras of people like Jeffrey Chappell. For the spiritually Enlightened, every chakra databank expresses the distinctive quality of that individual soul. It is also:

- Free from STUFF
- Large
- In good (not necessarily exactly equal, but reasonably good) proportion with all other chakra databanks
- Joyful
- Resourceful

What happens when you compare someone like Esther Hicks to someone like Jeffrey Chappell?

You already know that energetic literacy reveals a lollipop-like structure, rather than a well-proportioned cylinder. Well, there's also the matter of **energy frequency.**

An Enlightened aura carries a finer, higher vibration of energy than you'll find elsewhere. Technically, that's the Divine energy frequency. By contrast, Esther Hicks's vibration of energy frequency is clearly celestial, or astral, in nature.

Esther is enjoying a combination of spiritual addiction and being in a very close relationship with an astral being. Not all channelers become so identified with the one they channel. When that does happen, however, certain characteristics are common.

- Except for some Third Eye databanks, the rest of the channeler's chakra databanks will be small and weak.
- The channeler's personality will be minimized.
- Detailed aura reading of chakra databanks will reveal either habitual neglect of self or a large amount of STUFF, or both.

By contrast, a channeler's spiritual and psychic connection databanks will be vibrant. Expect these to be:

- Huge
- Different *in nature,* as if the chakra databanks come from a completely different personality than that of the person who hosts the channeled entity. (Which is just what's happening.)
- *Vibrationally,* the databanks about psychic connection will be different from the more human components of the channeler's aura, carrying an astral-level energy frequency.

What Else Happens with Channeling?

Any contact with The Other Side can seem equally good to a beginner at energetic literacy. Mediumship, channeling, working with spirits of any kind may seem like ideal ways for a humble person to have a conversation with God.

To the energetically literate, however, important distinctions can be made. Here are some basic facts of life about The Other Side.

- Astral frequency beings are different from God.
- Divine frequency beings, such as Jesus or Krishna or Kwan Yin, are *personal* aspects of God.
- Other aspects of God are *impersonal,* such as The Holy Spirit, The Great Spirit, The Loving Energy of the Universe, Spiritual Source.
- Some astral beings are at a high level of vibration, while others are not.
- And here's the most surprising fact: Anyone contacted through mediumship, angel contact, or channeling could be much less evolved than the human being doing that work.

Trance channeling is a distinct skill set. Besides Esther Hicks (who channels Abraham), other famous channelers are Jach Pursel (Lazarus), Jon C. Fox (Hilarion), Lee Carroll (Kryon), and Ron Scolastico, Ph.D. (The Guides).

For this sacred art, the channeler allows an entity or group of entities to take over his/her mind-body-spirit system. Afterwards, the channeler can't remember what was said.

During trance, the channeler's voice and facial appearance may alter. Certainly the channeler's aura changes. It shows the very strong imprint of whichever being takes over the channeler's body.

Dr. Scolastico has been a friend of mine for decades. Credit his training as a clinical psychologist or simply an instinct for balance, but Ron has always strictly limited the amount of time he spends channeling. He helps people as part of a well-rounded life. So Ron hasn't developed a high degree of spiritual addiction.

By contrast, spending huge amounts of time daily in a trance state can cause a channeler to become like a puppet, coming alive only when serving the entity. Stage 3 Energetic Literacy reveals that Esther Hicks has does have the pattern of spiritual addiction plus being strongly imprinted by the being she channels.

Co-creation is a different skill set from trance channeling. Anyone can choose to consciously co-create with a divine or celestial being. And since God costs no more to sign up with than any astral being, why not choose to co-create with the Divine? (An excellent resource for learning co-creation skills is www.teachingoftheinnerchrist.com.)

Divine Beings don't do trance channeling. Instead, perfected beings like St. Francis and Jesus will gently supplement your human knowledge, lighting up your aura but never taking it over. You will maintain your own sense of self.

This strengthens a person's aura, speeding the path toward Enlightenment. An Enlightened man like Jeffrey Chappell is always and only himself. Serenity comes from constant (and STUFF-free) co-creation with Spiritual Source. Esther Hicks has taken a different path, equally serene, but maybe not so great for her auric field.

Yes, it's a beautiful path to surrender totally, sacrificing your personal identity so that you can serve humanity. But no, Enlightenment doesn't necessarily come as a reward.

Esther's aura comes alive only when she's carrying the big presence of Abraham. Otherwise she's as quiet as a mouse, minimizing her own human presence.

If Esther Hicks worked alone, would she have had such a huge, successful career? I doubt it. The team is Esther and Jerry Hicks, after all. I'll read him soon. But first, aren't you curious about the entity group who speaks through her?

I was. So here comes my energetic literacy profile of Abraham. (As usual, you can see the photo used for this profile at the "Photo Supplement" online.)

ESTHER + ABRAHAM

Who is Abraham, exactly? At Abraham-Hicks.com, it says "Abraham is a name. A symbol. A feeling. Evocative - yet simple - like we want our names to be."

Elsewhere at the website, he is described as "a group consciousness from the non-physical dimension."

I'm not convinced this is true. As a healing practitioner, I have decades of experience with helping clients to clear out various forms of astral-level debris. So I'm intimately familiar with the difference between a group of entities versus one astral-level personality.

Based on my experience of energetic literacy at this level, Abraham doesn't read like a group of souls. Instead, this is one very distinct guy with a huge personal ego.

Check out what he does, using Esther Hicks' body and taking over her aura one chakra databank at a time.

Abraham: Magnetize Money Profile

*1. Root Chakra Databank: **Earning Money***
20 miles. "I want the power that goes with making money. "
Abraham's will of iron supports a very masculine quality of energy. While Esther channels Abraham, there couldn't be a clearer contrast between this forceful, even bossy, male presence versus Esther's meek-and-mild, girly-girlish self.

Abraham's drive to be rich is reminiscent of what I've found reading this same chakra databank in business tycoons like John D. Rockefeller. Yet there's something a little different about the quality here, which will be clarified especially in Chakra Databank #9 of this reading.

*2. Root Chakra Databank: **Saving Money***
20 miles. Such a keen intent to have and to hold! And this version of "to have and to hold" doesn't remind me of wedding vows. It's

more like, "I will accumulate enormous riches. I will fulfill my desires in a big way."

3. Root Chakra Databank: **Personality in Work Situations**
Out to the moon. "I show forth the glamour of the astral. Open up to my energies and I will make you feel inspired beyond your oldest dreams. I will bring you new dreams and fulfill them. There is no limit to the inspiration that I can bring you."

4. Root Chakra Databank: **Personality PROJECTED at Work**
9 inches. Glamorous, mild, service-oriented. "I'm a loving group of wise souls, assembled for the sole purpose of selflessly helping humanity."

5. Solar Plexus Chakra Databank: **Self-Confidence at Work**
Fills the room (expanding to exceed the size of any auditorium). Dominating the space.
"Nobody here can compete with me. I can answer any question, win any confrontation."

6. Solar Plexus Chakra Databank: **Handling Conflict at Work**
Fills the room (expanding to exceed the size of any auditorium). Strength is wrapped in the appearance of gentleness and kindliness.
There's also an undertone of contempt for the human-level people involved in his conversations. "I can outsmart any of you."

7. Heart Chakra Databank: **Emotional Intelligence at Work**
7 inches. Abraham has just enough interest in human emotion to find each person's greatest unmet need. Then he uses that vulnerability to gain power.
To an astral-level being, of course, all human needs scream loudly. (The ability to hide human pain from other humans is part of the illusion at Earth School. Astral beings aren't bound by that illusion.)

8. Throat Chakra Databank: **Communication at Work**
Out to the moon. A spell-binding combination of wisdom, compassion, otherworldly mystery... is mixed with a core need to control those who listen.

*9. Third Eye Chakra Databank: **Paying Attention to Human Life***
Out to the moon. And here, to this aura reader at least, Abraham turns scary.

Does he have his own human life to pay attention to? Of course not. Abraham is an astral-level entity, with his own drives and personality but no human body that rightfully belongs to him.

What would be the equivalent, for Abraham, of paying attention to his human life? Energetic literacy provides this answer:

"I aim to hook as many of you as I can, winning your obedience. I want you to feed me energetically through opening up your hearts and minds to my teaching. After your human life ends, I want you to come to my astral world and serve me."

*10. Third Eye Chakra Databank: **Connection to Spiritual Source***
4 inches. "Connect with me. Trust me. Let me into your life. I can inspire you like a version of God, only more comfortable."

Does living on The Other Side automatically guarantee that a being like Abraham looks heavenward, constantly praising God and singing like an angel in Handel's "Messiah"? Hardly.

Abraham behaves like other earthbound ghosts and psychic-level spirits who are encouraged by curious humans. These astral-level entities are vibrationally positioned a bit higher than human life, bringing them an advantage in terms of information and influence.

Research leads me to believe that Abraham wants power on earth, reaching down toward the human realm. Even though he's not in human form, he wants to soak up as much human energy as is possible.

Except for being "dead," Abraham has a lot in common with Andrew Carnegie, John D. Rockefeller, and other successful moneymakers whose auric fields I have researched in detail. They are highly effective, strong-minded personalities with an uncommon drive to succeed. Intense in their lower chakras, they engage powerfully to fulfill their ambitions.

In my opinion, Abraham greatly enjoys how he's positioned, having the knowledge and power of an astral-level spirit, while securely moving through the human energy system so generously provided by Ms. Hicks.

Meanwhile, what contribution is made by the channeler's spouse, Jerry Hicks? Curious? Let's use energetic literacy to find answers.

JERRY HICKS

According to his website, Abraham-hicks.com, Jerry lives "a fairy tale life." He's also an entrepreneur: "Yet, by the time he met Esther, Jerry had built a multi-million-dollar business operation engaging over 100,000 people. His success spring-boarded almost entirely from a chance reading of Napoleon Hill's *Think and Grow Rich*."

Before reading Jerry's aura from his website photo, I noted with fascination his insistence, that "I was never much interested in money. I was more interested in having a wonderful life… and being free."

It should be easy to tell how Jerry's aura supports such extreme financial indifference. Do your own detective work, if you wish, using your energetic literacy skills along with me. (See the photo used for this profile at the "Photo Supplement" online.)

Jerry Hicks: Magnetize Money Profile

1. Root Chakra Databank: Earning Money
Fills the room (expanding with the size of the auditorium). Does the size of this databank surprise you? Sure, Mr. Hicks talks publicly about being blithely indifferent to wealth. To my perception, Jerry's financial interest databank is way serious, nothing fairy-tale about it.
"I am very, very interested in making money. In fact, I expect it."

2. Root Chakra Databank: Saving Money
20 miles. Having money means validation for Jerry, validation that people in the past who didn't treat him nicely were wrong.
Wealth also means feeling secure, being on top of the world.

3. Root Chakra Databank: Personality at Work
Fills the room (expanding with the size of the workplace). Although charming, Mr. Hicks needs to control every aspect of his business.

4. Root Chakra Databank: Personality PROJECTED at Work
Fills the room (expanding with the size of the workplace). "I'm carefree. Money doesn't matter to me at all."

Tremendously nurturing, Jerry's kindly presence is like that of a favorite uncle: No demands, only giving and caring.

"I will restore your faith in how good people can be."

5. Solar Plexus Chakra Databank: *Self-Confidence at Work*

Fills the room (expanding with the size of the workplace). Jerry expects to be obeyed. He feels like a winner. He greatly enjoys modeling that kind of confidence, projecting it strongly to inspire all those who work for him.

6. Solar Plexus Chakra Databank: *Handling Conflict at Work*

Fills the room (expanding with the size of the workplace). So far, every part of Jerry's aura that I have read shows a will of iron. In this particular chakra databank, that will turns especially intense.

"I expect to win every conflict. Although I might appear to discuss other points of view, I will not compromise."

The quality here is a lock-and-key fit with his wife's corresponding databank. Remember Esther's spiritual surrender? She loves to submit, just as he loves to win.

7. Heart Chakra Databank: *Emotional Intelligence at Work*

5 inches. Jerry can be very protective, especially showing concern about his wife.

Otherwise his Emotional IQ scores pretty low. Like many a super-successful executive, Hicks notices just enough about people's feelings to manage them effectively.

8. Throat Chakra Databank: *Communication at Work*

Fills the room (expanding with the size of the auditorium). Mostly Jerry projects qualities like sincerity and humility, caring and spiritual focus.

However, the real gift of his soul at this chakra databank is finesse. He says just enough to get results, then steps back and allows others to respond.

Even though he'll persist quite vigorously to get the results he desires, Jerry communicates with the suave charm of a Fred Astaire.

Another business advantage for Mr. Hicks is his way with words, easily translating his message so that everyone can hear it. Big talent for creating that fairy-tale success!

9. Third Eye Chakra Databank: Awareness of His Human Life
7 miles. Jerry pays close attention to his likes and dislikes, desires and new goals.

Now that he is so hugely successful, Jerry has fun setting new goals for his success and meeting them. This material focus keeps him amused, preventing boredom.

10. Third Eye Chakra Databank: Connection to Spiritual Source
5 inches. Jerry believes in a benevolent God who wishes for him to become very, very rich.

The mystical side of his life is a light, fluffy, fairy tale kind of thing. Most of Jerry Hicks' aura has a completely different quality, being actively money-centered and very forceful indeed.

Long before LOA, Jerry Hicks was successful at business. Not surprising! He fits the profile of the mega-successful people we'll meet in later chapters.

It is, perhaps, surprising that his strengths are not in the direction of the Abraham-Hicks teachings. But perhaps Mr. Hicks sees his role as more of a business support. For that, his auric modeling is superb.

PRIORITIES, SET ENERGETICALLY

Looking for the exact opposite of spiritual addiction? You can find it in Rhonda Byrne and Jerry Hicks.

Chances are, long before they ever heard about LOA, these were ambitious people who were very focused on becoming very rich.

Such people need no dream boards to remind them to care about making money. Instead, LOA teachings have intensified their usual worldly focus.

I'm guessing that spiritual teachers like Byrne and Hicks would have naturally believed that anyone who used their spiritual principles would wind up with strengths like theirs.

It was like advocating a spiritual version of trickle-down economics. Since Jerry and Rhonda have such strength in their lower chakras, perhaps they assumed their spiritual techniques would create a trickle-down effect, with energy moving downward from the Third Eye Chakra to strengthen the rest of the aura.

Unfortunately, this cannot happen unless the practitioner *already* is strong there, long before beginning to practice LOA teachings.

Doesn't spiritual connection trump all? Theoretically, spiritual expansion would seem to form the whole basis for Law of Attraction teachings. But theory meets reality in each person's aura.

Inch-age reveals major secrets about who-you-be, the inner sense of proportion. Priorities related to belief do not necessarily translate into energetic realities.

But staying at the surface of perception, who can tell the difference? Without Stage 3 Energetic Literacy, it would be hard to tell how a person's thoughts about money are supported by chakra databanks.

Jerry and Rhonda may have no idea that most of their followers do not start out like them: Mega-ambitious, living mostly from the Solar Plexus Chakra down.

It's as though The Secret were a technique for how to run marathons. Jerry and Rhonda always had great form as sprinters, but many of their followers started out limping. When those followers took the advice given them, running miles every day, running harder and harder, it only worsened the original limp.

If you had a physical limp, eventually the pain from all that running would grow to the point where you sought medical help. A good diagnostician would find where the problem was, then help you fix it.

For prosperity problems, that diagnosis comes through energetic literacy. It can help each of us to locate our strengths, inspire us to heal our STUFF, and provide practical workarounds to stop the pain.

That's exactly what we're going to do. Only there's another kind of research we've just got to do first.

10. Does Salvation Bring Enlightenment?

Religion in the first millennium: What can I do for my God?
Religion in the second millennium: What can my God do for me?
—Melanie Matheson, Graphic designer for this book

Every religion has its distinctive beauty, in words and in auras. For some, "Enlightenment" is an eastern term, reminiscent of traditions sacred to millions: Hindus, Buddhists and Sikhs, yoga practitioners and meditators, mystical traditions thousands of years old.

For some, "Enlightenment" couldn't be more western. It means a period of idealistic rationalism, starting as early as the 1600s, dominated by Protestants, with Catholics and secularists developing their own versions as well.

How will "Enlightenment" be defined in the third millennium? Perhaps it will continue to mean what it always has, a kind of love song to God. Although definitions of "Enlightenment" vary, isn't it always an ideal of perfection?

Ever since I first encountered the concept, back in high school, my life has been motivated by the search for Enlightenment. In that, I know I'm not alone.

Have you, too, felt a yearning to become the best you could be, whether or not you called that "Enlightenment"? Has the meaning of that ideal changed as you have evolved? Or perhaps it has held true, despite all the other ways you have changed.

Either way, how beautiful! Your very individual sense of sacredness has shaped your spiritual ideals, and that alone deserves respect.

As energetic literacy becomes more widespread, we can check out the who-you-be aspect of each belief system. With our inquiring minds, we have the right to know the hidden consequences of any sacred teaching.

Patterns within chakra databanks might gloriously support, or starkly contradict, a particular spiritual teaching. For instance, what if a spiritual path were to promise Enlightenment yet, simultaneously, create patterns that disallow it?

Each belief system brings financial consequences, as well as spiritual impact. And I don't simply mean that attending church with old-money Episcopalians could be more socially advantageous than networking with new-money Baptists.

What happens when you do detailed aura readings on members of one group, then another? Patterns emerge. Certain chakra databanks tend to be bigger or smaller. Priorities favor some aspects of life over others.

Bottom line: Every spiritual path can result in some huge chakra databanks and others that are teensy.

After I did so much detailed research on LOA grassroots teachers, I thought it might be interesting to use the same Magnetize Money Snapshot on a contrasting group. Born Again Christians seemed especially intriguing, given their opposite way of relating to the concept of Enlightenment.

Surely you have heard the belief that America is a Christian nation, dominated by Christians, belonging to them, and where riches will flow if only you promise to give your life over to Jesus.

ENLIGHTENMENT — WHO CARES?

You know how there are two kinds of people. (What, you've heard this idea already?)

Some people seek Enlightenment. Others don't.

How will that simple choice impact a person's auric field? Results might surprise you.

Think of anyone you know fairly well, say, your neighbor Ferdinand. Probably you don't know, word for word, his definition of Enlightenment. But, if you think about it, chances are you can tell which type of person he is, Seeking Enlightenment or Indifferent to Enlightenment.

SEEKING ENLIGHTENMENT

People in this group seek a greater degree of perfection, perhaps aiming for a bigger version of self. That very personal goal could be religious, spiritual, physical, or psychological.

- As a member of this group, Ferdinand might practice prosperity teachings or success teachings, might be a Catholic, Buddhist, Jew, pagan, member of any religion, or be an agnostic.
- Ferdinand might go to AA meetings, where he's taking his personal growth one day at a time.
- Or he might regularly see a psychotherapist.
- Maybe Ferdinand's path simply involves eating health food or pumping iron at the gym.

Regardless of how hard someone like Ferdinand strives for perfection, his very seeking shows aurically. There will be a kind of openness in many Third Eye Chakra databanks.

INDIFFERENT TO ENLIGHTENMENT

What if Ferdinand belongs to this second group?

- He could be really successful, enjoying great professional standing or social prestige. Most of life's most successful people feel no need for personal growth. All that success proves to their satisfaction that "Anyone can succeed, if he has enough talent" (or similar ideas that are fun to generate, under the circumstances).
- Alternatively Ferdinand could be an atheist. This courageous belief system places responsibility squarely in human hands.
- By far the largest group of people with indifference to Enlightenment are religious Fundamentalists, whether Hindu, Buddhist, Jewish, Muslim, or Christian.
- In America, of course, the cultural conversation is dominated by Born Again Christians.

Salvation is one of the great benefits of being a Born Again Christian. In this belief system, Jesus Christ brings salvation. Once you agree to believe, you're saved, pure and simple. Deal closed.

From this perspective, seeking Enlightenment is unnecessary. Mere mortals can't do a thing on their own, while Jesus automatically fixes everything. Therefore, every day spent in personal seeking represents a pathetic waste of time. When will the spiritual surrender finally be done, and the saved life begin?

Aurically, anyone indifferent to Enlightenment shows rigidity at many Third Eye Chakra databanks. Strong beliefs about salvation correspond to inner qualities like security, comfort, and lack of curiosity.

Martin Luther might have been describing these Third Eye Chakra databanks when writing his great hymn, "A Mighty Fortress Is Our God." Many a true believer carries around auric patterns that look very much like Luther's famous lyric, "a bulwark never failing."

Born Again Auras

Researching the Born Again prosperity path, I probed photos of 50 passionate Evangelical Christians. Since they lead meetup groups online, photos are available for any energetically literate person to read in depth and detail.

Using the Magnetize Money Snapshot, I "interviewed" these grassroots leaders. As always, I began by exploring one person at a time, one chakra databank at a time. Afterwards, definite patterns emerged, a validation that every one of these Born Again leaders was exploring success differently from the other groups I researched.

What I found was remarkably consistent. All 50 were very security-conscious. All but one was rock-solid in terms of religious conviction.

Biggest for every single Fundamentalist was The Root Chakra Databank about **Earning Money.** The Solar Plexus Chakra databank about **Handling Conflict at Work** came in second. While **Connection to Spiritual Source** at the Third Eye Chakra was consistently solid but small.

Doing this research, my most inspiring subject was this young woman:

+ Fiona: *20 feet.* She has struggled hard in life. Now she surrenders to God to provide for her. A strong spiritual vocation pervades her whole life."

Usually what I discovered was far more mundane, such as these Root Chakra Databanks about **Earning Money**:

+ Floyd: *20 miles.* "I'm successful because I am chosen by God."
+ Felicia: 8 feet. "I work hard and get paid for it. Meanwhile I earn my way to heaven."
+ Fritz: *25 feet.* "I've always had money and always will. It's because my people are righteous, God-fearing folks."
+ Freddie: *25 feet.* Very confident and has an extremely outgoing personality. "I love being a success story for The Lord."

HANDLING CONFLICT WITH A GODLY ASSIST

When a Christian Fundamentalist truly believes, that includes the promise of salvation. Forever. Guilt need never arise again, as any mistakes will be forgiven. Another confidence booster is how rich blessings are considered inevitable. It's considered part of the bargain for complete surrender to God.

Many in this research group believed so fully, a strong faith trickled all the way down to the level of chakra databanks. Others didn't show quite the same degree of assurance. Here are examples of the variety I found, researching their Solar Plexus Chakra databanks about **Handling Conflict at Work**:

• Fabio: *7 feet.* Drops out of difficult conversations. Refuses to enter into arguments. "God loves a peacemaker."
• Fritz: *17 feet.* "I can win any fight. Nobody intimidates me, since I know I am right with the Lord."
• Francine: *14 inches.* Old anger is stuck, yet this woman doesn't believe she has any anger at all. "I used to get mad at things, but now I simply ask Jesus to take care of me."
+ Felicia: *4 feet.* "Why argue? Let other people get worked up. Meanwhile I think about God. And God always comes through."

Such consistency! Now let's explore the religious connection. For decades, I have been fascinated with auras of Fundamentalists of all kinds. When religion is so central to a person's life, it can lead to missionary fervor, political activism characterized by "The end justifies the means," even acts of terrorism.

Energetic literacy is at our disposal, remember. So we can investigate from the inside what happens in that very intimate databank about a true believer's **Connection to Spiritual Source.**

Researching this chakra databank, using newspaper photos over the years, I have found remarkably similar patterns among Fundamentalists in different religions. Although beliefs differ, there's a shocking sameness aurically, regardless of the Fundamentalist's religious preference, be it a strict and traditional Buddhist, Muslim, Hindu, Protestant, Catholic, or Jew.

Strictly following the letter of the law, that believer gains absolute certainty. Although rituals continue, spiritual seeking ends because that believer now has all the answers. So with rare exceptions, Fundamentalists of any kind usually show a rock-hard, very tiny experience at the Third Eye Chakra.

Really, would you expect something luscious and questing? Is the point of being devoutly religious to satisfy curiosity or to evolve? Of course not. In theory, you would expect certain things of a person who "has all the answers."

At the level of auras, however, will you find what you expect?

Thank energetic literacy for giving us the chance to distinguish an appealing belief (such as spiritual superiority to others) versus the size and quality in the relevant parts of a believer's aura.

Truth is, not a single one of the 50 Born Again leaders in my research showed a religious connection nearly as big as his or her drive to make money. In general Third Eye Chakra Databanks were extremely small, beautiful but small.

Among these religious people, my research turned up only one phony. Here's what energetic literacy revealed about Fargo:

- *Third Eye Chakra Databank,* **Connection to Spiritual Source.** *1 inch.* "It's pretty much B.S. Except I will play this game for the great social contacts."

All the rest of Fargo's peers were truly devout, although their size of spiritual connection wasn't necessarily larger than his. Here are some representative samples:

- Floyd: *2 inches.* "Mine is a solid, unquestioning faith."
- Felicia: *2 inches.* "God takes care of me. I don't need to worry about anything else."
- Fabio: *4 inches.* "I do all I am supposed to do. I enjoy preparing to live in the Kingdom of Heaven."
- Forrest: *1 inch.* "I feel sorry for people who aren't connected as I am, but it's their choice."
- Flannery: *3 inches.* "Sure, I used to worry about God and Hell. But now I feel taken care of, perfectly serene."

Although these patterns shocked me at first, on reflection they made perfect sense. Why would someone be motivated to grow spiritually after your place in heaven has been settled for all eternity?

Not only were Third Eye Chakra databanks small and stuck for the Born Again success seekers. Emotional self-awareness was tiny, as well.

Once I became curious about this aspect, I sampled my research group at random, exploring their Heart Chakra Databanks about **Emotional Self-Awareness.**

The size and quality here was a lock-in-key fit with that person's **Spiritual Connection** Databank at the Third Eye Chakra. In general, self-awareness was small and tight.

God lies in details, though, correct? Here are some:

- Fern: *2 inches.* "I use faith to handle my emotions."
- Felicia: *4 inches.* "Nobody understands me. That's okay, the Lord does."
- Fabio: *3 inches.* Old pain, locked in. Numbness. "Faith makes me cheerful. Any time I start to feel sad, I remember that I have been Born Again. Therefore, I have nothing to fear."

Not only does curiosity beget research. Research begets more research. After reading these fascinating samples of emotional self-awareness, of course I had to go back and do similar spot checks on that same databank with my LOA teachers.

For them, as well, the databank for **Emotional Self-Awareness** at the Heart Chakra was… closely related to the **Connection to Spiritual Source** databank at the Third Eye Chakra.

Why Everyone Wins

Since both groups were so different, you might wonder, "Who wins?" Is it LOA practitioners or their Born Again counterparts? Actually energetic literacy revealed a way that members of either groups could win.

Members of each group gained something distinctive, aurically, related to following that particular path. Christian believers developed lavish security and comfort. LOA believers were much more reflective about their lives. Beneath the required, cheerful façade, my random samples of the spiritual seekers showed emotional growth that was complex, if not brimming with Christian certitude.

Emotionally, my LOA subjects had experiences like these:

- Denise: *20 feet.* Acutely aware every time somebody hurts her feelings. Suffers a lot. Keeps trying to pick herself up emotionally.
- Dan: *25 miles.* There is so much anguish. "Every day is a struggle. At least I'm honest with myself."
- Doris: 25 feet. Pays a lot of attention to her feelings. Aware of many problems and conflicts, "but I hope I can work through them better because of my spiritual connection."
- Daisy: *14 feet.* "Curious about all the feelings within me. Wanting to use that power for spiritual purposes and wishing that I didn't have some of those negative feelings. Am I just not working hard enough? Somehow those terrible feelings just won't go away."
- Darlene: *40 feet.* Springboards from negative feelings by "Going spiritual," where she substitutes awareness of the transcendent for inconvenient emotions.

Different beliefs offer marvelous ways to grow. Aurically, there's no need to judge different paths as superior or inferior. Each of us chooses the *appropriate* path, given our current level of consciousness.

Still, by researching with energetic literacy, even more curiosity grew within me. I wondered, could there be a correlation between different patterns related to belief systems and concrete results for being able to Magnetize Money?

11. Which Auras Magnetize Money

It is popular mythology that you will be rich and happy if you do what you love. Nothing is so effective at disproving this nonsense as the undeniable fact that I would be living in a cardboard carton today if I played golf for a living.
Gene Bedell, *The Millionaire in the Mirror*

What if a belief system promised wealth yet, unintentionally, made wealth harder to attain than otherwise?

Every belief system has financial implications. Once I began researching financial style with energetic literacy, many ideas I had cherished for years were turned inside out. Beliefs that sounded good might not be good, not in terms of their consequences.

Which patterns developed in the auras of people who were megasuccessful? Were those patterns consistent with what I had been reading (and believing) for decades about "Think and grow rich"?

I didn't want to stop investigating until I found answers.

So far, I've presented my findings about LOA grassroots teachers and their Born Again counterparts. Also you glimpsed the contrasting patterns in the top LOA teachers and you have aurically sampled Enlightenment.

Based on this, maybe you have started to question the relationship between strong beliefs, auras, and financial consequences. We'll go into more detail about this later, especially practical ways you can Magnetize Money. Meanwhile, here's an energetic overview of true prosperity patterns.

What shows in the no-fibbing zone known as the human energy field? Successful people have large chakra databanks related to physical presence and interest in money. Powerful conflict resolution ability is required, along with other down-to-earth aspects of life.

Say goodbye to ideas like "Think and Grow Rich" or "Do What You Love and The Money Will Follow." Chakras from the ribcage down matter most for gaining wealth, not chakras from the forehead up.

IS THAT FAIR?

Okay, maybe these findings suggest that wealth requirements could be called materialistic. Spiritually how would that be fair?

"What you pay attention to grows stronger in your life." How often have you heard that saying? Well, that's fair, isn't it? Make the choice and then receive the consequences.

But let's get something straight. One very important nuance can seem confusing before a person has full energetic literacy. "Pay attention" isn't the whole story. The complete version goes, "Paying attention from which part of your energy field?"

- Paying attention *spiritually* creates big Third Eye Chakra databanks.
- Paying attention *materially* feeds databanks at the Root Chakra.

Again, every wealth seeker needs to solve problems. In your life so far, you've had your share, haven't you? Well, which approach did you take?

- Handling conflicts by taking *vigorous action* increases the functioning at your Solar Plexus Chakra databanks.
- Handling conflicts by means of *ideals,* ideology, or spiritually-based systems sounds wonderful but creates small, ineffective Solar Plexus Chakra databanks.

AM I CALLING SPIRITUAL LIFE "IRRELEVANT"?

Hardly. Spiritual life matters so much that it could be called indispensable… for spiritual life. When it comes to making money, however, spiritual interests are optional.

Bottom line: Those of us who want to make money must pay attention to making money. Actually making it. In tangible reality.

When we pay enough attention, that passion for wealth will show up aurically. Well meant substitutes, like thinking about growing rich, just can't do the job.

Admittedly, as my research findings added up, I wanted to protest. Okay, that's too dignified. I wanted to scream, cry, pitch a temper tantrum right on the floor, all the while howling, "It's not fair. Shouldn't life, or God, or somebody, reward purity of heart and spiritual focus?"

Maybe the lifetimes do add up, so justice does prevail. But adding up the complex karmas… would have to be another book. Here our job is to investigate how money works energetically. Because isn't it time for life's dedicated spiritual seekers to become more successful?

So let's revisit our findings, starting with the Root Chakra Databank about **Earning Money.** Of course, this databank matters enormously for anyone who wishes to Magnetize Money. Come to think of it, remember these rich folks?

- Bill Gates. *50 miles.* Flexible thinking, abstract intelligence, and technological thinking combine with extreme determination to win the game of financial acquisition.
- Donald Trump. *90 miles.* Feeling as though he possesses a version of the Midas Touch. His power of command over people and money can practically hypnotize them. Because he comes on so strong, and never flinches, "weak people" usually go along with his demands.
- Rhonda Byrne. *50 miles.* Intense determination and self-reliance abound.
- Jerry Hicks. *Fills the room (expanding with the size of the auditorium).* "I am very, very interested in making money. In fact, I expect it."
- Abraham. *20 miles.* I want the power that goes with making money.

Now let's compare this to our previous findings about grassroots teachers, passionate believers in the Law of Attraction. Again, we're reading the Root Chakra Databank about **Earning Money.**

- Grassroots LOA Teacher Dave: *5 feet.* Sure that he's an expert. "I have this money thing handled."
- Grassroots LOA Teacher Daisy: *6 inches.* "I have things on earth all figured out. They're simple."
- Grassroots LOA Teacher Denise: *4 inches.* Escapes from problems with reality and money by focusing on her favorite beliefs.

How about the same money-attracting Root Chakra databank for the Born Again Christians?

- Grassroots Born Again Teacher Floyd: *20 miles.* "I'm successful because I am chosen by God."
- Grassroots Born Again Teacher Fritz: *25 feet.* "I've always had money and always will. It's because my people are good, God-fearing folks."
- Grassroots Born Again Teacher Freddie: *25 feet.* Very confident and has an outgoing personality. "I love being a success story for The Lord."

Problem Solving to Magnetize Money

"Think and grow rich" is so appealing. If that really were how life worked, though, why not simply administer an IQ test early in life? The world's best thinkers could go straight to the head of the class, shortly thereafter to be awarded their rightful positions on the Forbes Magazine Rich Folks List.

No, at Earth School, wealth doesn't work that way. People who seek material success must, above all, make contact with external reality. When our good ideas don't instantly produce the desired results, we must use power circuits — get messy if needed — and fix things.

Handling Conflict at Work? Of course, this Solar Plexus Chakra databank would correlate with business success. And what have we found among the rich and famous?

- Bill Gates: *50 miles.* The man does have a hot temper. Under certain conditions, anger burns. Then Bill will project intense rage within the first three feet past his physical body. If you stand anywhere within that distance, you won't need aura reading to feel scorched.
- Donald Trump: *90 miles.* Enjoys using his authority. Telling people how things are going to be, and that's that. Playing this role makes Donald Trump feel good about himself as a "real man."
- Rhonda Byrne: *40 feet.* So many women shy away from using their power. But no problem for Ms. Byrne. She may

even welcome conflict. Certainly, she expects to win; intimidation may often be used as part of her approach. Compact, forceful energy in this chakra databank can be mobilized quickly to take decisive action.

- Abraham: *Fills the room (expanding to exceed the size of any auditorium)*. Strength is wrapped in the appearance of gentleness and kindliness. There's also an undertone of contempt for the human-level people involved in his conversations. "I can outsmart any of you."
- Jerry Hicks: *Fills the room (expanding with the size of the workplace)*. "I expect to win every conflict. Although I might appear to discuss other points of view, I will not compromise."

Effective! By contrast, look again at our sweet true believers and the Solar Plexus Chakra Databank about **Handling Conflict at Work**:

- Grassroots LOA Teacher Dave: *4 feet*. Defensive, pushy way of handling conflict.
- Grassroots LOA Teacher Daisy: *3 inches*. "The trick is to disengage, then flow and concentrate on God. This will get you whatever you want."
- Grassroots LOA Teacher Denise: *5 inches*. Blames others for her problems, sometimes people in her present and sometimes people in her past.

What do we find when we revisit the empowerment that results from being saved for all eternity? (Also being spiritually superior to all others, not that one is officially supposed to gloat.)

Again, we'll check out the Solar Plexus Chakra Databank for **Handling Conflict at Work**:

- Grassroots Born Again Teacher Fabio: *7 feet*. Drops out of difficult conversations. Refuses to enter into arguments. "God loves a peacemaker."
- Grassroots Born Again Teacher Fritz: *17 feet*. I can find my way in any argument. Nobody intimidates me, since I know I am right with the Lord.
- Grassroots Born Again Teacher Felicia: *4 feet*. I don't argue. I let other people get worked up. Meanwhile I think about God. And God always comes through.

WHAT ABOUT THAT SPIRITUAL CONNECTION?

Hey, it's still the most important part of life to me. If I had to choose between pursuing Enlightenment versus earning a living, I would choose spiritual wealth.

Yet which of us really needs to choose? Having a vibrant spiritual life is merely optional in order to Magnetize Money. Optional, plus that aspect must stay in proportion with the rest of our auras.

Let's re-visit what we have found so far in the Third Eye Chakra Databank about **Connection to Spiritual Source.** When I researched grassroots LOA teachers, they were practicing what they preached. A spiritual system brought them spiritual benefits:

- Grassroots LOA Teacher Dave: *90 miles.* Seeking the outer edge of spiritual experience, fascinated by exploring the limits of consciousness.
- Grassroots LOA Teacher Daisy: *Out to the stars.* "I long for heaven."
- Grassroots LOA Teacher Denise: *Out to the moon.* Denise would like to be a missionary for this kind of experience, it is so sweet.

That's quite a contrast to the experience of the Saved and Settled for the Third Eye Chakra Databank about **Connection to Spiritual Source.**

- Grassroots Born Again Teacher Floyd: *2 inches.* Mine is a solid, unquestioning faith.
- Grassroots Born Again Teacher Fabio: *4 inches.* I do everything I am supposed to do. I enjoy preparing to live in the Kingdom of Heaven.
- Grassroots Born Again Teacher Forrest: *1 inches.* "I feel sorry for people who aren't connected as I am, but it's their choice."

Whether somebody finds Salvation or seeks Enlightenment, certain Third Eye Chakra patterns do seem to fit right in with patterns for that respective group of true believers.

By contrast, when it comes to the Third Eye Chakra Databank: **Connection to Spiritual Source,** there's no uniformity in the big moneymakers we have researched:

- Donald Trump. *10 feet.* As the model for his relationship with Spiritual Source, this executive feels like Mommy's loveable favorite. Secure in his connection to the Divine, Donald takes it for granted. Inspiration is always there when he needs it.
- Rhonda Byrne. *4 inches.* This aspect of life has been handled. Now it's time to do my part and go claim success.
- Bill Gates. *50 miles.* What's really lovely about Bill's connection, at the time of this photo, is the self-aware presence of God.
- Abraham: *4 inches.* Connect with me. "Trust me. Let me into your life. I can inspire you like a version of God, only more comfortable."
- Jerry Hicks: *5 inches.* Jerry believes in a benevolent God who wishes for him to become very, very rich. The mystical side of his life is a light, fluffy, fairy tale kind of thing. Most of Jerry Hicks' aura has a completely different quality, being actively money-centered and very forceful indeed.

If you were to choose your spiritual path based solely on its money making, Root-Chakra-shaping, potential, you would definitely choose Fundamentalist Christianity over LOA. But if you wanted a faster rate of personal growth, gathering money mostly by chance, LOA might be your choice.

Of course, each one of us has more choices. We can combine big financial mojo with questing spiritual growth. We can enhance these strengths with the security that comes from having a relatively balanced, STUFF-free aura.

- Helping you to develop that… is the purpose of Parts Two and Three of this program. Resourceful Reader, if you want, I can help you to jump-start that kind of life.
- Otherwise I can confirm how well you're doing already.

CELEBRATING YOUR RESOURCEFULNESS

I do think it's important to pause for a moment in celebration of your resourcefulness, whatever your path or past has been. Remember, your aura is jam-packed with gifts of your soul, distinctive as fingerprints.

From the perspective of energetic literacy, everyone is a winner. Decisions that improve our ability to Magnetize Money even better can be made one day — and one choice — at a time.

It's fascinating to me, the degree to which everyone in this world can win spiritually. While completing this book's research on the Fundamentalist prosperity seekers, I suddenly flashed on a memory I hadn't thought about for years.

One of my 900+ media interviews has been with a very successful radio broadcaster. Joe was a talk show host on the biggest station in his market. In advance of our live interview, he had sent me photos from newsmakers in his big Midwestern city, un-named people well known to his listeners if not to me.

During the interview, Joe asked me to profile these local celebs, using skills of energetic literacy. It was standard media work for me then, doing that kind of interviews.

Only this particular one turned memorable with the third man I profiled. The fellow was remarkably stuck spiritually. His two-inch spiritual connection wasn't merely small but out of place in an otherwise dynamic aura. Picture it like a living room with one tattered old armchair among gorgeous contemporary sofas and lavish, up-to-date, window treatments.

Summoning all available tact, I told the broadcaster something like this, "What an interesting relationship this man has to his spiritual life or religion. It's as though 20 years ago he decided that he had figured everything out. Since then, he has never felt the need to check back. He considers that everything is handled."

Joe chimed in gleefully. "You're so right. That's my photo you're talking about, ma'am."

Yes, Joe was proud of his faith, delighted that he hadn't budged one inch in 20 years.

Religious certainty is a fine way to live. Joe is a shining, proud, example. From my perspective, Fundamentalists are a remarkably incurious group of people. But happy. And — take note, LOA followers — if my Magnetize Money Snapshots are correct, these Born-Again Christians are positioned to make way more money than you.

Hardworking LOA followers don't develop the auras of Rhonda Byrne or Jerry Hicks. Nor are most like Esther Hicks. To round out this chapter, here are Magnetize Money Snapshots on three more success experts who discuss the Law of Attraction: Deanna Davis, James Arthur Ray, and Brian Tracy.

I can cheerfully report that their auras are wonderfully different altogether. Maybe it's no coincidence that each of these writers has career specialties in addition to LOA teachings. Reading their success strategies, you'll find that (unlike Abraham-Hicks and The Secret) these leaders don't emphasize pure spiritual attraction as the 100% main way to gain wealth.

MAGNETIZING MONEY WITH A SENSE OF HUMOR

Deanna Davis, Ph.D., has written my favorite LOA book: *The Law of Attraction in Action: A Down-to-Earth Guide to Transforming Your Life (No Matter Where You're Starting From)*

Serious yet humorous, this writer has produced other self-help titles as well. See them at her website www.deannadavis.net. To read her aura along with me, you can find the photo used for this research at the "Photo Supplement" online.

Deanna Davis: Magnetize Money Snapshot

*1. Root Chakra Databank: **Earning Money***
50 miles. Fresh-faced and pretty, Deanna is lit up by ambition. Desires to succeed, to stand out, to help people all show here.

If you're familiar with Deanna's work, you know that humor is also a part of her brand. Humor and quirky practicality are also evident at this deep databank level.

*2. Solar Plexus Chakra Databank: **Handling Conflict at Work***
5 feet. That's not doing badly for someone so young. Determination to succeed pushes Deanna to overcome conflicts. Don't expect shyness here. When pressures threaten, she acts boldly to defend herself.

*3. Third Eye Chakra Databank: **Connection to Spiritual Source***
20 feet. A passionate, faith-filled connection lights up this chakra databank. It's a here-and-now experience.

As with so many who routinely co-create with their Spiritual Source, Deanna finds it relatively easy to recharge spiritually. Consequently, writing is inspired; daily living gains humility.

Does this writer brag, let alone write in books, about her gorgeous spiritual connection? Not that I've noticed. Deanna simply lives it.

EXPECTING TO WIN

Meet the President and CEO of James Ray International (JRI). A prolific writer and charismatic seminar leader, James writes about LOA and much, much more. His official website is www.jamesray.com. See the photo used for this profile at the "Photo Supplement" online.

James Arthur Ray: Magnetize Money Snapshot

1. Root Chakra Databank: **Earning Money**
90 miles. James brings huge sex appeal and charisma to his pursuit of wealth. He feels worthy of great success, paired with a child-like enthusiasm.

2. Solar Plexus Chakra Databank: **Handling Conflict at Work**
90 miles. Qualities like detachment, humor, and fearlessness can fortify his position during a conflict. Also, James is unusually effective at handling conflict because he projects a strong quality of victory in advance.

All by itself, this auric modeling can act as a superb deterrent. Who would be foolish enough to fight with such a winner?

3. Third Eye Chakra Databank: **Connection to Spiritual Source**
90 miles. James feels, and lives, with a clear connection to his Spiritual Source. No sentimentality, either. For this man, having that clear connection is simply a fact of life.

One reason why Mr. Ray projects such confidence in his own skin is this powerful spiritual connection. A secure connection helps him to relax all over, recharging his prosperity circuits with mega-watt charisma.

EARNING MONEY WITH FINESSE + BRAINS

The formidable Brian Tracy writes about LOA and much, much more. See his official website, www.briantracy.com. Find the photo used for this Magnetize Money research at the "Photo Supplement" online.

Brian Tracy: Magnetize Money Snapshot

*1. Root Chakra Databank: **Earning Money***
50 miles, when on his own.

If speaking, Brian's auric presence at this databank will fill the room, no matter how large, and still be spacious enough to overflow by a few inches.

A healthy respect for authority, a strong connection to reality, and the ability to be objective about that reality — qualities like these would make Brian Tracy extraordinarily effective even if his projection at this chakra databank were 50 inches, not 50 miles.

*2. Solar Plexus Chakra Databank: **Handling Conflict at Work***
50 miles. Brian is boss. Conflict doesn't shake him. This brings a kind of relief to anyone he manages or coaches. Firm, confident action is going to be taken... and with finesse. Brian Tracy is like the Fred Astaire of management.

*3. Third Eye Chakra Databank: **Connection to Spiritual Source***
50 feet. His spiritual connection is no mushy gushy thing. Nor is it dogmatic.

Brian Tracy lives like this: He has hands. He has feet. He has a clear connection to Spiritual Source. For him, it is just that simple.

Brian Tracy, James Arthur Ray, and Deanna Davis have written about various aspects of success, LOA included. Nowhere have I seen any of them emphasizing the deeply personal topic of spiritual connection.

That doesn't surprise me, due to what we've just seen in their related chakra databanks. Someone who is truly secure spiritually doesn't need to proselytize. Perhaps James, Brian, and Deanna assume that everyone else shares this gift for spiritual connection.

Well, not quite. Still, let's intrepidly keep on exploring which aura-level patterns help a person to Magnetize Money.

THE MAGNETIZE MONEY PATTERN

Success experts Deanna, Brian, and James teach differently, live differently, and write differently. Aurically, however, they have loads in common. All three show enormous strength at these money-related chakra databanks:

- Huge drive to make money at the Root Chakra.
- Unabashed personal power at the Solar Plexus Chakra

Teachings of Abraham-Hicks and Rhonda Byrne are, by comparison, far more faith based. Our research on grassroots LOA followers showed the consequences, huge emphasis on **Spiritual Connection** at the Third Eye Chakra, with weakness at these other two chakra databanks.

Ironically, our research found very different patterns for America's most aggressive and popular LOA leaders. Jerry Hicks, Rhonda Byrne, and Abraham have nothing in common, energetically, with their followers but somewhat resemble Deanna Davis, Brian Tracy and James Earl Ray.

Inspiringly, the three latter teachers haven't sacrificed an oomphy, glorious spiritual connection at the Third Eye Chakra. Great role models, these three success experts can inspire us all to use our full potential to Magnetize Money.

Of course we can aim for spiritual fulfillment as well as material wealth… especially if we don't make the mistake of *substituting* spiritual striving for material wealth.

Our next chapter may supply extra incentive for you to use your full potential for success and prosperity.

12. How Auric Modeling Can Help You Grow Rich

"The most important of all things to possess is Peace of Mind. There is absolutely nothing else in the world which is equal in value to that. Nothing else that life can offer is so important...."
— Emmet Fox, *Find And Use Your Inner Power*

"With Stage 3 Energetic Literacy, we know that peace of mind is more than mental serenity. Peace of mind, peace anywhere in your aura, will show in your auric modeling."
— Rose Rosetree, Writing in the Third Millennium

You're a broadcaster, you know. This has nothing to do with your winning the audition for a reality show. Like every person on earth, you broadcast energetic signals directly through your energy field.

When psychics read people, it's based on those energetic broadcasts. Without any training at psychic development, sensitive people of all kinds "pick up information" from those automatic broadcasts.

Say, for instance, you're visiting with Uncle Ralph. On this occasion, he's wearing a big, fake smile that would work perfectly in a beer commercial, especially if several alluring young women were present.

"How are you?" you say, locking eyes with him because you've always been fond of Uncle Ralph so you really would like to know the truth.

"Never better," he answers.

Man oh man, you sure hope he's lying. Because you can feel the sadness and loneliness, broadcasting loud and clear. No way can Uncle Ralph stifle that signal. Once an energetic broadcast reaches that strong a level of intensity, no fake body language can cover it up.

That's why we have sayings like, "Who you *are* is speaking so much louder than your words."

THIN SLICES

There's also a deeper form of energetic broadcasting called **"Thin slices."** It informs people at the subconscious level and tells them quite accurately about who-you-be, not just "How you feel right now."

Malcolm Gladwell wrote persuasively about thin slices in his bestseller *Blink*. In fact he named the term.

True, Gladwell didn't discuss energetic literacy in his research for *Blink*. Such a shame, because really it's the most direct way to process the subliminal messages that every person subconsciously broadcasts.

Nonetheless, Gladwell did an admirable job of describing "thin-slicing," how a person can make spontaneous decisions based on relatively little conscious information.

Snap judgments can be superior to information overload, as Gladwell persuasively illustrates. And, while praising simple, intuitive ways to sort through information, the bestselling author makes this important point: Training can refine intuitive ability, helping us to thin-slice far more accurately.

Even a beginner at energetic literacy will distinguish "Good vibes" from "Bad vibes," but why stop there? Developing more skill, one can read how each chakra databank sends out a signal.

Overall patterns become strong broadcasts. Some reassure a potential customer or employer. Some are intended to Magnetize Money yet do precisely the opposite.

Spiritual addiction is an example of counter-productive energetic broadcasting. Even if you dress for success, use the newest tricks to pace-and-lead with your body language, etc., that won't help a bit if the signal sent energetically goes like this:

"I'm barely here in my body and couldn't care less about human life."

No, that isn't attractive to customers. Even shiny new shoes can't cover up that kind of thin slice, either.

That's why I'm preparing you to tweak your energetic modeling so that it becomes effective at broadcasting the message, "Yes, I can Magnetize Money."

Ideas and workarounds in the following parts of our Program can help you become way more competitive in any business situation.

So, if you're serious about success — or you want to become more effective as a person for any reason at all — you need to understand clearly *why* it matters so much that you send out a congruent, strong signal through energetic broadcasting.

What is the name for how people broadcast these complex energy signals? You already know the technical term: Auric modeling.

By this point in our sequence of empowerment, you're ready to look more deeply into the meaning that auric modeling has for you and your financial bottom line.

Auras tell the truth about who-you-be, and there's no faking these energy broadcasts. Everyone reads them, too. Except usually this happens only at the level of auras, the subconscious mind. Auric modeling shapes what we learn from thin-slicing.

With conscious Stage 3 Energetic Literacy, you're ahead of the game. Even then, you won't constantly be reading auras. I hope. I certainly don't. Mostly a person with energetic literacy gets to be "normal."

Using skill at energetic literacy is like reading print words. Pity the read-a-holic who stumbles around reading newspapers constantly but never looking at people in the normal human way.

Similarly, constant aura reading would not be desirable as a substitute for engaging in life with your conscious mind. Trying to do this could, actually, throw your aura way out of whack, making it harder to Magnetize Money.

Still, today's success seekers need to remember that auric modeling happens as predictably as breathing. Here's more detail about the mechanics of auric modeling.

When you enter a room with other people, it's as if everybody strips off all clothing immediately and jumps into a large hot tub. Together, you proceed to exchange information. Sure, you're checking out everyone's naked body parts. Other people are checking you out as well. They discover exactly who-you-be.

No worries, this hot tub business is only an analogy. Any Wonderbra or toupee is safe for now. But your aura really is completely visible to others, energetically leaving you utterly naked. Who knew the children's song about Santa Claus really contained an element of truth?

He sees you when you're sleeping.
He knows when you're awake.
He knows if you've been bad or good.
So be good, for goodness sake.

However, the jolly, bearded elf isn't the one you need to impress so much as your potential customers, your boss, all the people you meet in the pursuit of success.

That naked aura of yours, with its hundreds of chakra databanks, reveals exactly who you are. It models your way of being as vividly as if you were some high fashion model strutting down a narrow runway (only maybe not so well paid, not quite yet).

Completely exposed are databanks like those I will read at the end of this chapter. But first, let's answer a practical question.

IS AURIC MODELING
ONE MORE THING TO WORRY ABOUT?

No. Remember, most of the news about yours is good. Your energy field is packed with chakra databanks, each one broadcasting a unique gift.

Think fingerprints! All over your body! (Unless you find that image frightening.)

Auric modeling is a great educational resource. Being with other people can bring you more than a contact high. It can teach you a different way to be. Each person models unique gifts, pain overcome, and life lessons learned. Spiritually, we're constantly teaching each other by personal example. And I don't mean how well we quote scripture.

When you meet someone whose aura inspires you, it's not only "I like that person." Your conscious mind may never figure out why, beyond Malcolm Gladwell's great concept of thin-slicing.

At the level of auras, however, you're going, "Yum, I like how that outrageous Donald Trump handles power." Or, perhaps, "Check out the fierce intellect, balanced wisdom, and feisty sense of humor on historian Doris Kearns Goodwin."

"Screen chemistry" is the name that Hollywood types give to auric modeling. Something about a particular star inspires viewers.

Behold Samuel L. Jackson modeling strength or Sting tossing sexiness into his songs as if his very life depended on it. Watch Amy Adams showing the world how to be vulnerable yet perky.

When a performer's auric modeling is intense, consistent, and likeable, voila! That's bankable star power.

Well, what about making yourself more bankable? Magnetizing Money requires that you succeed with certain basics of auric modeling. These can give you the chemistry of a credible person for your own line of work.

If you want to accomplish great things in your field, clean up your aura and make that great, too.

Consider Napoleon Hill, an inspiring example of auric modeling. You may already know that Andrew Carnegie invited the young journalist to interview outstanding business successes of the day. Agreeing, Hill was duly furnished with contact info. and letters of reference.

So generous! One of the richest men of his time (second only to John D. Rockefeller), Mr. Carnegie offered how much of a cash advance, exactly, to support the eager young man?

The extent of Carnegie's princely offer was to reimburse the writer's out-of-pocket expenses. Wow!

The journalist hardly came from a wealthy family that would finance his ambitions. And doing all those interviews took years, not weeks.

When you first learned of this strange start for *Think and Grow Rich*, did you appreciate the true weirdness of this real-life situation?

What kind of aura did that notable young man possess? Was Mr. Hill simply a gullible young idealist, lacking in street smarts? Did innate psychic ability tell him that eventually this book would sell 30 million copies? Or did his aura brim over with reckless courage?

Now that you're developing familiarity with that success secret known as "auric modeling," here's something else to ponder. What about Napoleon Hill commanded the attention of those 500 top businessmen?

Sure, Hill was given letters of reference to the country's power elite. Well, hello! That and ten cents would have bought you a fine cup of coffee, back in the day.

Much of Hill's research was done during the Depression. Then, as now, the rich and famous had plenty of groupies.

Do you think they were lacking for eager young men, seeking appointments and proffering impressive letters of reference or brilliant business plans or other reasons why "It's extremely urgent that we talk. Don't worry. Our appointment won't take long. Shall we plan for three hours?"

Napoleon Hill carried more than letters of reference. That is why he could Magnetize Money.

Hill brought auric modeling, just like all the other eager young men trying to get their foot in the door. Only Hill did his version impressively. Thus he managed to score depth interviews with the business world's richest and most influential leaders.

Auric modeling can become your secret of success as well as Napoleon Hill's.

You're going to do it anyway, broadcast a certain way of being. With today's energetic literacy, you can make sure that you broadcast something that attracts success.

Sure, you can develop the aura of a rich and influential leader. For inspiration, let's explore the auric modeling of amazing Napoleon Hill. And not just a snapshot, this time. Let's do a full profile.

Napoleon Hill: Magnetize Money Profile

1. Root Chakra Databank: *Earning Money*
5 miles. Behold the determination of a long-distance runner, not pushy but terribly insistent.

"I'm going to reach my goal with you or without you, but I'd sure like to have you keep me company."

Hill also possesses a rare quality of kindness in this chakra databank. Deep down he believes that earning money is a noble pursuit.

2. Root Chakra Databank: *Saving Money*
6 miles. Although I wouldn't call Napoleon greedy, he sure expects to possess loads and loads of money. (Note: He is not straining hard to make himself believe this. He simply believes it.)

3. Root Chakra Databank: *Personality at Work*

1 mile. Curious, questing, Hill has a strong personality with enough personal ego to keep him going but not so much as to arouse feelings of competition in ego-laden captains of industry.

4. Root Chakra Databank: *Personality PROJECTED at Work* (i.e. *While interviewing captains of industry for* Think and Grow Rich)

4 miles. "Personally, I'm at least as powerful as you are. But, notice, I also have a faraway look in my eye, a researcher's quality, because I am only gathering information. I would never, ever pose a threat to you in your business activities.

"No, I admire you from afar. I only seek to understand what makes you so great."

5. Solar Plexus Chakra Databank: *Self-Confidence at Work*

14 inches. Hill feels smart and capable enough to become successful.

Yet I believe he also carries STUFF related to cords of attachment to family members who have not been particularly successful. (This is what makes this confidence databank so small in Napoleon Hill, the kind of STUFF which can be healed but hasn't been, STUFF from family members who lack respect for Hill and his prospects for being successful in life.)

6. Solar Plexus Chakra Databank: *Handling Conflict at Work*

1 mile. Napoleon Hill brings a great deal of wisdom and skill at untangling conflicts for small groups of people.

Full dignity intact, Hill has a way of shifting the intensity of a potential argument into a research opportunity, as in, "We have so many capable and brilliant minds assembled here; let's get busy solving problems together. Together, we can succeed."

7. Heart Chakra Databank: *Emotional Intelligence at Work*

15 inches. Hill is curious, but not too curious, about how people feel. Mostly, he relates what he finds to ideas and theories.

Thus, Hill never appears to be emotionally invasive.

8. *Throat Chakra Databank: **Communication at Work** (e.g., When doing interviews with captains of industry.)*

6 feet. Forceful yet humble: "I'm an ordinary guy, not high-class and definitely not competing with you.

"I admire you without being smarmy. I'm here to receive wisdom from you, and would appreciate so very much if you would be generous with your time and advice."

9. *Third Eye Chakra Databank: **Awareness of His Human Life***

20 miles. Here is a secret of Hill's success as a reporter, as well as a person. He combines intense curiosity about life, slight detachment, and an exceptionally strong inner commitment to honestly monitor his human life in order to make it successful.

10. *Third Eye Chakra Databank: **Connection to Spiritual Source***

Out to the sky. Hill's spiritual connection sustains him in everyday life and motivates him to learn as much as possible.

It's a beautiful, natural, sense of the sacred in life. This man is fortunate enough to have a gift for feeling the presence of God alongside him during the activities of daily life.

Although Hill's spiritual connection databank is large in proportion with the rest, notice that his auric field is huge all around. Besides, "Out to the sky" is not "Out to the moon" or larger, like that of many an LOA follower.

The relative balance in Hill's aura, combined with the quality of chakra databanks, spoke louder than words, and enticingly.

Therefore, when captains of industry checked out his auric modeling, they would find someone they were able to respect. Hill is strong in the databanks that would have mattered most to them.

It also helps that Hill doesn't seem threatening, phony, or combative. Instead, his personality emphasizes qualities that are genuinely engaging. Carnegie chose the right man for this job.

And Hill had enough spiritual vision to accept the assignment, despite the stunningly stingy business deal offered him by Andrew Carnegie.

Summarizing Hill's Energetic Broadcast

That lovely, but out-of-proportion, Third Eye Chakra databank helps explain what Napoleon Hill emphasized in his prosperity system.

Through auric modeling, we don't merely show the world ways to be. Our energy systems are so fluid that a huge surge in one part of an aura can change all the rest. Then conscious thinking changes as well, based on which chakra databanks grow bigger or smaller.

Given his huge connection to Spiritual Source, while interviewing Joseph Stalin and other earthbound big shots, Hill wore the equivalent of lavender-tinted glasses.

Later he reflected on that lovely but slightly distorted reality and brought forth a lavender-tinted prosperity system. Why wouldn't he?

The man lived lavender, having considerably imbalanced Third Eye Chakra databanks. (Note that Hill had many such extra-large third eye databanks, not only the sample one I have read for you here).

Naturally a Napoleon Hill would emphasize "Think and grow rich." Energetically, that is exactly how he was positioned to attract success himself.

Had he possessed Donald Trump's aura instead, Hill would have emphasized something entirely different.

Bless his slightly off-kilter aura. Hill never anticipated those who would follow his lead, how later prosperity teachers would recommend practices that were downright dangerous, inviting a far more serious aura-level imbalance than he ever had.

13. Help from Your Highest Power

Many people are already aware of the difference between spirituality and religion. They realize that having a belief system — a set of thoughts that you regard as the absolute truth — does not make you spiritual no matter what the nature of those beliefs. In fact, the more you make your thoughts (beliefs) into your identity, the more cut off you are from the spiritual dimension within yourself.
— Eckhart Tolle, *A New Earth*

It's no accident that America's Civil Rights Movement was founded by a minister. Dr. Martin Luther King, Jr. gained strength from his spiritual connection. All of us can.

"We shall overcome." The famous song lyric from the Civil Rights Movement is one of the most power-packed sentences of the whole second millennium. Whenever your money magnet seems stuck, you might want to improvise a new version, such as:

- Yes, I *shall* overcome.
- Yes, I *can* overcome the problems that stall my success.
- Yes, I *can* heal the STUFF in my aura that attracts problems and disappointments.
- Even before all that STUFF is fully healed, I *can* do energetic workarounds that make me effective at taking action.
- And, yes, that *will* help me financially.

Who is your ultimate resource for gaining that strength, remembering love, finding your way whatever the obstacle?

It can be your Higher Power.

Only. Wait. And. Think. About. That.

Consider and reconsider that term. Popular use of "Higher Power" is an important second millennium discovery, right up there with "aspirin" and "weekends off."

During the first millennium plus much of the second, your only fully adult, major-league, socially-sanctioned option for spiritual help was "God." Which worked fine, provided that you felt comfortable with the official version at your local religious establishment.

In the 1930's, with the rise of Alcoholics Anonymous, a bold new alternative arose, the term "Higher Power" (HP).

Such a relief to so many was the notion that people could simply call on "a power greater than ourselves." It could be Nature or Science or even the 12-Step Group itself, so long as the designated HP was believed to be loving and caring.

What would happen to Alcoholics Anonymous and all the other 12-Step programs that followed if, suddenly, nobody could get help ever again from Higher Power? They'd quickly become Zero-Step programs with zero membership.

HP has inspired so much healing and financial improvement, you might wonder why I'm devoting a chapter to upgrading the term. If it ain't broke, don't fix it, right?

Certainly I'm not announcing that "Higher Power is dead," imitating the famous statement by Friedrich Nietzsche that "God is dead. God remains dead. And we have killed him."

Higher Power is very much alive, only maybe you have outgrown that particular frequency.

Yes, I'm convinced that, living in the third millennium, a person can do better than request help from Higher Power.

Why venture here? No topic could be more personal. Except wait a minute. *All* your choices about success and growth, even your values around making money, could be considered highly personal.

Besides, you're a Resourceful Reader. You can handle this exploration, whether you wind up agreeing with me or not.

WHEN YOU ASK FOR HELP

If your house were on fire, would you amble outside, wait until some random person stopped by, and mumble that you might need help?

Sure, somebody might wander over, someone who happened to be carrying a fire hose. But really, Resourceful Reader, surely you'd prefer to pull out your phone and dial 911 to get expert help fast.

Since there is no fire now, let's calmly consider what it means to ask for help, spiritual help. Sure, you can ask for help from your Higher Power. Yet, as someone who is developing energetic literacy, can you see why that might not be your best choice? First the good news about Higher Power. It brings help that you can trust.

Not everybody feels comfortable with the word "God." Grotesquely, in childhood, some of us were taught to fear God. Others suffered abuse from priests or ministers, or had other experiences that ruined the term for life. Many of us simply don't really believe in "a God." Yet we are willing to ask for help from a power greater than ourselves.

"Higher Power" to the rescue! With that language, we connect to a benevolent something-bigger while retaining self-authority.

And **self-authority** is one of the most important spiritual concepts of the late second millennium. It means "I did it my way" about religion and spirituality, or any other subject where you might have an opinion. Self-authority means that you get to be the main human decider about your life, nobody else.

It need not matter if certain members of your family tell you "We're praying for your soul," which makes you want to scream "Stop it." You're allowed to make your own choices about religion. You won't be jailed, not in most parts of the world, not in this third millennium.

With self-authority available, you can be curious about HP. Or you can be mildly indifferent. However you think about Higher Power, that is your business, nobody else's.

Self-authority is your right, living in this third millennium. Frankly, that's a much faster way to evolve, compared to giving your power away. Well, self-authority can even boost your earning power.

Self-Authority Switches ON
Your Ability to Magnetize Money

What isn't optional, if you aim to Magnetize Money? You definitely need self-authority. Here's how to make best use of yours. Starting right now, officially consider yourself the most important decision maker in your life. That's right, give yourself the promotion. You can do that right now.

It's easy to tell the difference between people who have self-authority and people who don't.

Gone are the brave mixed messages in nonverbal communication.

Gone is the big fake smile of forced cheerfulness, mingled with other body language of "I don't really wanna be here."

Alas, chronic ambivalence shows in many a hardworking follower of success teachings.

Self-authority can change that. It adds self-confidence. It subtracts resentment. Self-authority can even revitalize the tone of your voice.

Does strong self-authority show at the level of energetic literacy? Only everywhere! The presence or lack of self-authority can be read in dozens of chakra databanks.

So even for the sake of your auric modeling — the hidden factor behind your ability to Magnetize Money — you would want to claim your spiritual inheritance of self-authority.

And now you are invited to apply your full self-authority to a highly controversial question, "What's wrong with depending on your HP?"

THREE WORLDS, NOT TWO

For 10,000 years, an oral tradition from India has described three worlds of interest to all spiritual seekers who aim to gain prosperity. As chanted in scriptures like the Rig Veda, this understanding names three worlds. Notice that number. Three worlds, not two.

I emphasize this point because of my mathematical genius. Wait, not that. There's a serious reason.

In many workshops and websites, prosperity experts refer to only two worlds. Haven't you heard many otherwise sophisticated people use terms like these?

- The Human World
- The Other Side

Now hear this. "The Other Side" includes two different worlds. Each is completely different from the other, just as both of them are completely different from The Human World.

The Divine World is the highest energetic frequency, containing pure and concentrated vibrations of spiritual truth. The Divine is available as an *impersonal presence,* with names like The Universe, The Holy Spirit, The Great Spirit, God.

In addition, the Divine is available in personal forms, with bodies and individual identities and names. Some Divine Beings are *Ascended Masters* like Jesus and Buddha, while others are *Archangels* like Archangel Gabriel and Archangel Raphael.

Energetic textures in The Divine World are etheric, a.k.a., "spiritual" and "akashic" (as in a term you may have heard, "Akashic Records").

The Astral World is the middle frequency. Like the Human World, it contains more layers than a well-made croissant.

Although The Astral World definitely has higher vibrations than our Human World, the frequencies still are way lower than the vibes belonging to The Divine World.

So an astral being like Abraham could trance-channel prosperity teachings through someone like Esther Hicks whereas Jesus would not. By the end of the second millennium, humanity was evolved enough for this to not be necessary. No longer do Divine Beings need use people like puppets for trance channeling. (Anyone today who does trance channeling works with astral beings, knowingly or not.)

Besides "trance channeling," names used in conjunction with The Astral World are *guardian angels, spirit guides, ghosts, mediumship,* and *ancestor spirits.*

Energy textures in The Astral World are psychic, a.k.a. "celestial."

At the third vibration, **The Human World**, we specialize in perceptions that are material and physical.

Money is, of course, physical. For those of us who wish to Magnetize Money, whether we choose to be religious or not, it's rather important to admit the truth of this saying attributed to Jesus:

Render therefore unto Caesar the things which are Caesar's; and unto God the things that are God's.

Physical money is earned in the realm of Caesar, or whoever is politically in charge at the time. Money is physical. Physical money is not a kind of bonus attained by earning extra credit at spiritual life.

NEITHER HERE NOR THERE

You haven't always been human, you know. Before this life and after it, too, you will move back to The Astral World. There you'll enjoy life at whatever level of spiritual evolution you have attained.

Yes, The Astral World is home to evolving souls, where it contains heavens galore.

Here on Earth, haven't you seen plenty of churches, mosques, temples, etc.? Didn't you ever wonder why we have so many? Each religious organization serves people at a particular level of spiritual evolution. And you can be sure there is a corresponding heaven as well.

Plus, Astral World heavens are available for people who choose not to belong to any organized religion whatsoever.

Now, what if the most inspiring influence in your life is Abraham or Lazaris or other channeled beings? You'll go to a heaven at their vibration. Thank the Law of Attraction, pulling you in like a homing signal for your next trip back to The Astral World.

So why does a soul like yours or mine bother to incarnate at The Human World? You don't need me to tell you how annoying this place can be.

Two words: Spiritual evolution.

While living on earth, your usual set of light bodies (a.k.a., Your auric field) evolves due to being joined to a physical, earth-level body.

Between incarnations like this one, you hang out in your energetic body without the adorable, but slow-and-clunky, human one.

Astral living is so much easier. Psychic-level life is bliss, unless you're at a really low level (like those astral planes inhabited by souls with grotesque, blinding hatred or slimy sexual addictions).

Nothing hurts, because your body isn't physical. As for needing money, ha! Even your weight, trust me — no problem!

Living in The Astral World, you don't need money because you can instantly manifest whatever you want. Dead people don't pay mortgages. Simply imagine your dream house and, voila! Faster than you can say "Mega-mansion," it appears.

Hmm, does that sound a little like what is promised in the Law of Attraction? "Desire it and it will appear?"

Sure will, if you're living in The Astral World.

There we feel completely connected to God and each other. Really, there's just one catch. Souls don't evolve terribly fast. When life is one glorious day after another, we have no major problems to test our character. There isn't even time for worrying, since human-type time doesn't exist at this level.

Therefore, ambitious souls choose to incarnate in places where they can evolve faster. One great place to do that is The Human World.

However, one way to evolve *extra slowly* is to be neither here nor there, reluctantly living in The Human World but constantly wishing you could escape to The Astral World.

WIN THE GOODIES WHILE LIVING ON EARTH

To Magnetize Money here and soon, it helps to understand more about how that human evolution works.

From childhood on, we are taught to believe in the physical level of life as if it were the only reality that could possibly count. Watch babies and you'll see them staring inches away from people, checking out their auras. Or you'll hear babies laugh hysterically because they alternate touching their auras, then touching a solid version of their bodies. (To grownups, of course, it can seem as though babies are merely playing with their toes.)

By age five, most children become thoroughly convinced that earth's physical reality is all that matters... unless they are "developmentally disabled," autistic, etc. In that case, a child develops a more complicated perspective that may include more than the usual share of information from both the Human plus Astral plus Divine Worlds.

Otherwise, what is the standard basis for evolving at The Human World?

- We identify with our physical bodies more than our aura-level bodies.
- Therefore, we have fear and pain.
- Therefore, we feel more or less disconnected from other people and God.
- And those physical bodies of ours sure need money!

Manifesting money, or anything else, happens much more slowly on earth than at any psychic-level realm. Time, space, and gravity force us to push our way through obstacles. The Human World has economic laws like "supply and demand" and "diminishing returns."

Basically, manifesting our desires can be slow and hard… on purpose. In The Human World, few of us can simply desire and voila! In comes the money. No instant manifestation here — instead, we must hold fast to a goal and pursue it one day at a time.

If we wish to Magnetize Money, we must be able to handle that money. At least, we must be reasonably confident that we'll be able to handle it. Otherwise, ambivalence will sabotage our actions at the level of auric modeling, which will sabotage any practice done in the name of "Prosperity."

Every thought, word, and action in The Human World produces consequences. Sometimes this is called "**karma**." Physicists might define karma this way, "Every action causes an equal and opposite reaction." Sometimes these reactions come back to us quickly. Other reactions take months or years or even lifetimes.

Yes, your karma from this life is mixed with consequences generated way before now. Plus physical reality on earth must balance everyone else's karma, not only yours. Such a brilliantly designed school for each soul's evolution! Free will plus everyone else's intersecting karma causes life here to be like a crazy, unpredictable, tossed salad.

Karma on earth is so complex and confusing, nobody can figure it all out. Instead, practical people simply accept that *now* is the time of greatest power. This viewpoint can be wonderfully motivating.

In present time, we can aim to create the best karma possible. If we desire wealth, we can summon up purposeful thoughts, supplemented by powerful words, and take appropriate actions. We can do this daily, building momentum over the years.

When the message we keep broadcasting is realistic, consistent, effective, and decisive, we will get results way faster than otherwise. If money is what we desire, of course we will Magnetize Money.

Needing to focus that hard in a world of crazy, mixed-up karma — can that cause a soul to evolve super fast? You bet.

Back at asking for help from your Higher Power, where does that fit in? Asking for this type of assistance causes you to attract help from a higher vibration than your everyday consciousness. But how much higher?

Both the human and astral planes contain many layers of vibration. Think of notes on a piano — not that I'm saying each plane of existence is limited to 88 levels, the number of keys on a grand piano.

But continuing with our analogy, let's say that you are feeling "low" — corresponding to a note like a moderately Low C (one octave below Middle C). You may be recovering from an addiction. Or you hate your job. Or you don't even have a job. Choose an example that is up for you now, an aspect of life where you could use help.

What will happen if you ask for help from your Higher Power? You might attract help at the level of Middle C. Or if you're really lucky, a whole octave higher.

But why trust to luck? In the realm of spirit, absolutely every human being can live like a billionaire. Why on earth would you settle for help that is merely a tiny bit higher? Your request might attract something not so terribly great.

You could be magnetizing help that is the equivalent of one half-step higher on life's keyboard, a low C sharp that still counts as way below Middle C. In human terms, that could mean attracting the support of an AA sponsor who is just slightly into recovery. You'll get some inspiration, but not nearly as much as you need.

How high, vibrationally, is the best help that you could reasonably summon? Why settle for some lowish "whatever," when you could ask for — and receive — help like the very highest piano key?

FREE HELP FROM YOUR HIGHEST POWER

"Be careful what you ask for. You will surely get it."

When you ask for help from The Other Side, you will surely get that. But what kind of help will that be, exactly?

You might draw an angel, a guide, or an ancestor spirit. Any of these astral-level beings can be glorious — wildly impressive, actually, compared to a mere human.

But here's the funny thing about accepting help from some random astral-level entity. It could actually be lower in consciousness than you are. That adorable angel, the departed spirit of your Uncle Logan, could have consciousness like the lowest note on the astral piano keyboard, quite a growly low A.

Even so, in many ways Logan will know things you don't, since he has access to astral-level information. That includes full energetic literacy as his primary mode of perception.

Logan could be as sweet as an angel can be. Yet if you were hanging with him on the Other Side, vibrationally you might be several octaves higher. That's like having a college senior take advice from a second grader.

After asking for help from "A Higher Power," you could get someone like Uncle Logan (or worse). He or she will be very happy to accept your prayers. But why settle for whoever happens to be available? Why aim, or pray, so low? That's tantamount to a business plan where, in the space to write down your financial goals, an inexperienced business owner writes "Whatever."

By contrast, what happens when you ask for help from your **Highest Power**? (That's not High*er* but High*est*.)

Requesting High*est*, automatically your consciousness will attract help from the Divine Level. Remember, that's home to omniscience, omnipotence, the biggest love and spiritual light and nurturing power in all the Universe, free for the asking.

Sure, you can substitute the name of any Divine Being for the term "Highest Power." If you choose Jesus, Kwan Yin, Hercules, or Archangel Michael, your consultation fee will be exactly the same: Free.

Since you have self-authority, naturally, that request will bring in *your* version of the Divine Being. For decades, I have helped clients in healing sessions where I co-created with The Highest Power.

Who would choose? My client. Then we would receive help from that client's version of Buddha or Jesus, not mine.

Some of the names my clients have chosen have been rather ingenious, such as "The Loving Intelligence of the Universe." No worries. I only draw the line at the sweet, but relatively ineffectual, "Higher Power."

Since you have self-authority, Resourceful Reader, I can't persuade you to give Highest Power a try. But I do encourage you to think about the ideas I've presented and decide for yourself. To make this offer more enticing, here comes one of my favorite techniques for healing STUFF from auras.

REMOVING STUFF WITH YOUR HIGHEST POWER

As a healer, I help clients to remove several different kinds of STUFF:

- Cords of attachment.
- Frozen blocks of stuck energy resulting from traumas.
- Free-floating astral debris, such as psychic coercion and negative thought forms.
- STUFF that comes in due to talent, but not yet true skill, at being an empath.
- I even facilitate the occasional exorcism. (Last year, for instance, I facilitated 31 exorcisms out of more than 1,000 personal sessions.)

Removing different types of STUFF requires specialized techniques.

However, there is another big category of STUFF that can be removed relatively easily, no special skill set required. This STUFF is simply astral-level grime from minor traumas, frustrations, contact with difficult people, etc.

The following technique clears it nicely. Personally, I like to use it every 2-3 days. Once you learn the how-to's, it takes just a few minutes.

I would like credit my two inspirations for this technique.

Judy Lavine is a world-class medical intuitive and distance healer who works directly with Highest Power. (See www.judylavine.com.)

Dolly Parton is a singer you may have heard of. In her autobiography, *My Life and Other Unfinished Business*, she describes how she uses the upside-down part of this technique — yet more evidence of Dolly's brilliance, far as I'm concerned.

Your Highest Power Helps You Heal STUFF

Before you do this technique for the first time, read through all the instructions as a preview. Then actually do the technique, peeking with one eye as needed to go through the steps.

1. Sit comfortably on a chair and close your eyes. Let your attention turn inward. Notice something personal about yourself right now, such as an emotion, any physical sensation in your body, or the pace of your thoughts.

Any random choice is fine. Be sloppy, taking it easy throughout the entire technique.

2. Say aloud or think, "Highest Power, I command you to fill me and surround me with Divine Love, Divine Truth, and Divine Power."

3. Take a few deep breaths, then return to normal breathing. Notice how you feel. (Is there anything specific you are supposed to feel? Of course not. Different feelings can come up each time. No flashy experience is ever required.)

4. Ask your Highest Power to turn you upside down, then gently shake out all the STUFF in your aura that can safely be released right now.
Think about this happening in your own way, whether you pretend or imagine or visualize or feel.
You might have an image of yourself at a distance, as if watching it on TV, or you might feel something happening directly in your body. Make something up, one way or the other. (Sloppy is okay, remember.)

5. Whenever you feel that the job is done, ask your Highest Power to turn you right side up. (If you had an image of yourself as separate from your body, do your own version of turning that body right side up; then merge this separate version of self with your regular physical body.)

6. Notice how you feel now. Go back to the type of perception you had earlier, e.g., emotion, physical sensation, the pace of your thoughts. Notice any difference?

7. In your imagination, do a quick song or dance of gratitude to your Highest Power. Think cartoon, not serious — unless, with full self-authority, you prefer a very serious manner. Your choice.

8. Say out loud or think: "Thank you, Highest Power. It is done. It is done. It is done."
Have you guessed? You're saying one repetition for each of the Three Worlds.

DISENGAGEMENT VERSUS ENLIGHTENMENT

As someone who aims to Magnetize Money, it's pretty hard not to evolve fast at Earth School. Sometimes, though, a person will get off the program and have no clue.

Pity those born very rich. Most find it hard to fully engage in life. Maybe you've never thought of your financial struggles as a motivator for personal growth. Well, think of it now.

Have you ever met someone who was born with silver spoons for the baby food, plus a trust fund to match? I have. Lucky people like that haven't necessarily been so lucky at all. They can be relatively untouched by motivations like fear of poverty, the need to earn a living, etc. That means less incentive to engage fully in life.

I remember one period in my past, during the worst of my spiritual addiction, when I was really, really poor. I had a tooth in urgent need of a crown. Yet I had to wait a whole year before I could afford to see a dentist. Managing food and cheap rent was hard enough.

At the time, I tried to be a good sport, affirming like mad. I dreamt about being fully Enlightened, when all my problems (including the tooth) would be magically solved. In retrospect, that tooth was a godsend, keeping me more grounded than I'd have been otherwise.

Pain, poverty, weight problems: Difficulties like these can be gorgeous Earth School blessings in disguise. When we're getting so pie-in-the-sky that otherwise we'd waste our time here, ouch! On comes the karma-catastrophe.

Sure it stinks. But it works.

We start paying attention again as if life *really mattered.* Does it accelerate our evolution, or increase our wealth, to strive for detachment? I don't think so.

At the time of this writing, one popular way to detach from life is marijuana, medical or recreational. From the perspective of energetic literacy, pot is not the innocuous chemical that users claim. Nor is it a perfectly sensible drug to ease pain. (Hypnosis would be that sensible drug, as it is well researched, effective, and involves no chemicals whatsoever.)

Pot, like cocaine or heroin, moves a person's consciousness into an astral-level high… the particular level depending upon the drug taken, how often it's taken, and the state of the person's nervous system.

Not only is major STUFF deposited aurically whenever a person takes a drug like pot. The person starts identifying more with The Astral World. Becoming disengaged from life, not believing in one's Earth School curriculum, can slow evolution significantly, keeping a person from earning at full potential. (All addictions do that, not just spiritual addiction.)

By contrast, spiritual Enlightenment is the opposite of dysfunction and disengagement. In this high state of consciousness, a person is fully human, functioning without STUFF. So energetic literacy reveals gifts of the soul but not entrenched patterns of fear, pain, anger, resentment, sorrow, etc.

To verify a state of Enlightenment, you need full energetic literacy. You can't base your evaluation on outward behavior, such as possessing a happy mood, a perfect weight, flawless skin, or other surface-level attributes.

Remember our research on Jeffrey Chappell? A certain kind of detachment arises within any Enlightened woman or man. Only it's a joy-based, blissful form of detachment. Spiritual consciousness has grown so big, there's no reason left to sweat the small stuff.

To conclude Part One of our Program, here is a Magnetize Money Snapshot of an influential success expert, not Enlightened but radiating a contagious passion for life.

Alexandra Stoddard: Magnetize Money Snapshot

While Alexandra Stoddard doesn't teach how to earn money, she gives exceedingly good advice about how to spend it. You could call her a lifestyle coach or even, as she calls herself these days, a "philosopher of contemporary living."

No matter how much money you have magnetized so far, Stoddard can help you enjoy it. Learn more at her official website, www.alexandrastoddard.com. And find the photo used for this energetic literacy profile at our "Photo Supplement" online.

1. Root Chakra Databank: *Earning Money*

50 miles. In Alexandra's case, earning feels like attracting. There is no pushing, no conflict, no fuss.

"I work hard and always do my best. This attracts money."

2. Solar Plexus Chakra Databank: *Handling Conflict at Work*

35 feet. Negotiation and listening are such strong skills, Alexandra confidently expects to work out any conflict.

In fact, she doesn't expect conflict to arise. Her down-to-earth way of paying attention to life warns her quickly of any signs of impending conflict.

3. Third Eye Chakra Databank: *Connection to Spiritual Source*

90 feet. Qualities like love and beauty give a distinctive flavor to Alexandra's spiritual connection. She has the energy field of a born artist.

What a rock-firm, flexible, connection to Highest Power! No need for her to talk theology. She lives this glorious connection, shines it out through auric modeling.

One of the most splendid things about this altogether extraordinary woman is her human gusto. Alexandra's relationship to physical objects — beautiful things — is magical.

You can consider Alexandra Stoddard living proof. Way before Enlightenment, a person can be wonderfully present in human life. Choice can help make that happen, paying attention to human life as though it mattered.

That's different from cultivating detachment as a short-cut to self-realization. To sum up:

- Enlightenment isn't a mood but an integrated state of mind-body-spirit, where the nervous system is STUFF-free.

- Enlightenment does not mean spiritual addiction, where some Third Eye Chakra databanks are way enormous and the rest of the aura remains puny.
- Enlightenment doesn't happen because a well meaning person prays constantly or tries to think only happy thoughts. Instead, all the chakra databanks are fully alive, engaged in life, and animated by bliss.

Yes, it is possible to evolve so much at The Human Level that the quality of life changes for good.

Collectively, humanity is moving toward that, I believe. And I'm hopeful that, when historians look back on the third millennium, they will find that a couple of decades into it, the majority of humans achieved a permanent state of Enlightenment.

Could that state of fulfillment be your future? Could your drive to Magnetize Money help you to evolve extra fast?

Energetic literacy doesn't guarantee Enlightenment… but certainly makes it easier to evolve than settling for whatever happens to come your the way.

Caring about your progress toward wealth demands that one pay attention to objective reality. One is less likely to outsource one's life to be run by an astral being.

So many paths work for self-actualization. What doesn't seem to help much? Squandering a human lifetime on being homesick for heaven.

PART TWO
Magnetize Money
As Only You Can

To Magnetize Money, be here (fully) now. Then do what it takes to grow rich.

Do you believe that success can come to you because you are talented in some ways that others are not?

Or do you believe that you can attract success because you are willing to work hard?

People in that second group achieve far more than those in the first. You can read all about that, including supporting research, in "The Talent Myth: Are Smart People Overrated?" It's a chapter in *What the Dog Saw* by Malcolm Gladwell.

Turns out, you're more likely to become a star in the workplace — a high performer who earns what you're paid — if you are willing to work for results, not merely bask in your own specialness.

But what if you choose to do both?

- Suppose that you like yourself and believe in your talent.
- Suppose that you also like yourself as someone who works hard, that you are eager to do what it takes to achieve the success you desire?
- Suppose further that your auric modeling supports both ways of liking yourself. In short, all that liking is strong enough to produce genuine results in objective reality.

That's what it really would mean to **fall in like** with yourself.

Making that happen is the purpose of Part Two of our Magnetize Money Program.

14. Why You Are the Best

Be impeccable with your word.
— Don Miguel Ruiz, *The Four Agreements*

Of course your word can be impeccable. Your ability to communicate, like all the gifts of your soul, is programmed to work perfectly. You were made with every ability you need to live as the very best possible version of YOU.
— Rose Rosetree, Here (Helping you to Magnetize Money)

Although no human can be the best at everything, you can be the world's best at some things. Yes, you. Definitely.

That personal identity, stamped upon hundreds of your chakra databanks, is unique as thumbprints. It can help you to Magnetize Money. Only, help! What is your distinctive way of being impeccable, your wholeness as a person?

Resourceful Reader, that is your brand, your competitive advantage in the workplace. And there may be more to it than you think.

A Cool Analogy

Every time you look at a refrigerator, it can help you to Magnetize Money as a fully functioning, highly individual, person. Just allow that fridge to remind you of the following analogy.

Your own personal refrigerator, the one in your home right now, contains built-in compartments. For example, there are:

- A freezer, for the ice cream, convenience vegetables, all those chickens you bought on sale, plus any wedding cakes you feel the need to keep around.
- A tall shelf, perfect for orange juice containers, leftover casseroles, any large, bulky items.

- A meat keeper, or sushi keeper, or cheese spa, or hangout place to hold any wide, flat foods.
- One big shelf, towards the bottom, enshrining that precious broccoli, the lettuce and other vegetables.
- One or more big compartments, all the way at the bottom, to stash cherries, potatoes, important bottles of nail polish, any other items that require the least amount of cooling.
- Inside the door you have other fascinating, useful little compartments, such as a little egg nursery with built-in bassinettes.

Each appliance contains built-in locations with the perfect shape and temperature to store a particular kind of food.

What an improvement today's food keepers are, compared to the original "ice box." No mere one-size-holds-all food chest with a block of cold stuff at the bottom! Shelves and compartments within your appliance bring such versatility.

Unfortunately, many people live as though never instructed in the basics of modern fridge use. Take Joy, for instance. She does the equivalent of keeping her broccoli in the freezer.

Also the eggs. Plus tomatoes — and, trust me, freezing does not enhance their texture. Raw bacon, no it does not turn into flat protein popsicles. Lettuce, less said the better because frozen lettuce turns decidedly weird.

Yogurt? Sob! You cannot make "frozen yogurt" by sticking a normal container of the healthy stuff into your freezer. You get the idea. Joy's refrigerator contains many compartments for a reason. No one shelf is meant to store everything at an ideal temperature.

Have you guessed the point of this analogy? Spiritual addiction! Here it comes again, this time in vivid, tooth-tingling color. In terms of your aura, living with spiritual addiction is like storing all your food right in the freezer.

Other addictions do something comparable, making one fridge compartment serve as an overstuffed, out-of-balance and overused part of the whole energy system. Example are:

- A **sex addiction** emphasizes certain databanks in the Belly Chakra, as if cramming all your juice bottles into the meat keeper.

- A **gambling addiction** emphasizes certain databanks in the Root Chakra, comparable to tossing all your frozen dinners into the fruit compartment, right at the bottom.
- A **drug addiction** emphasizes certain databanks in the Third Eye Chakra, similar to shoving bacon, lettuce, tomato, and bread into the back of the freezer (where it will *not* make a very good sandwich).
- An **alcohol addiction** emphasizes certain databanks in the Third Eye Chakra, not unlike stuffing baloney and sardines into your ice cube tray.

Sadly, there is one great big difference between having an imbalanced aura versus Joy's wacko-style fridge use. Unlike weirdly stored food, Joy's aura-level imbalance won't be consciously clear to others... not unless her employer or customer has full energetic literacy.

Sure, this ability to secretly store things wrong can appear convenient, short term. Again, let's consider Joy, with her spiritual addiction courtesy of too much LOA. She'll appears fine at the surface level, especially with that great big, cheerful smile.

People with Stage 1 Energetic Literacy won't notice a problem, considering that Joy's vibes are wonderful.

Stage 2 Energetic Literacy might not reveal the problem either, because her chakras on the whole might qualify as "open."

Joy's hidden problem would show with Stage 3 Energetic Literacy, in the size of her chakra databanks, plus problem-related STUFF, and distorted patterns overall that amount to the syndrome I call "spiritual addiction."

Otherwise Joy may have no clue whatsoever about these hidden, subconscious-level, problems. Especially because noticing them would contradict her belief system. That is telling her, "When everything inside your fridge becomes well and truly frozen, every dream of your heart will come true."

Energetic Sub-Routines

With an aura way out of whack, a person may have scant motivation to overcome an imbalance... until hitting bottom. Then the sad pattern is seen: No job. Home foreclosure. No sex for the past three years. Ouch indeed!

Alternatively, a person can discover imbalance relatively early and choose to fix the problem then. And such a person might be you.

Certainly, it's helpful to know about problems that distort the functioning of one's energy field. So let's return to our analogy that compares an auric field to a well-working refrigerator.

Each of your major shelves — okay, chakras — is a like a big separate compartment. It can take over the functions that rightly belong to an entirely different compartment. When this happens, there will be no loudspeaker announcement like ,"Watch out for Joy's weird frozen block, what used to be yogurt but now has become a large and sullen, opaque mass. Can't miss it. The whole blob is topped with a sad, yellowish puddle of ice."

No, the capacity for self-delusion, combined with human versatility, nicely covers up problems like "fresh yogurt in the freezer." Eventually, however, imbalance intensifies until it can be ignored no longer.

- Sometimes STUFF causes a chakra databank to turn teensy, **under-functioning** at just a fraction of its potential effectiveness. Low energy alert! Enthusiasm mysteriously disappears for the related aspect of life.
- Sometimes STUFF causes **over-functioning** instead. A particular aspect of life is emphasized. Too much energy, even obsession. This problem, of course, can relate to addictions or other problems with overall balance.
- A third kind of problem can arise. I call it "an energetic subroutine." Let's continue to use Joy's situation for an example. Say that her fridge is built with a wide, slender shelf quite high up, a meat keeper.
  Usually Joy buys deli items, like cheese slices, and stores them quite nicely. With the shelf broken, however, she starts keeping these products somewhere completely different, perhaps all the way at the bottom, in her least-chilled compartment, the fruit keeper.
  Because that meat keeper stays broken, Joy develops a habit of always putting food in the wrong place.

Soon, Joy doesn't think twice. Routinely she keeps her cheese at the fridge bottom, then wonders how come it spoils so often. Hey, maybe she blames her deli.

ENERGETIC SUB-ROUTINES IN EVERYDAY LIFE

Here are examples of energetic sub-routines that sabotage success teachings. Each example is drawn from the aura of a real-life client I was able to help.

For your own protection in the workplace, learn to recognize these syndromes in people, everyone you do business with or, even, possibly, yourself.

- Third Eye Chakra functioning takes over to such an extent, Joe doesn't live in "reality" any longer. He's so busy affirming, he scarcely notices what is happening around him in the physical world.
(While he's on the job, Joe's co-workers can tell that he "isn't all there.")
- Some of Jenny's Heart Chakra databanks are working overtime. She tries so hard to "be happy and attract wealth through positive emotions." This results in a strained personality, making her seem like a phony and, even, arousing suspicion in others. Something funny is clearly going on.
(Ironically, Jenny's hard work to gain wealth couldn't be more counterproductive.)
- Because Jeremiah works in the mental health field, he figures he knows "all about" human emotions.
If only he knew what was really going on at the level of his own aura. Human emotions aren't made to be figured out but experienced. Many of Jeremiah's Heart Chakra's databanks have been outsourced to his Solar Plexus Chakra.

What does it feel like, having an entrenched energetic sub-routine? Let's go into Jeremiah's plight in a bit more detail.

Because emotions are more than ideas, Jeremiah's problem is not merely theoretical. At his Heart Chakra, he carries STUFF configured into an energetic sub-routine. Until this pattern changes, he will have a big blind spot emotionally.

Eventually someone may tell him, "Jeremiah, you only have thoughts about feelings. It has been years since you've had a real-life emotion."

Research has shown that emotional intelligence helps to build business success. Poor Jeremiah thinks he has it, but doesn't.

Here's another example of how life can suffer, due to an energetic sub-routine. Janet has been dieting for years. Until her weight is brought under control, she can't have much of a career. At least that's what she believes.

What if Janet were asked, "Are you in touch with your physical body?"

She might laugh. Or cry. She might tell you all she has learned about counting calories and carbs, reeling off entire pages from her memorized chart about glycemic index.

Except, with Stage 3 Energetic Literacy, the truth becomes sadly obvious. Aurically, Janet is only really alive from the bust up. She hasn't had an authentic, direct experience of her body for years.

Of course, all her energetic sub-routines can be healed. Realistically, Janet's weight problems may or may not be over. Definitely, though, she can focus on earning real money and, otherwise, getting a life.

Clients like Janet have shown improvement rather quickly. They needed help to rebalance, that's all. A bit of STUFF removal here, some validation there....

Resourceful Reader, even a minor problem with an energetic sub-routine could cause you to de-Magnetize Money. If you have a problem with an energetic sub-routine, Part Two of our Magnetize Money Program can help you identify the problem.

I will supply some energetic workarounds that are your next step to improving your auric modeling and, through that, your bottom line financially. You'll know that a healing technique has worked because you'll become more resourceful, and successful, in your attempts to Magnetize Money.

Other people may say they notice a positive change in you. Not knowing about auric modeling yet, they may give you today's "highest compliment" and ask, "Have you lost weight?"

WORK THAT REFRIGERATOR

You can't just think and grow rich. Nobody can. Money isn't developed exclusively from within your human self, like growing hair. Wealth requires an interpersonal flow.

Therefore, effective success teachings must improve how a person circulates socially.

What do your paying customers think of you? How about their real-world actions, needs, and desires? Are you willing to learn what they'll pay for?

Networking can help you pursue business contacts. But what will cause a new business contact to like *you* or read your emails or keep that shiny new business card?

Use all the circuits in your energy fridge. Auric modeling proclaims the truth of who-you-be. Over time, a better energetic balance can help you to broaden your social network.

Just like a top-of-the-line refrigerator, you were built energetically as a splendid appliance. Sure, you have circuits for getting along relatively well with your boss, anybody you supervise, any reasonable client. Should you be self-employed, you can use your full potential to attract and keep customers.

Let's call all these business relationships your **"Significant Other in Career"** or **SOC**. (Pronounced "sock.")

Using your full potential won't guarantee how any SOC responds to you. Even if you could wave a top-tier magic wand, phoenix feather and all, you couldn't *force* someone else to respect you. Nonetheless, you can *attract* more respect coming to you from every SOC.

Here's a real-life example of someone who uses his energetic potential to great advantage. Not perfectly, but very effectively for the purpose of becoming rich.

Supermarket super-owner Karl Albrecht has become the wealthiest man in Germany and the sixth richest man worldwide. This man knows how to Magnetize Money, a.k.a. lettuce, well enough to have gained an estimated fortune of $21.5 billion.

The Richest Man in Germany: Magnetize Money Snapshot

1. Root Chakra Databank: *Earning Money*

900 miles. Getting this man excited it isn't easy. Offer him some really fresh-looking asparagus and I doubt he would be thrilled... unless he could buy it in great quantity, at a great price, for his stores.

And, yes, I've peeked into Karl's Libido databank at the Belly Chakra. Sex is okay, but it no longer rings his chimes, either.

Money, however? Yum.

2. Solar Plexus Chakra Databank: *Handling Conflict at Work*

90 scary miles. Karl doesn't strike me as physically dangerous. Rather, the quality of this databank suggests that he would be totally legal and civilized in his ruthless way of punishing any wrongdoer.

If you work for this man, you really, really don't want to wind up on his "Bad List." But in terms of using his circuits effectively to get what he wants, he's doing fine (and doing it in a way that helps him to Magnetize Money).

3. Third Eye Chakra Databank: *Connection to Spiritual Source*

2 inches. Mr. Albrecht's relationship to Highest Power appears to be one of polite indifference. Related Third Eye Chakra databanks ("Spiritual Growth," "Envisioning with Help from Spiritual Source") are likewise puny. Don't think for a moment that that Karl's success has come from hard work with a dream board.

However, the supermarket king does fine at other Third Eye Chakra databanks — ones related to his very human, personal life.

Altogether Karl Albrecht is making fabulous use of his inner appliance. That aura-level refrigerator of his is in excellent shape.

Using the gifts of his soul to accomplish what he values most — anyone can do that. Just like him, we have been built with the auric equivalent of a first-rate refrigerator.

You or I might make choices that are kinder, gentler, more spiritually delicious than those made by Mr. Albrecht. But make no mistake. Energetically this man knows how to work his fridge.

15. No More Frozen Lettuce

Avoid believing things are better than they really are when you are on a peak, or worse than they really are when you are in a valley. Make reality your friend.
— Spencer Johnson, M.D., *Peaks and Valleys*

Sure you can clean up your act, at the level of auras. You can sort out, shelf by shelf, what is kept in your energetic refrigerator. Use the best techniques you can find, including the energetic workarounds in this chapter.

Meanwhile, don't be like Joe, mentioned in our last chapter, that patient success seeker who blames every money problem on his temporary lack of perfection, so he keeps on trying to affirm his way to success.

For pity's sake, American bills say "In God we trust," not "God approves of your having money only if you are perfect in every way."

Never put your work success on hold until you attain perfection. Do an energetic workaround instead. Right now. This chapter is full of them.

Point by point, I will describe how well-functioning chakra databanks can help to you to Magnetize Money.

Here's what I recommend. Read the whole chapter. Then choose one of these energetic workaround as a priority and play with that technique for a week. Continue to experiment, one workaround for a week at a time, just a few minutes per day.

That way you'll know which technique changes what.

Depending on your personal growth areas, your priorities and resources, you might also choose to accelerate the process of Magnetizing Money by hiring some consultants. And I don't necessarily mean business coaches. Find the healers and therapists who are right for you, specialists at permanently healing STUFF from blocked chakra databanks. Even if you don't give a hoot, personally, about having your aura be balanced, consider it a business investment.

Your human consciousness is one of the most powerful tools on the planet. Here come ways to direct that consciousness in ways that make you a stronger magnet for success.

Interact More Effectively with Your SOC

Most of us make money through some kind of interaction or service related to other people. (Resourceful Reader, remember, I'm continuing to refer to these people as "Significant Other in Career" or SOC.)

To interact most productively with any SOC, you need a strongly functioning **Root Chakra**.

All 50 databanks in this chakra support your reality-based social behavior. When they function well, while you engage with others you will seem like a credible adult who is fully present in the situation.

Also, with a lively Root Chakra, you will seem important to others, or at least worth noticing. An impressive thin slice of your personality will create your first impressions.

A common mistake: Trying to adjust your energy with positive thinking, affirmations, etc. Any inner activity to strengthen yourself spiritually will be a poor substitute for the basic human job called "Be present in the here-and-now."

What's your energetic workaround?

Be Here. Be Here. Be Here.

Early in your business conversation, pay attention to at least three things about your SOC on the level of physical reality. You could notice clothes, the room where you are, the pace of the conversation. Notice anything, so long as it is objective and physical.

By paying attention at this level you strengthen your energy presence at the Root Chakra.

Afterwards, for the rest of your conversation, pay close attention to what is said and done on the level of reality. That's where business contracts are signed, right on the surface of life.

Okay, those with energetic literacy know that Root Chakra and surface are not the *only* places where business is transacted. Never ignore this material aspect, however, not if you aim to magnetize material-level money.

With a well-working **second chakra,** you'll be plugged into the energy dynamics of any conversation. Realistically, you need accurate information as you improvise any here-and-now conversation.

A common mistake: Trying to force another person to submit to you, energetically.

For example, a person who wants the best possible energy dynamics might misuse a technique like "**Pace and Lead.**" This body language-based technique is often recommended for sales. Say that Money Magnetizer Tyrone starts to subtly copy physical positions, tempo of gestures, or tone of voice of his client, Tina.

After entraining with Tina, he then tests the connection by initiating new gestures. When Tina starts copying him, Tyrone "knows" he has increased his chances of making a sale.

If you think about it, you have surely been on the receiving end when someone tried to control you with "Pace and Lead." Well, how much did you enjoy that?

Even if you didn't know exactly which gimmick the sales person used, you could probably feel that you were being manipulated.

With all respect to Tyrone and the really good product he is trying to sell, sneaky isn't good. Trevor's intent to trick customers may work in some cases. But it will definitely show in his auric modeling and detract from his credibility. You can be energy smart without ever once being energy coercive.

Strength in Belly Chakra databanks will improve your ability to engage the energy with any SOC. When you have full energetic literacy, you can take an accurate peek whenever you wish. Find out exactly what's going on.

Before then, what's your energetic workaround?

A Super-Quick Energetic Hello

At the start of your conversation with the SOC, take a minute or less to check out the nonverbal aspect.

- Who speaks *first?*
- Who speaks *more?*
- Does any *feeling* develop within you about the energy dynamics?

Compute this with any skills you possess for energetic literacy.

Only do all this very briefly. Immediately return to paying attention at the surface of regular human reality. That way, you will continue to be effective.

Even a very quick notice can tell you if the energy flow is going well. Or not.

What if you're not sure? Count whatever you have received as valid. Over time you'll build confidence.

Whatever you learn, aim to make this conversation work the best it can. Be willing to adapt your timing, your words, to improve the energy flow.

At the surface level of body language or pacing, take on just a bit of the style of the person you're talking to. And be sure to consciously set an intention before doing this. *"I don't aim to manipulate. I aim to communicate."*

Automatically, you'll start flowing better with your SOC.

WHO WANTS TO BE TREATED LIKE A NOBODY?

For your greatest success, each SOC must represent more to you than an income stream. Unlike you — but totally like himself or herself — that SOC is an individual.

When you appreciate that deeply enough to show energetically, your speech and actions will shift in subtle ways that add up to repeat business.

Which part of you is designed to assess and repair these power dynamics? It's your **Solar Plexus Chakra.**

When this chakra works well, you'll feel stable, balancing your needs along with the needs of others. Databanks in your Solar Plexus Chakra can also help you to stay punctual, mindful of details, and flexible.

A common mistake: Sensing the individuals around you takes a bit of work. This work need not be hard, especially if your Third Chakra is functioning well.

Before then, you may sometimes relate to the viewpoint immortalized by Charles Schulz in *Peanuts*, " I love humanity; it's people I can't stand." And then, alas, you may try something that may seem like an energetic workaround but actually creates an energetic sub-routine.

Even the most spiritually-oriented prosperity teachings can encourage us to depend on theories about universal benevolence, rather than engaging with a SOC directly. In theory, who doesn't adore concepts like these?

- "When I look in your eyes, I can behold the Divine in you.'"
- "The only thing you need do is *feel good now*."
- "So long as I stay positive, there will be no problems."

Unfortunately, spiritually-based (Sixth Chakra-based) concepts like these can distract us from using our Third Chakra circuits. These power strengths are indispensible, especially when real-life conversations contain more than one point of view.

Your SOCs may not consciously know when prosperity shtick is being thrust upon them. But most human beings are surprisingly good at sensing the presence or absence of an authentic connection.

Ironically, making a super-human effort to draw from some universal source of benevolence won't work nearly as well as humble, everyday, human paying attention.

To. One. Conversation. At. A. Time.

What's your energetic workaround?

The Power-Enhancing Two-Step

While talking with that SOC, ask yourself occasionally, "How is the idea part of this conversation going?"

Do you agree with the SOC's point of view? If not, what can you do about it?

During any conversation, you have an energy presence, not merely an agenda. If you wish, your point of view can be supported by auric modeling with a powerful presence.

What flows through your intellect energetically? Whether the conversation is easy or difficult, personal power galore is available. It pulsates through your Third Chakra, the one at the ribcage.

Don't block that energy with shallow breathing, tensing up your body, or a rigid posture.

Still not feeling fully resourceful yet? Inwardly take a step back from the conversation. Take a deep breath. Then, privately (and quickly):

1. Notice how the conversation is going.

2. Ask inside, "How can I persuasively present my point of view?"

3. Commit to not only talking. Listen.

4. Commit to not pushing. Listen.

5. Ask yourself, "How important is it that I be right, and that this person agrees I am right? Is there a way, with integrity, that I can simply show this person respect?"

Often it helps to remember that your goal is to Magnetize Money, not necessarily convert every person to your point of view."

Okay, step back into that conversation. Engage with your full self, all your life force energies ablaze. Whatever the outcome of this particular conversation, you are building a cumulative social strength, alternating a healthy give-and-take while keeping full power engaged.

CONNECTING EMOTIONALLY WITH YOUR SOC

A big smile can bring you a long way socially, especially in any group devoted to practicing LOA. But let's get real. Using full energetic literacy, it becomes clear: Authentic emotional connection isn't about looking happy. Or looking anything that you don't feel. Or even, necessarily, about how you feel at all.

How does your SOC feel? That's the primary thing to notice in business dealings.

Until your **Heart Chakra** works well, however, you won't really know. Theories or affirmations can fix your business relationships about as effectively as Monopoly money will buy you a real-life railroad.

Strong emotional connections at work require emotional intelligence (EI). It helps you to name the emotions of other people, connect with those people emotionally, then reason and solve problems based on a strong emotional connection. EI is well documented as indispensable for business success.

But EI isn't the sole requirement for having productive workplace relationships. Energetically, what about the who-you-be while you wield that EI?

We've all seen the mega-bright, hollow smile of an overworked positive thinker. It's about as subtle as a 10-foot Frosty the Snowman blowup ornament, out on the lawn to help everyone celebrate Christmas, like it or not. Sure, a smile beats a frown or a snore. Still...

Auric modeling reveals every imbalance. At the level of energetic truth, each person's who-you-be shows up as clearly as a decorated Christmas tree. Electric lights will either twinkle or not. Who would knowingly display a string of bulbs that doesn't quite light up?

Bring on the energetic workaround!

At Home on Your Range

Over the years, I have done extensive research into individual gifts at the Heart Chakra databank for **Emotional Self-Awareness.** Each person is unique in that way. By analogy, think of the range of a person's singing voice. Not everyone sings like Mariah Carey, larking her voice across four octaves.

According to Broadway legend, when the classic musical "The King and I" was created, actress Deborah Kerr was named as the star. She had charisma, acting talent, beauty, and a lovely voice... far as it went. Songs composed for Kerr needed to be restricted to her very small vocal range. So they were.

(Try singing "Getting to Know You" and you'll hear what I mean. Or find the movie version of the musical and hear delightful Deborah herself.)

Tiny though Deborah Kerr's vocal range may have been, she sang those notes beautifully. Emotionally, everyone can do that much. Regardless of your natural range, you can perform with verve and zest.

So move from potentially great to the real thing. Exercise your range of emotions and experiment with EI at the same time.

- While with your SOC, move away from surface reality for this two-second technique.
- Ask yourself, "What is this person feeling emotionally right now?"
- Find words for it. Be sloppy. You're not on trial here, just warming up your emotional voice.
- Consider whatever you learn to be valuable information. Just for a second, let yourself feel the impact emotionally.
- Now bring yourself right back to the here-and-now conversation.

Some people will always have more emotional range than others, but there's no need to compare yourself to anyone else. You can sing beautifully within the range you've got, so use it.

Energetic Communication with Your SOC

Throat Chakra alignment can boost your effectiveness, too. Your **fifth chakra** can become a major force helping you to Magnetize Money.

Energetic literacy brings many useful discoveries related to databanks here. Energetically powerful communication brings an oomph that most people haven't developed yet. (What's the big exception here? Throat Chakra power is common among the very rich and successful.)

For starters, let's recognize a common problem revealed by energetic literacy. Might you be storing old patterns of grief, rage, or fear in your Throat Chakra? If so, don't think you can hide it. On the level of auric modeling, everything shows, remember?

I don't point this out in the spirit of "Blame the victim." Instead, I want to remind you, a person who seeks real-life results in the world: Resourceful Reader, you never leave home without your aura.

One client of mine had a Throat Chakra problem that drastically limited his success. Jose carried patterns of STUFF on the theme that went, "Why bother to speak up for myself? Nobody ever will listen."

Energetically, this "Why bother?" stuck out like a sore thumb. If clairaudient, you could hear it, too.

I even heard it literally. Via my voice mail. At the time, I had one of those voice-activated machines where the caller could leave a message of any length. Afterwards the machine would click off.

Except poor Jose. He couldn't manage to leave a complete message. The man's voice was so soft, my machine would register "Nobody's there" and hang up on him, mid-sentence.

Jose chose to heal this pattern from the inside out. Once he moved out some rather discouraging cords of attachment, Jose regained his ability to communicate just fine. We have stayed in touch, so I can verify that Jose is now able to leave a complete voice message whenever he wants.

However, it is also possible to use energetic workarounds to fix communication problems from the outside in. Admittedly, this can take a bit more resolve and patience. Still it can be done, and done 100% as do-it-yourself. Want to try? Here's your energetic workaround.

Heal One Nonverbal Problem at a Time

Self-fulfilling prophecy is a term psychologists use for negative beliefs about life that come true. If you find a discouraging pattern to your conversation with others, find a quiet moment when you can reflect on your life. Then ask yourself, "What is the pattern?"

Here are examples of patterns that might be related to Throat Chakra databank problems:

- People treat me as though I have nothing to say.
- People act belligerent for no reason.
- People say that I have a chip on my shoulder.

Energetic STUFF causes patterns like these. Then the patterns turn into self-fulfilling prophecies. After a while, you expect the negative outcome and, thus, the old pattern plays "Gotcha" time and time again.

As part of the cycle, a person develops nonverbal habits, like the way Jose felt so sure that nobody listened to him, and therefore he let his voice became inaudible.

But nonverbal behavior can be changed. You can stop any game of "Communication Gotcha." Make use of this simple fact: Throat Chakra blockage can link directly to habits at the body language level.

Once you identify a pattern, you can find how it shows nonverbally. Just do a bit of research:

- Pretend that you're talking to some SOCs and record your voice. Listen afterwards, as if you were a contestant for the reality show, "American Idol of Non-Verbal Confidence."
- Or playact near a full-length mirror. Every once in a while, stop the action. Move over just a bit so you can catch the full-length body language.
- Even better, get a friend to make a video — one that you definitely won't post on YouTube. Role play yourself in a work

setting. Record. Play it back. Watch objectively. (Even better if your friend is kind, watch together and discuss.)

Whichever "Gotcha" habit shows from your research, working persistently, you can change that. Tone of voice, physical posture while speaking, facial expression — any of these may sabotage how you speak to SOCs.

Resolve to change those habits, one by one. For instance, if your voice trails off mid-sentence, resolve to speak faster and louder. You'll have to find your own part of this workaround. And you will, so long as you refuse to give up.

WHEN IN DOUBT, CONSULT YOUR HUMAN SELF

Personally, I wouldn't dream of neglecting my **sixth chakra.** Neither would you, right? Yet energetic research on the rich reveals that, contrary to most prosperity teachings, the spiritual side of making money is quite optional. A gorgeous, glorious Third Eye connection to Highest Power isn't necessary at all (not for making money, anyway).

Only there is one major exception. When somebody aims to Magnetize Money, one databank at the Third Eye Chakra *must* work well. It's called "Awareness of Your Human Life."

How are you doing at that one? When you need help with career, or have doubts about your own performance, whose opinion do you seek?

Consider your own perspective, informed by checking in with reality as well as introspection. "Your opinion" means the wisdom generated by *you,* the human being who lives within your skin. Here and now and wonderfully human.

Just as some prosperity seekers confuse spiritual addiction with Enlightenment, sometimes there's a confusion related to time. Did you ever try to be your *future* self while earning money in the *present?* Okay, few of us put it that way. Yet we squander some of our loveliest aura-level resources by doing things like this:

- Trying very, very hard to always consult my guides.
- Wishing that I were Enlightened.
- Asking myself, "What am I meant to learn here?"
- Wondering "What would Jesus do?"
- Golly, there's even a book out now with the title *What Would Napoleon Hill Do?*

Any of these habits is tantamount to giving away your self-authority, which won't help a thing. Certainly it won't make you rich.

Major money makers don't emphasize otherworldliness. (Consider Esther Hicks + Abraham to be the exception that proves the rule.)

Instead, successful people consult themselves. Perhaps they trust their personal Angel Committee to whisper into their ears, so the input will seem like their own thoughts.

Your Angel Committee can that for you, too. Just ask. Change your old Spiritual Agreement by saying aloud one time:

"Dear Angel Committee, from now on I choose to be in charge of my life. I choose to value my own thoughts and feelings. Unless there's a life-or-death emergency, send your advice to me in automatic mode. That way, I'll receive it as my own thoughts and feelings. I am now committed to making my human self the primary authority in my human life. Thanks."

Yes, handing power back to yourself can be that simple.

But what if you have the habit of not valuing your perfectly human and worthy opinion? Whom can you consult, if not your guides? Bring on the energetic workaround!

Your Power of Attention in the Here and Now

In any business situation, stay focused on what is happening. Not what could or should happen.

Use all your marbles. Use them here and now, willing to be part of human reality rather than trying to fix that reality, manipulate it, or escape from it.

While you're at work, don't do E.F.T. or Reiki; try self-hypnosis or pull out a pendulum. Don't attempt a walking meditation. Don't keep affirming your life's purpose.

Whenever one person in a conversation detaches through practices like this, it shows to everyone else on the level of auric modeling.

Save spiritual practices and healing sessions for outside of work. Ordinary human reactions of yours in the here-and-now can greatly improve the credibility of your auric modeling. Without a divided mind, your opinions and actions will bring better outcomes.

DOES SUCCESS REQUIRE ABSOLUTE PERFECTION?

Most of the world's richest people aren't Enlightened yet. Energetic, perfection is not required to Magnetize Money.

What if you're extra ambitious? What if you wish to become wealthy and also be a nice person with great relationships? No, you're not asking too much.

To Magnetize Money, however, remember to consistently do the practical things for business. As your part-time job, sure, choose one ongoing energetic workaround or do occasional consultations with a practitioner you like who has skills for removing STUFF. In short, solve one problem at a time and enjoy the cumulative benefits.

And who decides which improvement to focus on first? That's you. Self-authority to the rescue!

Whenever a new client comes to me for help with healing STUFF, I'll ask, "Which aspect of your life do you want to improve today."

About half my new clients have figured this out, which is great. They set intentions like "More confidence" and "Better communication." But the other half say things like, "Tell me. What I am supposed to heal first?"

How flattering! Except what self-respecting emotional or spiritual healer wants to take over a client's personal power?

Resourceful Reader, use your self-authority in life. When you choose your focus for healing (or anything else) listen to your own interests, your hunches, your common sense. Surely these deserve to be held at least as high as the notion of meant-to-be.

Truth is, efforts to Magnetize Money take time. Personal development takes time. And, no matter how resourceful you may be, your time isn't infinite. So why not give yourself the benefit of a time share? Do a bit of self-improvement daily, then turn your attention out toward objective reality — that fascinating place where money is made.

For inspiration about how imperfect you can be, yet still manage to become wildly successful, let's close this chapter with a profile of Tycoon T. I'm keeping him anonymous for reasons that will soon become obvious. Here's one clue to his identity: The man is among the hundred richest people in the world according to Forbes Magazine 2009.

His aura is huge and powerful. Sure, it contains some STUFF that might make you or me cringe. But does Tycoon T. sit around lamenting his lack of perfection? Or does he simply get on with his life and do what it takes to grow rich?

Tycoon T.: Magnetize Money Profile

1. Root Chakra Databank: **Earning Money**

500 miles. "Ambitious" doesn't really do T. justice. Nor does a simple word like "competitive." Energetically, this guy is more like a conquistador. Money is an enduring symbol of power, so he aims to win financially. And I mean: He. Aims. To. Win.

2. Root Chakra Databank: **Saving Money**

80 miles. Saving may not be much fun, compared to the conquest of earning. Still this tycoon *needs* wealth — not so much for its own sake as for all the options it brings. He's careful, wily, and extremely serious about maintaining his financial reserves.

3. Root Chakra Databank: **Personality at Work**

100 miles. This very forceful personality expects to be so respected, he's treated more like a god than a human. Make that a god with lower-case "g."

Actual worship isn't required, but Tycoon T. does consider himself a different kind of human, way more important than ordinary mortals. His personality combines surface skills for connecting to people with a core that needs to stay in control. Employees at any level of management, get chummy with him at your own risk!

4. Root Chakra Databank: *Personality PROJECTED at Work*

500 miles. The personality construct chosen by this executive is fascinating. He aims to make an unmistakable impression on every business contact.

After making that impression, he doesn't want to spend a lot of time hanging around, possibly smudging the polished silver of his well-crafted image.

So he hits business associates hard with his presence, then gets away as fast as he can, as if saying, "On to bigger, more important people!" That urgent exit becomes part of his glamour.

With this glamorous image, much like bottling a fine wine, care has been taken to creating the finish. The desired aftertaste after meeting Tycoon T. goes like this: "What a genius at understanding people! No wonder he is so successful!"

5. Solar Plexus Chakra Databank: *Self-Confidence at Work*

A variable 500 miles. You could boil T.'s self-confidence down to this motto: "I can out-think you. I can out-maneuver you. Just try to defy me! I'll bring you down to your knees."

Does working with other people necessarily have to involve competition? Does third millennium business require the spirit of old-fashioned jousts, with gauntlets tossed down at the slightest provocation?

Maybe not for you or me, but that urge to compete certainly sets the tone for Tycoon T.'s special brand of confidence.

6. Solar Plexus Chakra Databank: *Handling Conflict at Work*

20 miles. Focused rage. Once a situation flips the switch, and conflict can't be avoided, kaboom! The man has a temper that could scorch lawns.

7. Heart Chakra Databank: *Emotional Intelligence at Work*

90 miles. T. cares more about noticing how people feel... than about the people themselves. He loves to influence people's emotions as part of winning wealth.

The tycoon's type of emotional intelligence is clean and keen. He won't actively coerce, which would take away the sport. But he sure does love to control.

8. Throat Chakra Databank: **Communication at Work**
90 miles. Don't expect the words to be flashy. Instead, pay attention to the breathtaking confidence of the speaker. Although he may not own the lands of an emperor, Tycoon T. does possess an emperor's sense of command.

9. Third Eye Chakra Databank: **Awareness of his Human Life**
50 miles. Here is a man who knows what he wants. To T., human success is the goal of life.

10. Third Eye Chakra Databank: **Connection to Spiritual Source**
3 inches. God? Puhleeze. Theologically, as well as commercially, T. is a self-made man. He needs no deity to transmit messages. Life means "I figure out what I want. Then I get it."

What's the closest T. comes to interest in God? That would be having others treat him as a god — not because he needs that but because, when it happens, he finds it so very interesting.

So you're no Tycoon T.? Hooray! Sure he has big bucks, but he also must live with himself.

Meanwhile, your prize is that you get to live with yourself. As you master the secrets to Magnetize Money, you can gain wisdom along with your wealth. Never does your life have to feel like a consolation prize.

16. Network Smarter with Energetic Literacy

Most wealthy people have a wide variety of interests and activities. In fact, there is a substantial correlation between the number of interests and activities that people are involved in and their level of financial wealth.
—Thomas J. Stanley, Ph.D., *Stop Acting Rich… and Start Living Like a Real Millionaire*

Networking is beloved by many a seeker of wealth. One reason is simple. The more successful people you know, the better connected you'll be.

For sheer quantity of connections, any of the following resources could prove indispensible.

- An antique Rolodex.
- Even more retro, plain index cards.
- A software system, such as Jeffrey J. Mayer's ACT!
- Blogging with a large blogroll.
- Maintaining a website stuffed with reciprocal links.
- Social networking as a way of life.
- Secretly hiring people to praise your business at review websites.

In terms of energetic literacy, networking is a Root Chakra builder. The same thing happens when you don't aim to network but, instead, strive for a great social life, seeking the maximum quantity and quality of social connections (as rich people do).

Social contact can also help a person recover from spiritual addiction, provided the talk doesn't center on spirituality.

Yes, for many reasons, Root Chakras can be strengthened by conversation at the most superficial level, the realm of "Hello" and "How do you spell that last name?"

Energetically, your impressiveness to others is directly proportional to having a strong presence at the Root Chakra. So networking makes more sense than ever.

At the level of databanks in your first chakra, you can get results in a week, spending just 10 minutes daily for social outreach.

Of course, this will build Root Chakra strength only if you can bring yourself to *enjoy* these superficial conversations and do them honestly. (Back at hiring people to praise you online, do you think anyone's auric modeling can really get away with that?)

In *Success is a Journey*, Jeffrey J. Mayer modifies the usual networking advice, which can degenerate into a kind of numbers game. He suggests cultivating business friendships only with people you actually like. Networking Jeffrey J.-style, you still might gather thousands onto your life list as an avid networker.

But do you really have time for that cast of thousands? With Mayer's concept, you must cultivate relationships with your networkees by calling or emailing every single one several times a year.

Certainly everyone knows (or should know) that any new business card has an expiration date of three days. After that, don't bother to contact that person unless you're delivering money. For other business purposes, your smokin' hot lead is now cold as yesterday's pizza.

Of course, all of us have been victims of hit-and-run networking, with a business card slapped into your hand right before the busy networker rushes on to the next hot prospect.

One way to distinguish yourself as a networker is to set an underlying intention to share prosperity, rather than grab it. Although that intention may be private, it matters at least as much as your visible speed at slinging cards or your dedication to Jeffrey J.-style follow-up.

NETWORKING TO MAGNETIZE MONEY

Mayer's *Success is a Journey* was published in 1998. Much as I admire the author and book, his thinking is very second millennium: For success, you simply make the right moves.

Presumably, nobody who matters is going to be energetically literate. Back in the day, before energetic literacy was common, success teachings focused on externals like these:

You had to mind your manners.

Grooming mattered immensely, of course.

Wearing status labels could help. Clothing should certainly appear costly.

Other than that, who cared what you were like as a person, so long as you kept active and stayed out of jail?

Hello! That's different now. In the third millennium, it matters that you bring your aura to every networking event.

Will your efforts really Magnetize Money? Today, that depends largely on your underlying auric modeling. So let's use third millennium street smarts to increase your effectiveness as a networker.

GO-GETTING IN THE THIRD MILLENNIUM

Attention, busy networkers of the 21st century and beyond. Has your lifestyle caused your auric modeling to turn earthbound? Maybe it's time to develop your upper chakras.

Networking sure will not fix that for you. Think about what it means energetically, being a go-getter. Do your efforts at career advancement mostly emphasize the going forth and getting?

Then your auric modeling may show smallish development from the Heart Chakra up. In physical terms, that would be the equivalent of body building like crazy, but only from the waist down.

Imagine having legs like tree-trunks, abs of titanium, an impeccably muscled butt. Gorgeous, except from the waist up… what if your energy bod has pretzel- stick-like chest and arms? Maybe a small pretzel nugget for the head?

Seriously, everyone needs some spiritual practice or technique for emotional growth, practiced daily.

Choose as many as you wish. But, for balance, aim for a total time of 30-60 minutes each day. Any of these could strengthen your auric modeling from the Heart Chakra up:

- Prayer
- Meditation
- Visualization
- Self-hypnosis

- Aura reading
- Face reading
- Skilled empath merge
- Contemplation or analyzing your emotions
- Emotional Freedom Technique
- Angel work
- Tai Chi
- Qigong
- Yoga
- Reiki
- Energy Medicine
- Healing Touch

Just make sure not to overdo. For most people, 30-60 minutes per day is plenty. After that, you're flirting with spiritual addiction, that dreaded lollipop life, so counter-productive if you desire to magnetize the kind of money which counts as valid currency here on earth.

TIME FOR YOUR HUMAN LIFE

Meanwhile, what about you Resourceful Readers with the opposite problem? Are you still working your way back from spiritual addiction? How much time do you spend daily on your various woo-woo activities?

To calculate the time allocated, include all activities like those listed previously.

Then add in every minute when you supposedly are doing regular human things but secretly wish that you could be more religious or spiritual.

Add every minute that you affirm or dream or visualize how rich you aim to be some day.

All dream board time counts, too, of course.

Add it up. Then cut it out, okay? At least cut it *down...* 30 minutes per day, maximum.

The secret is out. Some of you prosperity seekers have been far busier networking with angels than with real people.

Yes, You Can Upgrade Now

In the rest of this chapter, I'm going to share my very favorite energetic workarounds for networking. They can greatly expand your credibility for business communication of all kinds.

Each workaround is designed to wake you up from inside, transforming you energetically. Given the value of auric modeling, that could be like mining gold.

Effective networking isn't only a matter of rules. Sure, you can learn tricks of body language to appear extra interested in your networkee, such as "Pace and Lead," which was discussed in our previous chapter.

You can train yourself to use Emotional Intelligence or work hard to become a better listener. But how far will that go unless you also develop true emotional sensitivity? That's a different matter entirely.

A Networking Oops

One tip I especially like from Jeffrey J. Mayer's *Success is a Journey* goes like this:

Each time you speak with a person, try to ask three questions of him before you start speaking about yourself. This will show that you are interested in the person and the things that are going on in his life.

Except, oops! Several pages later, the success coach warns:

This is one of my biggest pet peeves: I'm talking with someone and he or she asks: "How are you doing?" or "What's going on?" So I answer, and instead of asking a follow-up question, the person says, "Well, what else is going on?" The conversation goes on this way for about 45 seconds and it's apparent that this person has absolutely no interest in any of the things that are going on in my life.

Hold on. Maybe those people were just following the rules. Jeffrey J.'s rules.

Hence my idea that successful networking requires more than following *anyone's* rules.

Reading Jeffrey's book, it's obvious that this man has a big, open heart. If you tried squeezing a page of his book to draw out the essence of Jeffrey J. Meyer as a person, your hand might drip from the honey of his contagious friendliness. (Note: I do not generally recommend literally squeezing book pages as a technique of energetic literacy.)

But what about those clueless networkers, so frustrating to Jeffrey J. Mayer? How to explain networkers totally unlike their mentor? These well meaning wealth-seekers push so hard to follow success teachings, yet ironically they turn their customers off.

In them, you might find Heart Chakra databanks like small, over-salted peanuts.

You, Resourceful Reader, have the right to show the world something markedly different. Maybe your auric modeling at the Heart Chakra could become more like a s'more, cookie plus chocolate and a marshmallow center roasted to a delicious state of goo.

Want sweeter Heart Chakra databanks? It's not just a great investment in your career but helpful for *enjoying* all that extra money you manage to magnetize. So try the following energetic workaround.

INCREASE YOUR EMOTIONAL SELF-AWARENESS

There's great energetic power in paying attention to your very own personal feelings. Notice, I don't mean dwelling on those feelings incessantly... which would be a great way to de-Magnetize Money.

Besides, realistically, who has an extra 40 hours a week just to wallow in feelings?

I'm going to give you some good, quick techniques for more Emotional Self-Awareness. Whether you choose the beginner's version or the more advanced method, you can make it a daily exercise that grows with you. And, once learned, neither workaround will take more than two precious minutes of your time.

Gone are the days when paying attention to emotions was synonymous with analyzing your emotions, their causes, and all related childhood traumas. In the third millennium, we can make use of the principle of "No keeping lettuce in the freezer."

Remember, energetic sub-routines happen when someone develops habits of using one chakra to do the job of another. Each part of your aura has its own specialties and, thus, its own language. Thinking about your feelings shouldn't be confused with feeling them.

A classic French saying puts it beautifully: "Le coeur a les raisons que la raison ne connait pas."

In other words, your emotions have reasons that, to your reasoning intellect, could seem simple verging on stupid. Fortunately, you don't need to *understand* your emotions for an exercise like the following one to be effective.

Emotional Self-Awareness, The Basic Technique

Use this technique to find and name whatever emotion(s) you have right now. Read through all the instructions as a preview. Then do each step in order, peeking with one eye as needed to go through the full sequence.

1. Sit where you won't be interrupted. Close your eyes. (This starts to turn attention inward, rather than paying attention to external reality.)

2. Take one long, slow deep breath. Then return to normal breathing. (This breathing part keeps you alive. Joke! Still, jokes can be helpful for this particular technique. Feeling relaxed will help you continue to go deeper within.)

3. Choose to be interested in your emotions. Feel around or put the question to yourself directly, in words, "What emotion or emotions do I feel right now?"

4. Say out loud whatever you get, e.g., "I feel miserable. I also feel optimistic. I feel silly, too."

5. Open your eyes.

If this technique was easy for you, congratulations. If not, I can help you to work your full emotional range. So keep reading.

To the extent this technique seemed difficult, congratulate yourself. That would mean you have just diagnosed a problem akin to lettuce in the freezer. Consider the possibility that you have been overfunctioning in some other part of your aura to compensate for underfunctioning in your Heart Chakra.

If there's a mix-up, can you sort it out? Sure, and that would be smart. A well working Heart Chakra isn't optional, not if you want to Magnetize Money as part of a balanced life.

Consider people you have met through work, success seekers who pride themselves on how well they read potential customers yet it seems to you they have zilch self-awareness.

Can't you tell when they're fooling themselves? True emotional self-awareness isn't the same as using the latest gimmick or doing good old wishful thinking.

By regularly practicing the previous energetic workaround, anyone can get the hang of emotional self-awareness. Let's refine the experience you just had.

Answers like the following are common with my new clients. Although not a bad start, none of the following "names" for emotions really counts as emotional self-awareness:

1. I wish I had better feelings.
2. I am richly blessed.
3. I'm trying to be in touch with my emotions.
4. I'm remembering how I felt on the first day of school.
5. I want to feel happy all the time.
6. There's a grey sky but I just know if I keep waiting long enough the sun will come through.
7. Belly ache!
8. I notice a slight ache in my Heart Chakra.
9. I want more money, and I want it bad.
10. Those cars on the street sure are loud.

Answers like these aren't terrible. They're quite close, actually, though not yet totally successful. For convenience, let's refer to all these answers as "Something interesting, but not quite the name of an emotion in the here and now."

Before I supply our next workaround, let's take a brief interlude for perspective.

EMOTIONAL COURAGE

Emotional self-awareness, done well, requires a kind of courage. What isn't required? Trying hard to manufacture a feeling. Being human, you always have at least one, no trying required.

Sometimes people are scared to make contact with these simple unadorned feelings. Or people can be simply be used to energetic sub-routines that disallow any direct emotional experience. Common sub-routines involve substituting thinking energy (from the Solar Plexus Chakra) or spiritual energy (from the Third Eye Chakra) or sexual energy flows (from the Belly Chakra), or physical awareness (from the Root Chakra). Anything but regular human emotions!

When your Heart Chakra databank for **Emotional Self-Aware-ness** works well. it's simple to name basic human emotions. Although they have hundreds of names, human emotions fall into four basic categories:

- Happy
- Sad
- Scared
- Angry

Let's use this understanding to solve problems with our earlier examples.

1. *I wish I had better feelings.* Making a wish is not an emotion. But you're close. How do you feel emotionally when you're making that wish?

2. *I am richly blessed.* Statements about prosperity are not emotions. Reciting any religious credo or philosophy does not count as emotion, either. Answers like this may be symptoms of spiritual addiction, so you might wish to re-read Chapter 6 before returning to this exercise.

3. *I'm trying to be in touch with my emotions.* Have I got
    good news for you. If you have been doing this hard kind of
    work, forget it. Be sloppy instead, and simply pay attention
    in a relaxed manner.

    "Trying to be in touch with my emotions" really means
    "Using my intellect to figure out my emotions."

    That effort is doomed to failure since intellect is a com-
    pletely separate compartment of your aura. Feelings are
    feelings, thoughts are thoughts, and bunches of lettuce are
    not ice cubes.

4. *I'm remembering how I felt on the first day of school.*
    Strolling down memory lane is different from paying
    attention to your feelings here and now. If you can't easily
    pay attention in the present, ask yourself, "How does that
    memory make me feel now?"

5. *I want to feel happy all the time.* Aha, a desire for the future,
    perhaps! Imagining your future, however, is not the same as
    paying attention to your feelings here and now.

    Be brave. Tell yourself something like, "That's nice, dear.
    Now, how do I actually feel right now?"

6. *There's a grey sky but I just know if I keep waiting long
    enough the sun will come through.* Images are a very com-
    mon response, when people start using this technique.
    But images are not an emotion. So follow up with a ques-
    tion relating your image to emotion, e.g., "When the sky is
    grey and I keep waiting, how does that make me feel?"

7. *Belly ache!* Sure, in English we use the word "feel" to include
    physical sensations as well as emotions. But this exercise is
    about emotions. So follow up any physical sensation by
    taking another deep breath or two.

    Then remind yourself that before you were paying attention
    to your body. Now, however, you're going to pay attention to
    your emotions.

8. *I notice a slight ache in my Heart Chakra.* Nice try, but for most people chakras do not have emotions or physical sensations. Instead, there's some confusion as you are developing your energetic literacy.

   Emotions, physical sensations, perception of energy — these are all related to different chakras (Heart, Root, Third Eye). For best result, don't mush them up.

   Returning to our technique, take another deep breath. Remind yourself that before you were paying attention to your aura but now you are going to pay attention to your emotions and find a simple name or two for what you are feeling emotionally.

9. *I want more money, and I want it bad.* Oy, you're so close! Not to the money yet, so keep reading. But you have very nearly landed on an emotion.

   Take another breath and ask yourself, "When I want the money, how does that make me feel?"

10. *Those cars on the street sure are loud.* So what's new? When you hear all that racket, how does it make you feel? (Why become aware of outer sounds during a technique like this one? Often it's simply lack of practice at going within. Doing this Emotional Self-Awareness technique on a regular basis can help.)

Emotional Self-Awareness —Advanced Version

Resourceful Reader, let's explore more of the riches of your Heart Chakra. The following workaround can fine-tune your Emotional Self-Awareness. Plus, it's interesting!

As usual, read through all the instructions as a preview. Then do the technique, peeking with one eye as needed to go step by step.

1. Sit where you won't be interrupted. Close your eyes.
2. Take two long, slow deep breaths. Then return to normal

breathing. (Do not try to save time by taking two long breaths at the same time. Yes, jokes still can help you relax into a simple awareness of your emotions.)

3. Choose to be interested in your emotions. Feel around. Or put the question to yourself directly, in words, "What emotion or emotions do I feel right now?"

4. Say aloud whatever you get.

5. Eyes still closed, listen to what you just said:

• Was it one or two words, actual here-and-now emotion words, like "happy" or "ecstatic"? Then skip to Step 8.

• Or was it, "Something, but not quite the name of an emotion in the here and now"? Then continue with Step 6.

6. Take another long, slow deep breath and return to normal breathing. Ask yourself this follow-up question: "How does what I just said make me feel?"

7. Say aloud one or more emotion words, whatever occurs to you.

8. Open your eyes and consider yourself successful.

More Help with Emotional Self-Awareness

For the past 15 years, in my healing sessions, I have usually led clients through one of the many exercises I have developed for emotional self-awareness. That form of self-honesty is essential for helping just about anyone meet success goals, be they financial or emotional or spiritual.

At first, it surprised me how often new clients had trouble with something so simple. Although I have some of the smartest clients in the world, many needed a lot of coaching for making contact with their own emotions.

Eventually I began to connect some dots. How did a client's skill at emotional self-awareness correlate with the strength in that client's Heart Chakra databank for **Emotional Self-Awareness**? Perfectly!

Most people assume they are doing fine with emotional self-awareness. Yet they're not.

Unless they use Stage 3 Energetic Literacy, how could they tell?

All inner experience feels like energy. At Stages 1 or 2, the mechanics of inner experience can seem like one big mush.

Only Stage 3 Energetic Literacy reveals problems like energetic sub-routines and STUFF in different chakra databanks. Before developing that basic human skill, many prosperity and success seekers sabotage their success and don't know it. Despite working hard, they're neglecting their true emotional lives.

Instead they keep busy *explaining* those feelings, *analyzing* them, *improving* them. Routinely they substitute input from different chakra databanks, clueless about what they're doing. Ironically, they may pride themselves on superior emotional wisdom.

Some of my clients with this problem have been professional therapists or energy healers. Talented at it, too!

In our first sessions, they considered themselves, rightly, to be experts at understanding the human heart. Only, in terms of our fridge analogy, these healing professionals lived with the equivalent of lettuce in the freezer.

Soon those clients were back in balance. They succeeded at a really important kind of networking: Being in touch with your own human heart.

Do you suspect that you might have a similar problem? Don't let that discourage you. Remember that STUFF can always, always, always be healed.

What if you're not sure how well you really do with emotional self-awareness? Think about what happened with the techniques in this chapter. They're a pretty accurate indicator of your current level of skill.

Was it easy? Did you find at least one name-of-emotion? Then consider that you are doing well, and better than most. (Even if you weren't thrilled with all the names you came up with, emotional self-honesty does makes life better.)

But if you had problems or any kind of struggle; if you hated doing the techniques as much as if they gave you jock itch (particularly troubling if you're female), here is what I suggest.

Do one of the techniques in this chapter twice daily for six weeks. (According to many therapists, that's how long it takes to form a new habit.) And here are some Do's and Don'ts that may help:

- DO any "Emotional Self-Awareness" technique very quickly each time.
- DON'T make it into a big deal that involves 10 minutes of agony.

- DO be fascinated with whatever emotion(s) you name. Allow yourself to feel whatever you feel.
- DON'T judge what you feel.

- DO welcome any human emotion that you notice within yourself. This is part of your humanity.
- DON'T bring in spirituality, religion, or prosperity techniques to shift your emotions into something supposedly better for prosperity purposes. (Ironically, one can develop patterns of denial out of love for God or depth of faith. Yet won't religion be lived more fully with more self-honesty and less STUFF in chakra databanks?)

- DO your technique no more than six times per day.
- DON'T wallow in your emotions the rest of your day, becoming like one of those very serious actors who is always being an A*C*T*O*R. Emotions are only one compartment in the refrigerator of your aura. To Magnetize Money best, use all your compartments.

At this point, Resourceful Reader, you may be saying, "Fine. Except how can I expect to live as a happy person, or an effective money magnet, or even a decent refrigerator, considering the hideous toxic environment where I have to work?"

I would love to help you solve that problem. Next!

17. Money Magnets in a Toxic Work Environment

If you direct your focus into knocking things down to get ahead, you may find your-self living, well, in ruins.
— Laura Day, *How to Rule the World from Your Couch*

Nobody I have met likes to be used by others. (Unless you would be the surprising and saintly exception.) No, we humans generally prefer to be respected.

Failing that, at least we hope not to be "Duh-ed." As customers, we expect to be treated as though we're always right. As employees, we crave appreciation.

None of this ought to be considered unreasonable. Which makes it all the more galling if you don't get to work in… Paradise.

What can you do if you happen to dislike your current job? How to cope if you can't stand certain people at work? First, know that you're entitled to feel that way. Lying to yourself won't help a thing.

Next, how are you going to change this situation? It's hard to do auric modeling that sings "Magnetize Money" when secretly (or not so secretly) your job makes you want to vomit.

On the level of energy, a toxic work environment does the equivalent of caking mud onto your money magnets. Soon they can't attract so much as a single iron filing, not one pathetic dime.

What, you're still acting like a professional although that's really hard under the circumstances? Score yourself some character points. Apart from that, let's be honest. Energetically your loathing still shows.

Toxic patterns from a workplace can leave energy deposits that stay with you for days, even decades. Technically, these bits of STUFF are known as thought forms, façade bodies, psychic coercion, etc. Of course, they can be healed. But learning that skill set is… another book.

Here let's emphasize what to try first, something good and sticky.

How to Make a Positive Attitude Stick

You can't nod and smile at your boss one minute, then scowl as soon as she leaves the room and — well, certainly you *can*. Many of us have. Only you can't do this and expect it to really stay secret. Those grumbles and scowls stick around in your aura, especially if done every day.

Blame auric modeling, if you must. Even the best kept secrets about negativity show subconsciously. At that level, your boss will get the message. So will your customers. Even the most superficial idiot-creepy-obnoxious-lazy co-worker can pick up a vibe.

Besides that, globs of negativity in your aura will attract people and events of like quality. Thank the Law of Attraction. Fortunately, our next energetic workaround is based on a way to use LOA to help you prosper, even when your career circumstances stink.

Who would argue with trying to keep your attitude positive while in the workplace? Not somebody with a positive attitude, right?

Be discerning, however, in how you attempt to create that virtue choice known as "I insist on having a positive attitude at work, no matter how badly certain people here creep me out."

Positively awful coping strategies include:

- Attempting self-hypnosis in the midst of activity (something that professional hypnotists wouldn't advocate, incidentally).
- Muttering affirmations under your breath.
- Fake-smiling.
- Staring hopefully into a loathed person's eyes while trying to persuade yourself, "I find you so very, intensely, sweetsie-weetsie loveable."

Sometimes you have been on the receiving end of all this, true? Such brave attempts!

On the level of auras, they add a thick gloss of denial, comparable to Vaseline. Were you fooled one bit?

And I can assure you, at the level of auras, forced positivity does not count as a lovely look.

Does that mean your only alternative is to be sullen, resentful, and obviously disgusted? No, there's a specific energetic workaround, and it's coming right up.

Turn Your Aura Authentically Positive

In the past, did you like the result of affirmations? Then you'll love the results from this technique.

If you possess skills of energetic literacy, go forth and check out specifics. For instance, do a simple before-and-after picture on yourself. Check out some of your chakra databanks before you do this technique. Afterwards read those very same databanks.

For describing this six-step technique, I'll use the example of Valerie, a work colleague you can't avoid dealing with. When you do the technique, substitute the name of your own "Valerie."

1. Find one authentic good thing, *long term,* about "Valerie."
There must be *something* about Valerie's workplace effectiveness that you sincerely could love. Or like. Or, at least, can tolerate for a few long minutes.

One resource is the 5,000-year-old art of physiognomy, reading faces for character. You can use the power of face reading to help you deal with Valerie.

Find some redeeming quality any way you choose. Once you have located it, while you must deal with Valerie, be on the lookout for how well she does that whatever-it-is.

2. Find one silly, whimsical thing to enjoy about Valerie, *just for now.*
This short-term good thing can be something you discover as a delightful surprise, one day at a time. And I mean that as in "Have fun treasure hunting for today's interesting detail" rather than a 12-step program's very serious "day at a time."

Your short-term good thing could be as simple as finding your favorite color on the clothes Valerie is wearing today. Go ahead, enjoy that tiny patch of blue on her collar, be that a designer look or an ink stain.

Computers need to have their screens refreshed sometimes, and you deserve it, too.

3. To the extent you must pay attention to Valerie as a person, focus on these two good things as much as possible — either the long-term good thing or the one for now.

4. If your cute, post-modern sense of irony kicks in, down to the internalized eye-rolling, stop! Forbid yourself to go there. Instead, refocus on one of those good things about Valerie.

5. Of course, mostly focus on your work, the objective work linked to your performance evaluation, commissions, etc..

6. As a secondary focus, don't consider Valerie at all, not even that long-term good thing or the now one. Pay attention to YOU. You are, or can become, the most important person in the room.

CAN YOU TELL FRIENDS FROM ENEMIES?

Speaking of survival skills in the workplace, do you know this important one? Everybody is not your friend.

Some people are actually enemies. Sure, they can count as enemies even though they don't necessarily carry weapons or challenge you to duels.

Evaluate the relationships you have now and the new ones, too. Ask, "Friend or foe?" Invest your best efforts in life dealing with the friends, not the foes.

Trying hard to compliment people like Valerie is doomed to failure. Forced praise fools nobody.

Even genuine praise won't necessarily work, as in "Valerie, I'm going to overlook your despicable character and annoying manicure and, instead, make a big deal about the tiny thing in you that I do find acceptable, since today you are wearing a surprisingly tasteful, though streaky, blue spot of color on the collar of your hideous shirt."

If you think that Valerie doesn't know you dislike her, you're fooling yourself. In *Five Minds for the Future*, Howard Gardner tells an instructive story:

> Mahatma Gandhi kept reaching out to Hitler; the Indian leader wrote a letter to Hitler, addressed "Dear friend," calling on him to change his tactics and promising him forgiveness in return. In turn, Hitler remarked, "Shoot Gandhi, and if that does not suffice to reduce them to submission, shoot a dozen leading members of Congress [Gandhi's political party]."

Energetic literacy can show you clearly who isn't a friend. Faking, prevarication, malicious deception, etc., can be read in depth and detail. That's helpful since the proverbial "wolf in sheep's clothing" is a very common problem.

Let's be realistic. In your life so far, of the people who did you harm, who thoughtfully prefaced it with a verbal announcement?

Instead, consciously or not, people with a strong personal agenda can project a misleading façade that is distinctly different from the true sentiments within.

For instance, for an article in *The Washington Post,* I was asked to profile a Virginia politician who was running for governor in a way that suggested that, as a public servant, he would be kind, disinterested, and modest.

Profiling Marshall Coleman, I described him as having "a killer instinct… aggression… being more attracted to the campaign than to actually serving."

Reporter Hank Stuever had actually met Mr. Coleman. After hearing my profile, he laughed his head off. Hank was very familiar with the sheep coat routine.

Energetic literacy can include three amazingly accurate lie detector tests: Reading verbal integrity, action integrity, and spiritual integrity. Until you have developed this skill set, use the following energetic workaround.

She Loves Me, She Loves Me Not

One skill of energetic literacy is super-easy to awaken. Within two minutes of meeting a person, you can tell if *you* like that person. You can also tell if *that person* likes you or not.

To find out, here's all you need do. During or after the conversation, simply take a moment to ask yourself:

1. Do I like this person?
2. Does this person like me?

For instance, consider Vaughn, from the Accounting Department. If he doesn't like you now, he probably never will. You could smile at Vaughn, throw techniques at him, even shower him with tasteful, expensive gifts. Such a waste!

In movies, it's different. Think of all those romantic comedies. Velda and Virgil meet cute. They bicker. Amazingly, they still fall in love by the end of the movie. For joy!

Sure, that happens all the time... in movies.

In reality, courting people who don't like you is a singularly bad investment. For every person who dislikes you, there are a hundred others who would like you a lot, given the chance. Why waste time on those who don't appreciate you?

So, what's the rest of your energetic workaround? Choose to spend as little time as possible with those who don't like you. That isn't being negative but smart.

Rumor has it, Jesus Christ was a pretty loveable guy, too. But the lifetime did not end well, remember? Your job in life need not involve making everyone love you. Quit that volunteer work and you will gain a clearer aura, better social intelligence, and far more energy to help you Magnetize Money.

MORE HELP FOR A TOXIC WORK ENVIRONMENT

Sometimes we disregard inner warnings because we think that we need a particular job or work relationship so badly. Due to desperation, or habit, we can fall into toxic business relationships.

For example, Vincent came to me for a session related to his bogged-down career. He asked me to cut the cord of attachment to his boss, Vicky. **Cords of attachment** are energy structures that develop at the level of auras. Automatically, a cord will be created when you agree to accept a job. Or hire an employee. Or decide that a certain customer's business is worth pursuing, no matter what.

Once a cord of attachment is formed, it's permanent. After the relationship ends, that cord of attachment will linger until the last minutes of your life.

Each cord of attachment contains a sequence of energies between you and the cordee, highlighting a pattern that has been especially troubling to you as a person, given your overall patterns of STUFF.

Although the contents of a cord of attachment can change over time, alterations go in one direction only, bad to worse.

Whatever becomes stuck in your cord of attachment recycles within your aura and subconscious mind, repeating 24/7. Naturally this can become a kind of portable toxic workplace.

Yet, with skills, you can remove cords of attachment. With Vincent, I used the method called "12 Steps to Cut Cords of Attachment®" to permanently remove his cord to Vicky.

Removing this cord of attachment, here is the pattern I found. It dated from his initial job interview. (When I read out these cord items to Vincent during our session, he could relate to them all.)

What Was the Real Lesson?

VINCENT: Eager to help you as an employee. Intuitively, I feel that I could be a great fit here.
BOSS VICKY: Gracious. Super charming.
VINCENT: Uh-oh. Something about you doesn't compute. Stab of fear.
God, don't let me get hurt in a job again!
Oh, I'm just being silly.
I'm supposed to have trust. This situation is a spiritual lesson for me to learn more trust.

Yes, Vincent's belief system for attracting prosperity included his strong faith. He believed in searching for signals about what was "meant to be." Disregarding his gut feeling about this new boss, trying hard to do what he was "supposed to," Vincent accepted the job.

That job turned into a nightmare. Vincent's cord of attachment developed a second chunk of recycling anguish, summarized below. (This, of course, was removed along with the rest of the cord. And again, Vincent told me that he related to every item of Cord Dialogue that I validated for him during the session.)

More of Vincent's Cord Items with his Boss from Hell

BOSS VICKY: Scolding you. Insulting!

VINCENT: I feel used. I feel criticized.

I feel that you can't wait to get rid of me. You want to squeeze out all my ideas, plus all the work and energy you can extract. Then you plan to dump me.

You monster!

BOSS VICKY: Slimy. Dishonest. Using people while putting on a big show about "my great business plan, my high ideals for the company, etc."

Absolutely selfish.

Energetic flows like these really are like portable toxic workplaces. If you constantly worry about work, you're probably not making it up. I have gone into detail about Vincent's cord of attachment so that you can appreciate the potential of this little known healing specialty, something you could learn to do for yourself.

Beyond learning a quality method to cut cords of attachment, there's something else you can do, starting now.

Prevent problems. Use your basic street smarts. Use them along with all your fancier success and prosperity skills. If Vincent had done this, he never would have accepted a job with Vicky. He wouldn't have developed that horrible cord in the first place.

Sure, Vincent was "meant" to learn something from the relationship with Boss Vicky: Just say "No."

Perfectionism Will Slow You Down

In your efforts to Magnetize Money, some of us idealists can unwittingly set ourselves up for big trouble. So involved are we with taking the lemons life offers, busily turning them into lemonade. Meanwhile, we loveable but silly idealists may neglect juicy, sweet fruits that are right in front of us, ripe for the picking.

Gorgeous oranges and glorious mangoes may be readily available. It's okay to notice them, rather than devoting yourself to the somewhat limited art of lemonade cookery.

What if this advice comes late, since you're now in a toxic work environment? Consider your options realistically. If you can't fix the workplace, stay as long as you must. Just don't consider yourself doomed to stay in that job forever.

No, you do not have to believe that everything happens for a reason and, therefore, you must remain in that horrible job until you either become a saint or die of chronic tooth gnashing.

Minding Your Own Business

For pity's sake, leaven your idealism with common sense. Take inspiration from third millennium Catholics in Italy. Sure they're Catholic. Yet, mysteriously, their birth rate has become one of the lowest in the Western world.

Even if you believe in the infallibility of the pope, does he really know what it's like to wake up at 2:00 a.m. to feed Baby Girl #14? Who is the pope to ban contraceptives?

In our third millennium, you will find plenty of passionate Catholics who happen to use birth control. Maybe they can't tell the pope, "Mind your own business." But they can tell themselves which advice to take, and have a good life as a result.

Go ahead. Use your free will. If you must cope with a toxic work environment, remember that one of your smartest moves can be to say "No." Here are some practical variations on that theme:

- Somewhere between what would Jesus do and what would Machiavelli do… what would *you* do to improve the situation at work?
- When something at work goes wrong, begin with objective problem solving, not repairing your dream board.
- For heaven's sake, cut your cord of attachment to anyone at that job who is driving you crazy. Either learn a quality skill

set for yourself or hire someone for an hour and get the job done. (This practitioner, for instance, has helped many a client to not get fired.)

- So long as you're stuck in a difficult job, be sure to make the rest of your life count. Find at least 10 minutes a day, every day, to do something you really enjoy.

- Develop a plan to improve your career. Consistently take action toward your goal. Even 10 minutes a day will help.

- However, do not do this by sneaking around while on the job, paid by *someone* else to do *something* else.
  Sneaking will distort your auric modeling, which reveals a person's ethics quite clearly. (In Part Three of this Magnetize Money Program, we will be upgrading your skill sets for energetically effective goals and plans, a fine alternative to sneaking around at work due to desperation.)

- Wasting time at work may seem like a fine revenge, given a toxic workplace. Not really. Truth is, wasting time will dull out your aura and create lousy karma.

- Do extra work related to your current job, not less. That's how you'll keep your money magnets working properly.

Even if you must stay at a job that is less than ideal, *you* don't have to turn toxic. Do what you need to do. Then get out as soon as you can, all on your own terms.

A job is, essentially, a way to sustain yourself materially. Like a meal, it doesn't always have to be gourmet. Nor does eating have to become the entire focus of your life.

Live honorably while reorganizing your career and you'll become well positioned energetically to Magnetize Money at a better job.

18. Balance Give-and-Take...
Or Else

Giving and receiving are different aspects of the flow of energy in the universe. And in our willingness to give that which we seek, we keep the abundance of the universe circulating in our lives.
— Deepak Chopra, *The Seven Spiritual Laws of Success*

Before you get rich, must your aura contain a perfect balance of give-and-take? If I said "Yes," I'd be lying. (And horrors, lying is so bad for the aura!)

Most of us know how to divide human beings into two categories:

- Givers
- Takers

Actually, Resourceful Reader, to Magnetize Money we need three categories:

- Givers
- Takers
- People who balance give-and-take

Whichever type of person you want to be, you can give yourself that kind of life. Or take it for yourself. Or give-and-take it for yourself.

Before you choose — which I'm going to ask you to do before this chapter is done — let's remember another interesting fact of life. If you wish to magnetize major amounts of money, your realistic options drop down to two:

- Being a taker
- Being someone who balances give-and-take

That's right. To gain financial success in this world, you don't have to be a taker but it sure helps. And you can't be purely a giver. Sorry, but it's true.

The Pacemaker Principle

In your heart, certain cells play the role of "Pacemaker." They establish a rhythm. This pace is followed by the rest of the cells in your heart, which helps you to stay alive.

Sometimes a patient with heart problems is given an artificial pacemaker. It does the job of setting a pace for your heart, also allowing you to stay alive.

When it comes to a heartbeat, nobody can survive with "whatever." Each of us needs to set a definite rhythm, have a well-patterned heartbeat.

Biologically, another rather important rhythm is called "Breathe in and out." Not optional, right?

Give-and-take is a third, essential, life rhythm. Only this one is not purely biological. You have an established pattern for this, whether conscious or not. If the balance is off, of course that will impact both your auric modeling and your finances.

If you don't like what you have right now, go ahead. Change it. Become your own pacemaker.

FINANCIAL FLOW

You can't be a softie in personal life (habitually giving without expecting a thing in return) yet somehow become a totally different person at work (e.g., strong and commanding, always preferring to take).

Okay, maybe you can think of exceptions where a big giver made piles of money. Marilyn Monroe comes to mind. But she didn't get to keep that money for long, did she?

With energetic literacy, there's always more to learn about how people tick. Each individual is extraordinarily unique at the level of auras, so there can be exceptions to my rule that earning money requires strong auric modeling as a taker. Still, my conclusion about the importance of taking is based on a lot of research.

I had to research this particular topic. Meaning that, personally, I needed to. My natural inclination, and habits, and STUFF, used to make Rose Rosetree's motto "Give 95% of the time. Receive last, and even then, be sure to add generous quantities of guilt."

For decades into my career, this pattern limited my success. As my work became better known, however, I got "lucky." I began receiving emails galore requesting free help with aura readings, empath coaching, etc. My husband and I don't live on air, nor do we own the Bill and Melinda Gates Foundation. Therefore, I had to learn how to say "No."

Eventually I sorted out basic concepts like "Professional services require payment." This paired up with "Friendships require give-and-take in healthy balance." Once I became clear about this, my business income doubled, then continued to grow.

Your income may grow, too, when you learn the lessons of my give-and-take "interviews" with the Forbes Magazine list of "The 50 Richest People in America. "

When photos weren't available, I went on to the next picture on the Forbes list. Strictly speaking, my scope of research became "The 50 richest people in America with photos available for the article in Forbes Magazine 2009." Especially for this research, I developed the following prosperityprotocol.

The Give-and-Take Snapshot

1. Heart Chakra: **Emotional Giving**
This chakra databank relates to qualities like openness to other people, caring, and emotional generosity.

2. Heart Chakra: **Emotional Receiving**
This chakra databank reveals a person's patterns with receiving praise, interest, admiration, and other emotions from significant others. Both positive and negative emotions count here.

3. Throat Chakra: **Intimacy in Close Relationships**
How close is considered "too close"? Quality and quantity of social connection, both, can shape patterns of intimacy.

Before you read a summary of my findings with The Give-and-Take Snapshot, want to take any guesses about how well the super-rich do intimacy?

First, the Bad News

Altogether my research revealed much to admire... and even more to increase my compassion. What didn't I find, alas? Nobody (and I mean nobody) in this group gave more than he or she took.

Only two showed an equal balance. More on them soon.

That's right. Nobody out of the whole crafty, cash-laden crew, came close to what *you* probably do, which is to give early and often.

Sure, over the decades I have used energetic literacy to research plenty of humbler folk. Most people give more than they take. During these years, I have also researched plenty of the rich and/or famous. Many are lovely, some not.

I have been hired to do face reading at parties with budgets of half a million dollars or more. Some of these partygoers show, through their auric modeling, great willingness to take emotionally but not such a great willingness to give. One incident in particular sticks in my memory.

Give-and-Take at the Party

Arnold was a trim 40-something attorney, impeccably dressed. His wife Angie was glamorous, gorgeous, and groomed, staring with fascination as I read her man's face. He had to go first, of course.

As I summarized talents and potential challenges, Arnold listened intently. Okay, to be more accurate, he smirked and preened.

His adoring Angie was so attentive, she reminded me of a cheerleader. I practically expected her to leap up and do cartwheels.

When Angie's turn came, I really wanted to help her feel good. She didn't appear valued much by her high-powered husband.

To avoid boredom, he began walking around the den. This was, of course, no ordinary den but a mega-mansion version, stocked with very expensive-looking toys. Arnold picked up one trinket at a time, as if shopping.

Meanwhile, I was telling Angie things like, "That huge curve to your eyebrows suggests that you focus on emotions when dealing with people."

Angie would hold up her mirror as if seeing her surgically perfected face for the very first time. Angling and posing as if in wonderment, she would ask big, strong Arnold for advice. "Arnold, honeeeeey, am I like that? What do you think?"

Arnold, clearly, couldn't care less. He kept on oogling the nearby toys, ignoring his wife.

Warren Buffett sets a far better example of prosperous give-and-take. Emotional *giving* delights him; he finds it easy. Emotional *receiving* doesn't overwhelm him, as he is used to being appreciated. This rich man balances both sides of life.

And when it comes to intimacy, the man has finesse. Very loving to his significant others, Buffet knows how to manage his less important emotional investments, scaling down closeness to the appropriate level for each relationship.

Who was the other big winner with my give-and-take profiles? Meet "Aden." (I'm keeping him anonymous because this relatively favorable research is still not entirely flattering, as you'll soon see.)

Aden: The Give-and-Take Snapshot

1. Heart Chakra Databank: ***Emotional Giving***
90 feet. Huge presence to this man!
Aden's kindness is powerful, mostly, because he lives so passionately. This uncommonly zesty guy hugely enjoys giving to his favorite people.

2. Heart Chakra Databank: ***Emotional Receiving***
90 miles. Not just an altruist, Aden expects to receive abundantly. Emotionally, that means being shown both obedience and loyalty.
This mega-billionaire demands the highest standards of behavior.
"Anyone can be replaced." (Yes, you read that right.)

3. Throat Chakra Databank: ***Intimacy in Close Relationships***
19 feet. Intense, very human. Big moods, living large.

Don't be discouraged by Aden's "Anyone can be replaced." Beliefs like this aren't required to Magnetize Money. But do consider Aden's insistence on receiving. That's not so optional.

EMOTIONAL PERILS OF WEALTH

Let's get real. To judge from their auras, most of the mega-rich are emotionally impoverished.

Starting these profiles, I expected nothing of the kind. Net worth numbers like $40 billion (for Gates) or $37 billion (for Buffet) sound great. But what are the social consequences of having so much wealth?

The resulting attention can be crazy making. Think how your entire family might suck up to wealthy old Auntie Annette. Then multiply that suck up factor by what, a zillion?

Every one of America's top 50 wealthiest must deal with that unpleasant kind of interest. It's compounded daily, through flattery, groveling, and otherwise fake behavior. Besides the family members, the friends, the gold-diggers, how about all the rage from underpaid employees worldwide? Professional jealousy and competitiveness can also be directed at these highly visible targets. Ouch!

One of my most touching research subjects was a top billionaire whose financial standing had dropped significantly in recent years. Sure, he still made the top 50 wealthiest people in the U.S., but how much happiness did that buy him?

Antonio: The Give-and-Take Snapshot

1. Heart Chakra Databank: **Emotional Giving**
6 inches. Disillusioned, bitter.

2. Heart Chakra Databank: **Emotional Receiving**
90 miles. "Other people never give enough for it to feel real. Certainly they don't give enough to make me feel better about my bad luck."

3. Throat Chakra Databank: **Intimacy in Close Relationships**
9 inches. "Nobody really understands me."

GIVE-AND-TAKE WITH MEGA-MONEY

Antonio has hit bottom emotionally, with a ratio of give:take of 6 inches:90 miles. But what about other mega-billionaires?

The findings below are typical for America's wealthiest. First names throughout are fictitious, of course, allowing these folks to cling to whatever privacy remains in their lives.

Alex: The Give-and-Take Snapshot

*1. Heart Chakra Databank: **Emotional Giving***
3 feet. Believes himself to be very generous. Has a completely different standard for giving than for receiving.

*2. Heart Chakra Databank: **Emotional Receiving***
100 miles. Enjoys every bit of status, money, etc. as a form of emotional feeding. It strokes his personal ego.

*3. Throat Chakra Databank: **Intimacy in Close Relationships***
3 inches. Tells his closest people what he thinks they want to hear.

Adolfo: The Give-and-Take Snapshot

*1. Heart Chakra Databank: **Emotional Giving***
18 inches. "Everybody has a price, and I hate to overpay."

*2. Heart Chakra Databank: **Emotional Receiving***
50 miles. "Gaining people's respect and adulation is standard operating procedure for me. I require it, really."

*3. Throat Chakra Databank: **Intimacy in Close Relationships***
19 feet. "I really prize those close relationships. With all my responsibilities, it's so helpful to be able to get the attention I need."

Of course, the quality of this chakra databank suggests that Adolfo does way more than his share of the talking in these so-called "close relationships."

Ahmed: The Give-and-Take Snapshot

*1. Heart Chakra Databank: **Emotional Giving***
8 inches. "I have such contempt for ordinary people. Unfortunately, so few extraordinary people are available to take the time for relationships, even with me."

2. Heart Chakra: *Emotional Receiving*
90 miles. "You get used to it after a while. What a bore, how people think they can flatter you in order to get your money."

3. Throat Chakra Databank: *Intimacy in Close Relationships*
4 inches. "There will always be some people kept around to help me let off steam, but they're disposable. They know it and I know it."

CUDDLING UP TO A SOLID GOLD COIN

Intimacy does appear to be a common tradeoff for high financial status. When the mega-rich make their bargains with reality, financial stability can be trusted somewhat, but people?

Andy: The Give-and-Take Snapshot

1. Heart Chakra Databank: *Emotional Giving*
14 feet. Everything and everyone has a price. "I give only as a shrewd investment."

2. Heart Chakra Databank: *Emotional Receiving*
40 miles. He feels he deserves people's adulation. In an odd way, he doesn't even take the star treatment personally:
"Life has been good to me. I expect life to continue to be good to me."

3. Throat Chakra Databank: *Intimacy in Close Relationships*
6 inches. Intimacy? Now that's a tough prospect. Andy believes that "Expressing what I want" means exactly the same thing as "Getting close to a friend."

Arthur: The Give-and-Take Snapshot

1. Heart Chakra Databank: *Emotional Giving*
9 inches. "I don't trust people much. Mostly they're takers."

2. Heart Chakra Databank: *Emotional Receiving*
100 feet. "People come at me constantly, so noisy, heckling me. It's only so much sentimentality. As if I would fall for that!"

3. *Throat Chakra Databank:* **Intimacy in Close Relationships**
3 *inches.* "If I haven't known you for 30 years, or you aren't a blood relative, forget it. Even then, I have my suspicions. What do you really want from me?"

Andrea: The Give-and-Take Snapshot

1. *Heart Chakra Databank:* **Emotional Giving**
8 *inches.* Trusting people is hard, to put it mildly. "So many people try to get into my life just because they want my money."

2. *Heart Chakra Databank:* **Emotional Receiving**
40 *miles.* "Sometimes it's overwhelming, all the admiration and adulation. I can't tell if it's real or false. I do my best to survive."

3. *Throat Chakra Databank:* **Intimacy in Close Relationships**
4 *inches.* "It's hard for me to let down my guard. So many people are takers."

Anabella: The Give-and-Take Snapshot

1. *Heart Chakra Databank:* **Emotional Giving**
12 *inches.* "I don't have to be so generous to others, except I'm a nice person. Others in my position wouldn't be so kind."

2. *Heart Chakra Databank:* **Emotional Receiving**
1,000 *feet.* "I feel the pull on me of so many people, flattering and asking and demanding and whispering. It's overwhelming, how much I have to take in."

3. *Throat Chakra Databank:* **Intimacy in Close Relationships**
10 *inches.* "There are so few I can trust. Most people only pretend to be interested in me. They always want something."

INSPIRATION FROM ENLIGHTENED MILLIONAIRES

Lovely and evolved people do sometimes make the mega-rich list. Most of them just aren't lovely or evolved *emotionally,* not compared to the rest of their talents. The billionaire's major life skills lie elsewhere.

As I researched away on these Give-and-Take Snapshots, I did encounter some lovely surprises. Magnificent qualities kept me going. I even found a few mega-successful people whom I would consider spiritually Enlightened.

For them, every chakra databank I read was strong, STUFF free, and joyful. Enthusiastically, I went on to survey additional databanks too, and every single one contained that celestial razzle-dazzle I adore — the blissful, balanced quality that is humanity's destiny.

Enlightened rich people are surely the real winners in life's give-and-take sweepstakes.

Bill Gates has already been read in detail. Now meet Sergey Brin, among the spiritually wealthiest on earth.

Sergey Brin: The Give-and-Take Snapshot

1. Heart Chakra Databank: Emotional Giving
90 miles. Emotionally very generous, based on inner happiness.

2. Heart Chakra Databank: Emotional Receiving
100 miles. "I live in a generous world where I am always rewarded beyond what I give. I am so grateful for this."

3. Throat Chakra Databank: Intimacy in Close Relationships
14 feet. Authentically friendly, interested in people. Enjoys getting close to others.

Talk about enjoyable! Let's continue with Donald Bren, the real estate tycoon.

Donald Bren: The Give-and-Take Snapshot

1. Heart Chakra Databank: Emotional Giving
50 miles. Huge networker. Enthusiastic. Really loves people, especially socially important, influential people.

2. Heart Chakra Databank: Emotional Receiving
95 miles. "Life is absolutely thrilling for me. It's one big flow of energy."

> 3. *Throat Chakra Databank:* **Intimacy in Close Relationships**
> *80 miles.* Identifying with the joy and energy in the lives of others, as well as his own life. "I feel huge joy everywhere."

Finally, I was touched and inspired by profiling Steve Jobs. It's well known that the founder of Apple computers has brought the world iTunes, iPod, and iPad. But did you also know that Jobs bought Pixar from George Lucas?

So Jobs is partly responsible for "Finding Nemo" and "Toy Story." No wonder this man is one of America's most beloved business successes. Yet another reason could be his auric modeling. True, Jobs suffers far too much to be considered Enlightened quite yet. Even before all the STUFF is cleared out of his aura, Steve Jobs is impressive, exceptionally thoughtful for someone who has earned so much cash.

Steve Jobs: The Give-and-Take Snapshot

1. *Heart Chakra Databank:* **Emotional Giving**
5 miles. "I feel very lucky to have the people in my life who are close to me."

2. *Heart Chakra Databank:* **Emotional Receiving**
100 miles. "I'm an acquired taste. It's an honor that so many people have acquired it, but I would be a fool to depend on anyone's admiration, except for genuine liking that comes from the people I know well."

3. *Throat Chakra Databank:* **Intimacy in Close Relationships**
5 miles. Having these special people in my life keeps me sane, or what passes for sane. (A sense of humor is evident in this chakra databank, as well as others.)
Wow, a lively sense of humor — imagine finding that in someone so rich!

How will you choose to balance give and take? Only you can decide what would be a healthy balance. By living that, day by day, your accumulated choices will show up in your auric modeling. Financial consequences will flow accordingly.

Despite balancing your give -and-take, wealth can bring challenges to close relationships. One of my "interviewees" put it eloquently. Reading his chakra databank about Intimacy in Personal Relationships, here is what I found in Albert's Throat Chakra:

"Of course, I take all that big closeness with a grain of salt. I have seen too many careers end. Suddenly all the alleged friends evaporate. Although I enjoy what I have now, I no longer expect it to last."

No, we can't take it with us — neither the mansions like castles nor the "friends" who come along so eagerly to be bought or rented.

What can we take along? Soul growth is cumulative. (Energetic literacy even allows us to peek at the luscious details.)

Beyond this, consider carefully as you design your own balance sheet in life. To Magnetize Money, it is *required* that you feel totally comfortable with receiving from others.

Beyond that, if you have learned to balance give-and-take; if you insist on striving for true intimacy; if you manage to keep a sense of humor through it all — which may not seem like asking for majority shareholdings in the moon — wow, nonetheless!

You will have accomplished something extraordinary for spiritual evolution. Clearly, that's something most of America's Richest haven't yet been able to buy.

But how well do you really balance give-and-take? Let's not just assume, not when we can quiz.

19. The Financial Flow Quiz

Win/Win is a frame of mind and heart that constantly seeks mutual benefit in all human interactions... Win/Win is based on the paradigm that there is plenty for everybody, that one person's success is not achieved at the expense or exclusion of others.
— Steven R. Covey, *The 7 Habits of Highly Effective People*

There's no avoiding it. When your goal is to Magnetize Money, you've just got to learn how to take.

Balancing give and take would be lovely, though optional. But you can't avoid this fact of life here at Earth School: To Magnetize Money, you definitely need good circuits for taking, both emotionally and materially.

Financial flow is a money-related term for this. Which habits do you have? Answer TRUE or FALSE to the following seven questions.

1. Before I receive, I must give.
2. The more I give, the more I will get.
3. Because of my financial situation, I must give more than I receive, more than is fair. That's just how my life is right now.
4. At this time in my life, I am able take more than I give, which is just fine with me.
5. There's no point in asking for what I want. Love from my significant other means he or she will anticipate whatever I need. If I have to ask, it's too late. He or she wouldn't understand.
6. Provided that I keep on doing good, I will receive my reward eventually.
7. If short on cash, I should tithe or donate seed money to my church. Then God will pay me back with abundance.

Financial Flow Quiz – Keeping Score

You did great on this quiz. Every answer was correct… or at least useful for diagnostic purposes if you're seriously interested in being able to Magnetize Money.

Some perfectly good answers can decrease your odds at earning big wealth. Why? For one thing, answers about give-and-take aren't just answers. Beliefs about giving run very deep, creating patterns about expectation. Therefore, every answer you just gave could be linked to a self-fulfilling prophecy.

That's a belief so strong that, automatically, it pulls support from your subconscious mind and sets up auric modeling all over your energy field. This, in turn, evokes subconscious reactions from others.

Even a lukewarm, slight, belief that blocks your financial flow will activate support from the whole Universe, both microcosm and macrocosm.

If you believe strongly enough, you will magnetize many life experiences to support your choice. Sometimes this process is called **synchronicity**, meaningful coincidence. Another term could be "dooming yourself to relative poverty for the rest of your life."

Yes, hello! Financial consequences flow from all your answers, even if they are based on emotional or spiritual or religious or social aspects of your current lifestyle.

So remember this.You can always change your mind. A strong position could be modified without having to be discarded altogether. Changing some of your answers to our Financial Flow Quiz could help you to Magnetize Money as never before. So let's consider your options and beliefs related to financial flow.

1. Before I receive, I must give.

If TRUE: Some of us love being the one who always gives first. Certainly this sequence sets up a fine rhythm that can help a person to feel worthy of receiving.

However, this belief has a downside. Automatically you'll block your **luck** — things that come to you freely without your first giving a thing.

Besides, what happens when you interact with another person who also, rigidly, needs to always give first? Both of you will be stuck energetically. Most likely, neither of you will receive much.

If FALSE: Belief that you can receive without first giving in any particular situation, couldn't that improve your financial flow? Today could become your lucky day... because you feel worthy to receive, whether or not you give a thing.

Of course, Earth School does include universal laws, such as karma. This inevitable cause-and-effect dynamic produces consequences from every thought, word, and action.

So, if you routinely take without giving back much at all, neither in advance of receiving your windfall or afterwards, your long-term prospects may not be great.

2. THE MORE I GIVE, THE MORE I WILL GET.

If TRUE: When you're in a glorious flow of giving, this belief can set you up to receive money galore. Say that you have talent for a particular kind of work. Giving is easy, even delightful. Of course, wealth can grow that way.

Even when you contribute at work or at home *without* huge enjoyment, strong resolve to give can help you build long-term success.

Writers who make a really convincing case for this include two of my favorites, success expert Brian Tracy and prosperity expert Emmet Fox.

Unfortunately, giving can also be done in situations where a person would be a fool to expect any immediate return on investment. Think of enabling a drunk or pouring water into a leaky bucket. Giving makes a grand choice but a tragic reflex.

If FALSE: So you believe in evaluating your business investments on a case-by-case basis? That's smart. In *Never Give Up*, Donald Trump offers some wise words about this:

> Sometimes you work as hard as you can on something, and it doesn't work out. The question is: How do you know when to give up?

I usually tough it out longer than most people would in a similar situation — which is why I often succeed where others have failed. I also know that sometimes you have to throw in the towel.

Maybe you failed, but you probably learned something valuable. Chalk it up to experience, don't take it personally, and go find your next challenge.

3. BECAUSE OF MY FINANCIAL SITUATION, I MUST GIVE MORE THAN I RECEIVE, MORE THAN IS FAIR. THAT'S JUST HOW MY LIFE IS RIGHT NOW.

If TRUE: Certain financial scenarios involve giving more than you receive. You know it. Maybe the recipient knows it, too. Only *you* can decide if giving that much, really, is worthwhile in the long run.

- What if your main strategy to Magnetize Money has been to marry rich, so your whole life is focused on making that happen?
- Or what if Grannie Gaack holds the promise of inheritance over your head, bringing all the joy and gaiety of a lead balloon?

Does that person's money mean that much to you? How much are you willing to sacrifice?

To make life choices wisely, let's get one thing straight. Nobody can really force you to give more than you agree to give. Therefore, if you have agreed to an unfair amount of giving, you might ask yourself why. On some level you do have a choice.

Dare to consider your options realistically. Could you be receiving more than you think, some kind of secondary gain or deeper personal agenda?

Or might you be living an outdated belief or fantasy? Not every experiment must be followed through to the bitter end. (Remember Angie's "dream marriage" to Arnold in our last chapter?)

Even if you don't change a thing about your external situation, an honest assessment might free up your financial flow. As for the belief about "I must give more than I receive," that is totally negotiable.

If FALSE: What could be the opposite of the "I must give" belief? "I never give more than I choose to give." This alternative could be very empowering, leading to much greater flow of wealth.

Think of a buffet-style restaurant, set up as "All you can eat." Doesn't it feel great to take what you wish? You're not necessarily being greedy, merely enjoying a certain abundance.

Refusing to sacrifice to the point of pain — that hardly disallows healthy amounts of giving. In fact, to an outside observer your behavior might appear identical to the behavior where your answer was "TRUE."

For instance, you might seem to treat Grannie Gaack just the same way as in our first scenario, perfectly polite, only now you are secretly laughing your head off over the lead balloon aspect.

Check out her arm muscles, lifting that heavy thing!

4. AT THIS TIME IN MY LIFE, I AM ABLE TO TAKE MORE THAN I GIVE, WHICH IS JUST FINE WITH ME.

If TRUE: Resourceful Reader, a yes to this notion can really help you to Magnetize Money.

It doesn't make you ethically questionable, like some bank robber.

If only you knew the whole story, you might be awed at how much you have already given, in this lifetime and countless others as well. Being truly willing to accept the payback, why not?

If FALSE: So it isn't okay with you, receiving more than you appear to give right now?

You can Magnetize Money on the pay-as-you-go plan. However, you might want to reconsider. Karma from your past actions doesn't only have to be bad, you know.

5. THERE'S NO POINT IN ASKING FOR WHAT I WANT. LOVE FROM MY SIGNIFICANT OTHER MEANS HE OR SHE WILL ANTICIPATE WHATEVER I NEED. IF I HAVE TO ASK, IT'S TOO LATE. HE OR SHE WOULDN'T UNDERSTAND.

If TRUE: Many a lifestyle is based on this form of give-and-take. The technical term for it, alas, is "co-dependence."

You may not have to go back far in your family tree to find ancestors who were co-dependent in ways that limited financial flow.

Possibly this kind of emotional dynamic was compatible with making a great deal of money. But probably not.

If you enjoy living with our Belief #5, it can be a sweet surrender. Personally, though, I would encourage you to explore how much sweeter your life could be without this belief. It heads my list of joy-sucking ways to live, especially the version that substitutes "God" for the term "significant other."

If FALSE: You do believe in asking for what you want? What, you call that "communication"? Excellent.

That's certainly how I would prefer to be treated on the receiving end, since omniscience isn't one of my virtues.

Co-dependence in personal relationships has a way of leaking into workplace relationships as well. The opposite choice, direct communication, can make it way easier to Magnetize Money.

6. Provided that I keep on doing good, I will receive my reward eventually.

If TRUE: Maybe you were brought up to believe this as central to your religion. You might even have been promised an "eternal reward."

While it's true that good karma flows from every generous thought and action, note the horrible implications in Belief #6. Fie on that sad word "eventually"!

Tomorrow never comes, unless you count ideas like "Eternal reward." Maybe Belief #6 isn't the easiest way to Magnetize Money.

If FALSE: What would the opposite version be? "If I keep acting selfish and creepy, it will never catch up with me."

That Opposite Version of Belief #6 may seem strange, yet for many a millionaire it apparently works just fine. Of course, the person's conscious justification might be quite different, such as "My family has always been rich, always will be rich. How could we not, given our genetic superiority?" (This language comes directly from one of my Give-and-Take Snapshots, actually.)

Using energetic literacy to profile the very rich, I have found many variations on this Opposite Version of Belief #6. What I have not found, however, is anyone who keeps around this kind of STUFF... and also is happy.

Personally, I prefer a different alternative, "Of course, I always do my best in life. I claim the consequences of my past good karma NOW."

Can you see how a belief like this could improve a person's bank balance? (Maybe the person's emotional balance as well!)

7. IF SHORT ON CASH, I SHOULD TITHE OR DONATE SEED MONEY TO MY CHURCH. THEN GOD WILL PAY ME BACK WITH ABUNDANCE.

If TRUE: **Tithing** means that you give 10% of your income to your earthly source of spiritual inspiration. The ancient custom of tithing is just plain beautiful, as well as good karma.

Many a prosperity writer (including two of my favorites, Catherine Ponder and Florence Scovil Shin) has described amazing spiritual demonstrations that began with giving to charity

Televangelists Oral Roberts and Joel Osteen have built their careers, in part, by inspiring the faithful to give, and give generously. In fact, Roberts was the first Protestant to popularize **seed money**.

"If you want God to supply your financial needs, then give SEED-MONEY for HIM to reproduce and multiply," Rev. Roberts wrote in *The Miracle of Seed Faith*.

How is seed money different from tithing? According to America's first televangelist, "In tithing, you give *after* you have made the income. In Seed-giving, you give *before* in expectation of return."

In 1987, Roberts warned viewers that God would "call him home" unless they sent him $8 million in contributions. (As a result, his loyal viewers contributed $9.1 million.)

Regardless of your religious affiliation, Belief #7 can awaken the power of self-fulfilling prophecy, as well as set up superb karma. Beyond that, any positive action in concert with your Highest Power can raise your vibrations, helping to improve the overall quality of your energy field.

If FALSE: If funds are low, instead of requesting a heavenly bailout, you might prefer to figure out how to earn more money. You might choose to evaluate your career, the path you're taking, and how your skill sets could bring you more money.

Instead of needing more idealism, you might need less. For instance, consider the story of Abe, one of my clients. He refused a promotion and quit his job because he disapproved of the emotional dynamics of his office manager.

But was Abe's job to do therapy on the office staff? No, he was a nurse, sent out on assignments away from that somewhat dysfunctional office. Abe was the one who suffered through months of unemployment, while his imperfect boss stayed very comfortably employed.

You might choose to question reflexive giving (of money, or free mental health services, etc.) as a way to fix your finances. An alternative to Belief #7 might be, "When short on cash, I solve human-level problems as best I can."

Tithing and seed money are lovely, but not when used as attempts to bribe God.

HEALING THAT GIVE-AND-TAKE BALANCE

Are you worried yet? Many a prosperity seeker is terrible at taking. Most success seekers need help with it, too.

But I promise you. Dysfunctional give-and-take patterns from your past and present can be changed. No time is more powerful than the now. Nor is any memory more powerful than your own consciousness in the present moment, complete with your buzzing-bright aura.

Sure, you can improve your God-given ability to take.

- Co-dependence is a good problem to rule out — or solve. Many books offer excellent advice, starting with *Codependent No More*, by Melody Beattie.
- Being a Highly Sensitive Person (HSP) can require some skills, too. Otherwise, you'll be at a disadvantage with highly

insensitive persons. Effective resources begin with the pioneering psychotherapist who discovered HSPs in the first place, the great Dr. Elaine Aron. *The Highly Sensitive Person* was written for the 1 in 5 people with the lifelong gift of sensitivity. (Aron's website is www.hsperson.com.)

- Empaths can also have problems with give-and-take. Did you know that every talented but not-yet-skilled empath constantly pulls in STUFF from others? Splat, it goes right into your aura, messing up all your gifts and especially your circuits for give-and-take. Effective techniques require subtle but effortless shifts of consciousness. See www.empoweredempath.com.

- All three skill sets — those for empaths, HSPs, and co-dependents — can prevent problems with financial flow. To heal patterns from the past, you might also need a few professional sessions to heal old STUFF from cords of attachment, etc.

So many good options! Before you avail yourself of a single one, however, try the following energetic workaround.

Right Your Balance of Give-and-Take

It's never too late to balance these two Heart Chakra databanks:
- **Giving to Others**
- **Receiving from Others**

Patterns of imbalance can creep up on us. Over-giving, you might often worry that "I need to give more." Over-taking, you may feel as though "I never have enough."

With either imbalance, however, there's a surprisingly easy remedy. To heal that deep balance, *don't go deeper. Go surface.*

Do a reality check, based on objective life.

Make a list, folding the paper in half lengthwise. Use each of these headings for one of the columns:
- Things I have given
- Things I have received

For context, think of a particular situation that bothers you now, related to business or your personal life or both.

> For three minutes, write on that topic. Write fast and free, whatever pops into your mind. Emphasize the objective facts: Hours, favors, money, you name it.
>
> How do the two columns compare? Can you draw any practical conclusions about how to handle this particular relationship from now on?
>
> Following up can impact your way of living… all the way down to evolving your Heart Chakra databanks.

Objective Truth Can Set You Free

Energetic literacy can support your balance of give-and-take, but never let the literacy itself become a distraction. In this regard, energetic literacy is exactly like all your other success and prosperity skills. None of them is meant to substitute for common sense about how to handle objective reality.

For 16 years, my client Alice worked for the "Acme Accounts Association." It seemed to her like a great success story. Alice had worked herself up from receptionist to account manager, hourly employee to salaried.

Alice was proud of herself. Except, slowly, success turned ugly for this hardworking new account manager. Over a period of three years, impossible amounts of work were thrown at her. Alice kept trying to catch them.

She knew the meaning of hard work. Besides, she was no quitter. Working far into the night, Alice often slept under her desk.

How did she keep herself going? Alice used prosperity principles. All that giving had to come back to her, right? Plus, she knew what she wanted. Keeping her goals clearly in mind, this gal insisted on staying focused on the positive.

According to the prosperity teachings Alice believed in, she was doing everything right.

Except her work load never became more manageable. Alice's requests to hire support staff were ignored. Inevitably, an emergency came up with one of Alice's big accounts. She was blamed for the problem.

The big boss called Alice into his office. He told her, "We'll let it go this time, but you must promise us this will never happen again."

"I can't promise." Alice blurted out. To her own surprise, she added, "I quit."

Following this incident, Alice booked a healing session with me. Recounting her sad tale, Alice expressed amazement that she had resigned. "I still can't believe it," she told me. "Acme has been my life for over 16 years."

Fortunately, I could help Alice to cut her cord of attachment to that big boss. His rage and her over-giving made a toxic brew. As is typical for these energy structures on the level of auras, imbalances from the cord of attachment were flowing through Alice's subconscious mind 24/7. No matter what happened later in her career, this pattern would have kept on replaying subconsciously for the rest of her life.

Except now it wouldn't. After having the cord removed permanently, Alice went on to research career alternatives. I supplied the perspective of energetic literacy to help her evaluate whether work choices could support all her chakra databanks, not only the ones about giving. Never again did Alice want to equate "My job" with "Give 98%, Receive 2%."

Right before out session ended, my client's voice turned thoughtful:

"You know, Rose, after six months, I could have told they didn't appreciate me. And they never would. If only I had paid attention!"

As for you, right now, have you been paying attention to financial flow at work? That means objectively paying attention, not the subjective version, living as Alice used to do. Never let *what you want* become a substitute for *what is.*

For inspiration, let's conclude this chapter with a full Magnetize Money Profile of Ingvar Kamprad. One of the richest people on earth, he's also one of the most Enlightened.

Had Kamprad been Alice's Big Boss, I doubt that she would have had to sleep under her desk. But if she had, at least Mr. Kamprad could have found a way to make it relatively comfortable. The man is, after all, the founder of IKEA.

Ingvar Kamprad: Top 10 Give-and-Take Databanks

Ever wonder where the name "Ikea" came from? Many billion dollars ago ($22 billion, to be exact), the world's fifth richest man decided to combine the initials of his first and last names, the name of his family farm, and the nearest village.

Find Ingvard's photo used for this profile at the "Photo Supplement" online.

1. Root Chakra Databank: **Earning Money**

50 miles. Although money remains a passion, for him, wealth isn't an end in itself. Not at age 83, when this photo was taken and he still works in the family business along with three sons.

He wants to earn buckets of money, helping people along the way. That's a deep intent for sharing the wealth he earns. In this way, Ingvar Kamprad's relationship to wealth is very different from anyone else I have read on the list of "The World's Billionaires 2009" from Forbes Magazine.

2. Root Chakra Databank: **Saving Money**

10 feet. Kamprad famously frequents cheap restaurants and his home furnishings come mostly from a certain inexpensive furniture chain.

Aura reading suggests, however, that frugality is simply a habit that runs on its own momentum. Ingvar is a saver by nature, just as the nature of peanut butter is sticky. To him, saving money is what responsible people do. Naturally he saves.

Note: Because of the lack of STUFF here, the lack of proportion in this databank is doesn't disqualify Kamprad from being considered Enlightened. Same with the relatively small Databank #1 noted earlier. The entrepreneur is designed this way to do his life work.

3. Root Chakra Databank: **Personality at Work**

900 miles. I'm reading Ingvar at 83, remember. Earlier in his career, all these databanks might have been even more powerful. Still, I'm struck by the personality of this self-made billionaire, reading him in our photo from 2009.

Under his management, don't expect to get away with a thing. Business is personal. Ingvar cares so much, he watches over it as a regular guy might watch over his family, meddling at every opportunity. Reminds me of words from my son at age 12, "I annoy because I love."

4. Root Chakra Databank: *Personality PROJECTED in Work Situations*

900 miles and exactly the same as he is the rest of the time. Mr. Kamprad doesn't do fake façade.

5. Solar Plexus Chakra Databank: *Self-Confidence at Work*

900 miles. Confidence for Kamprad isn't egoism so much as a commitment to work hard combined with his religious devotion.

If ever a man was a success story for Max Weber's book on *The Protestant Ethic and Spirit of Capitalism*, that man would be Ingvar Kamprad.

6. Solar Plexus Chakra Databank: *Handling Conflict at Work*

900 miles. Kindness emanates from this databank, provided that his worker is trustworthy. If you're a slacker, don't expect Ingvar to waste time on you. At his stage in life, how patient does he have to be with managers or employees who don't shape up?

Power Integrity at Work, a related Solar Plexus Chakra databank, is squeaky clean. And just as big. So a great advantage for Ingvar Kamprad is that he can lead by example.

7. Heart Chakra Databank: *Emotional Giving at Work*

900 miles. Giving is a frictionless flow. Ingvar feels full from within, so he can share goodwill with no strings attached.

8. Heart Chakra Databank: *Emotional Receiving at Work*

900 miles. Gratitude is mixed with discernment. This guy is nobody's mushy old fool.

Instead, he has lived long enough to take a great-grandfatherly interest in others. In his case, appreciation is amplified by an extremely wide-awake consciousness.

Ingvar can read people at any level he chooses, receiving a delightful Divine presence in every moment. If people are actually nice to him, that's like sauce on his Swedish meatballs.

> 9. *Third Eye Chakra Databank: Paying Attention to His Human Life*
> *900 miles.* You bet Ingvar pays attention. He is so loving this life. Sensuality, fun, playfulness, appreciation, living in the now... exuberant qualities like these make every day a holiday.
>
> 10. *Third Eye Chakra Databank: Connection to Spiritual Source*
> *900 miles.* What a pleasure it is to read the aura of this Enlightened man. I find this chakra databank particularly delightful. It reveals that a glorified quality is developing within Ingvar Kamprad's state of Enlightenment. The presence of God grows ever clearer and more vivid.

In case you ever doubted whether a modest and sane person could Magnetize Money, behold this extraordinary man.

Ingvar Kamprad has brought beauty into the lives of millions, with stores in 36 countries. Not everyone loves Ikea furniture, but any wealth seeker can be inspired by this billionaire's integrity and financial flow. He does give-and-take with perfect balance.

20. Energy Secrets of the Seriously Rich

We're neither pure nor wise nor good. We'll do the best we know.
— Richard Wilbur, "Candide"

You bet, I wanted to interview the 50 richest people in the world, and not just their balance of give-and-take but the most nitty gritty databanks of all, the Magnetize Money Snapshot.

No letters of introduction were forthcoming from Andrew Carnegie, but I had something just as useful for third millennium research: The most current annual list from Forbes Magazine, from 2009, complete with a good clear photo of each interviewee.

Add energetic literacy and research away — that was my plan. I wanted to investigate what made these rich people tick. And research I did, using the Magnetize Money Snapshot on all 50 of these high achievers.

A surprising number of the world's richest turned out to be related to Sam Walton, the late founder of Wal-Mart.

- There wasn't just his son Jim Walton (#11 with $17.8 billion).
- I also got to use energetic literacy on Alice Walton, the richest woman in the world ($17.6 billion).
- Tied for 12th place was Christy Walton ($17.6 billion also, which explains being tied for 12th place but not why Forbes doesn't also consider her, too, a contender for "the richest woman in the world.")
- Robson Walton made the list too, definitely male, and apparently managing to survive quite nicely on $17.6 billion.

Back in the day, when Napoleon Hill did his word-literacy version of interviews, he chatted up Joseph Stalin. Traveling no farther than my pink office in Sterling, Virginia, I also got to interview some truly strange and frightening people. Of course, I'm not going to quote their names when sharing results of my research.

PROFILES OF THE SERIOUSLY RICH

What do all these wallopingly-super-seriously-rich people have in common? Definitely not what you'd expect from reading *The Secret!*

Given all you know so far about energetic literacy, are you really surprised? Still, you can never predict the quirky nuances of any individual's auric modeling.

In the profiles that follow, I used the Magnetize Money Snapshot as an instrument to explore the most important components of business success. (To refresh your memory about the three databanks chosen for this research, see Chapter 5.)

Note: As with the profiles in our last chapter, I needed photos to "interview" these Forbes superstars. So I skipped the few who had no picture available via Forbes and continued down the list. Thus, my interview list is really the 50 richest people worldwide in the Forbes list for 2009 who had photos available.

OFTEN SPIRITUALLY DISAPPOINTING

Mega-money-makers don't necessarily shine spiritually. Out of my collection, only 1 of the 50 had an especially vibrant **Connection to Spiritual Source** databank. Among these fabulously wealthy individuals, Birgit Rousing is notable for many reasons.

This 85-year-old Swedish widow handles the family business along with her three children. Her father-in-law founded the packaging company Tetra Larval. It brought his family a vast fortune.

So the $9.9 billion didn't come into her life through sweat or scheming.

Still, in the grand bakery of life, Ms. Rousing is hardly some fluffy popover.

Birgit Rousing: Magnetize Money Snapshot

1. Root Chakra Databank: **Earning Money**
90 miles. Sees the business as a way to help people. Plus, it's a way to honor her late husband, etc. Birgit has chosen to let his passion become her passion.

2. Solar Plexus Chakra Databank: **Handling Conflict at Work**
90 miles. When business decisions are tough, Rousing may seek inspiration from her husband's memory or consult with her children. Clearly, she allows decency, dignity, and feminine energy to soften her business decisions.

3. Third Eye Chakra Databank: **Connection to Spiritual Source**
Out to the moon!!! In her everyday life, Birgit relies on intuition and inspiration.

Apart from this woman in charge of Tetra Larval, you won't find too much sweetness and light among the world's 50 richest.

Regarding spiritual connection, Birgit Rousing's 49 financial peers are quite a materialistic bunch — exactly opposite to the LOA volunteers I read for you in an earlier chapter.

Here are typical readings of the **Connection to Spiritual Source** databank.

- Billionaire X: *4 inches.* X really, really doesn't like having anyone tell him what to do. That includes "a God."
- Billionaire Y: *1 inch.* Instead of spiritual connection, Y's inner life emphasizes emotions directed toward human beings — hatred, envy, etc. When Y needs extra zing, she feeds on THAT.
- Billionaire Z: 2 inches. This self-made billionaire feels sure he has a very special relationship with The Lord, a relationship that requires no further exploration. It's like owning a valuable wine, kept in the cellar.

Curious to learn more about our Billionaires X, Y, and Z? Okay, here come the other two databanks in their Magnetize Money Snapshots.

Billionaire X: Earning and Fighting

1. Root Chakra Databank: **Earning Money**
Out to the stars. Receives huge spiritual inspiration in terms of action items. Becomes especially excited about translating his golden touch into making money.

2. Solar Plexus Chakra Databank: **Handling Conflict at Work**
Fills the room. If there's a conflict and you are involved, first you will feel his displeasure. If that doesn't get to you, X's next step is to nudge you with an icy cold shoulder.

Manners are very refined for this man, but it's always clear who's on his Good List or his Bad List. And those bad guys "will get what they deserve."

Remember, huge inchage of these chakra databanks goes with X's **Connection to Spiritual Source** of just 4 inches. Previously, you have seen symbolic diagrams of auras with spiritual addiction and Enlightenment. What version would correspond to the kind of auric modeling from Billionaire X? See Figure 9, on the opposite page.

Billionaire Y: Earning and Fighting

1. Root Chakra Databank: **Earning Money**
Out to the stars. Y's sense of self-importance is matched only by her sense of entitlement.

2. Solar Plexus Chakra Databank: **Handling Conflict at Work**
90 miles. This highly effective executive doesn't just triumph over her enemies. She gets even. She always gets even.

Interestingly, this databank shows a very low threshold for conflict. Ms. Y may imagine grave insult where none has been intended at all.

Gender aside, Figure 9 is also a fine symbolic representation of Y's auric modeling. Instead of calling it "X and Y's auric modeling," let's go for a more universal label: Focus on material life.

Billionaire Z: Earning and Fighting

1. Root Chakra Databank: *Earning Money*

Out to the sky. Imperialistic! It's not merely that Billionaire Z feels superior to most people. Rather, he considers himself part of an elite group that deserves to wield ultimate power in the world.

2. Solar Plexus Chakra Databank: *Handling Conflict at Work*

Out to the sky. He delegates the dirty work. Actually, it's very important to Billionaire Z that the surface of things must always appear tidy and professional.

Similarly, Z's manners are always classy, a point of pride. "Of course, I have contempt for people. That's fine. It doesn't show.'

FIGURE 9. FOCUS ON MATERIAL LIFE

SPECIAL TALENT FOR MAGNETIZING MONEY

Every single top billionaire has the golden touch. It shows as part of this person's strength at Root Chakra databanks like the one about **Earning Money.** In my research of the world's 50 richest, nobody — and I mean nobody — had a small showing here.

However, some of these billionaires are especially talented this way, possessing something akin to The Midas Touch. You might think of them as the ultimate "Money Magnetizers." Just don't assume that talent like this equals being "a nice person."

No, I don't think it would be prudent to refer to these fellows by name. Let's just call them "A" and "B."

Billionaire A: Magnetize Money Snapshot

*1. Root Chakra Databank: **Earning Money***
Out to the stars. His electrical presence signifies an uncommonly strong gift for making money. Whenever Mr. A thinks of a new way to earn money, it works. His intuition is uncanny.

A intuitively knows exactly where money is to be made. Following up, he gets great support.

*2. Solar Plexus Chakra Databank: **Handling Conflict at Work***
Out to the sky. To Billionaire A, either you flow with him, enjoying the allure of great power, or you are a nothing.

Working with him is like being an iron filing in the presence of a strong magnet.

So this way of avoiding conflict could be admired or considered scary, your choice.

*3. Third Eye Chakra Databank: **Connection to Spiritual Source***
1 inch. This guy is having such fun, achieving away. Why would he possibly have room to pay attention to anyone "more important"?

Incidentally, Mr. A isn't the most arrogant billionaire from this list I have interviewed energetically. Compared to many of these ultra-successful money makers, a guy like Al Capone might seem meek.

Here's a complete 10-point profile of our next billionaire, down to all the lurid details except for his name.

Billionaire B: Magnetize Money Profile

1. Root Chakra Databank: Earning Money

90 miles. Serious determination drives this self-made billionaire. Even though he's already the richest man in his country, don't expect that to satisfy him. This chakra databank screams out "I'm not nearly satisfied yet. I need more."

To Billionaire B, money is more real than people, and far more interesting.

2. Root Chakra Databank: **Saving Money**

90 miles. Having money brings an immensely thrilling kind of pride. Beyond that, wealth brings Billionaire B his sense of identity.

3. Root Chakra Databank: **Personality at Work**

40 miles. Such a no-nonsense personality! He will not like your jokes. He will not even want you to talk to him unless he has directly asked you a question.

Are you kidding? Don't ever, ever try to engage his personality in a friendly, fun way. Billionaire B is not a fun guy.

4. Root Chakra Databank: **Personality PROJECTED at Work**

100 miles. Billionaire B could have written the book on *Winning through Intimidation.* (Just for laughs, I did a quick energetic literacy comparison with the real author of that bestseller, Robert Ringer. Aurically, Ringer is no slouch. Yet Billionaire B could squash Mr. Ringer like a bug.)

The personality projected by Billionaire B sends a very clear message. I doubt that anyone who has experienced this man personally — even from the far edge of the room — would ever need a direct warning to obey him. B's chakra databank communicates most forcefully, "Don't you dare cross me."

5. Solar Plexus Chakra Databank: **Self-Confidence at Work**

40 miles. "Self-confidence" seems a mild word to describe Mr. B's overwhelming sense of self, a kind of sunbathing in his huge ego.

One great thing about the aura of this tycoon is that he makes an unforgettable imprint through auric modeling. Being in his presence, you quickly would learn how it feels, living large.

Aurically, he's much more like a king than most real-life political rulers I have read. Mr. B communicates an unmistakable sense of "My way or the highway. (And once you hit that highway, you had better run for your life.)"

6. Solar Plexus Chakra Databank: *Handling Conflict at Work*

50 miles. Scary! Just reading this chakra databank made me shiver. Cruelty is definitely part of this man's way of handling conflict at work.

It's one thing to watch a TV actor play "cruel." This is the real thing, from a man who would relish the excuse to teach anyone a violent lesson.

Gee, I have a hunch that Billionaire B doesn't encounter many discipline problems at work.

7. Heart Chakra Databank: *Emotional Intelligence at Work*

30 feet. Given the rest of B's aura, this chakra databank seems small. But I can assure you, the size is perfectly adequate.

Cold-hearted in every single chakra databank, Billionaire B is the kind of person you wouldn't *want* to understand you.

To the extent he can read people's hearts, it's about practical things like "What is this person emotionally capable of doing for me?" and "Does he scare easy?"

8. Throat Chakra Databank: *Communication at Work*

40 miles. Once again, "Ruthless" sums it up. Even his voice quality must creep people out.

9. Third Eye Chakra Databank: *Paying Attention to His Human Life*

Out to the moon. Talk about sizeable egos! No wonder Billionaire B appeared so ambitious in his Root Chakra databank about **Earning Money.** He's still growing his empire.

That job isn't nearly complete yet, thank you. The man wants more power, more deference, more money, more everything.

Why is he so insatiable? The main reason that shows here is that B feels he richly deserves everything he has now... plus much, much more.

10. Third Eye Chakra Databank: **Connection to Spiritual Source**
2 inches. "Basically, God is stupid."
The very notion of a Higher Power seems laughable to this tycoon. Or would seem laughable, had he a sense of humor.

FOLKS WHO CARE A LOT ABOUT MONEY

All in all, the world's wealthiest are a mixed bouquet, just like the neighbors you have right now. Okay, they're richer.

The other point of difference is how intensely every single one of these billionaires is driven by the need to be rich.

Otherwise, some are disgusting, others moderately tasteful, and some really quite lovely.

Of course, there's nothing to prevent someone with huge solid Root Chakra databanks from developing more in the higher chakras or, even, becoming Enlightened.

Now let's close this chapter by profiling one of my favorite energetic interviewees. Meet Alice Walton. According to the *Forbes Magazine* ranking, in 2009 she was the richest woman in the world. (See the photo used for this profile at the "Photo Supplement" online.)

Alice Walton: The Magnetize Money Snapshot

1. Root Chakra Databank: **Earning Money**
90 miles. What great sport it is for Ms. Walton, earning money. It's fun. It's easy. For her, making money has always been easy.

2. Solar Plexus Chakra Databank: **Handling Conflict at Work**
90 miles. Totally sure of herself, Alice laughs at people who give her a hard time. (Then she fires them, of course.)

Alice Walton's aura suggests that she doesn't demand the constant presence of yes-persons. Imagine! She actually enjoys having discussions; she isn't above taking advice or changing her mind.

However, this Walton heiress does demand being treated with the respect due a great personage, someone ultra-important like Queen Elizabeth or Oprah.

3. *Third Eye Chakra Databank:* **Connection to Spiritual Source**
Out to the sky. Very connected spiritually, Alice has been that way all her life.

Yes, the world's wealthiest can be sweet, just like Alice Walton. They can even be spiritually Enlightened, like Ingvar Kamprad. Just don't think that big money guarantees any of that.

Resourceful Reader, no amount of money can buy a strong spiritual connection.

However, as we'll see in Part Three of this Magnetize Money Program, maybe your free will can.

PART THREE
The Best Wealth Workshop in All the World

*I challenge you to find a better workshop than the one called "Living on Earth."
Ironically, many capable people strive so hard to be super-human, they forget
they signed up for this workshop.*

However you have lived in the past, now is your time to become truly
effective, unapologetically wealthy and healthy and happy and powerful. As a human.

Let's explore how to live to the fullest, projecting full strength
through your auric modeling. Combine this with appropriate actions
to Magnetize Money and you can succeed as never before.

21. How Big
Does Your Ego Have to Be?

"When I'm asked about how I turned Chrysler around, I always make the point that I didn't do it by myself — a lot of smart, dedicated people did it. Actually, since according to Time magazine my ego is as big as all outdoors, I should probably take credit for having done all of it by myself."
— Lee Iacocca,
Quoted in *The Little Book of Business Wisdom*, Peter Krass, editor

The best workshop in the world is living in this world... as though life mattered and you cared a great deal about your human self.

Serving others is a vital evolutionary project for each individual. Equally important, however, is looking out for yourself.

Everyone on earth can be a World Server, uplifting humanity. None of that service will be diminished if you also claim fulfillment in your human life.

When new space frees up to incarnate on earth as a human, how great an opportunity is that? Fistfights may break out in heaven, for all I know.

Certainly, experts who have traveled to other dimensions will tell you that incarnating on earth is considered a highly desirable spiritual opportunity. As one of my regression therapy clients put it during a session where she relived her Planning Meeting to incarnate here this time, "Hooray, Earth! That's where the big growth happens."

Well, if you're going to live here, why not play the full game? Go for wealth. Aim for happiness. Eat the food that suits your body; don't just feed your ideology.

But what about the tricky matter of having a human ego? Nothing is more personal than how you feel about that very human thing, your personal ego.

Are you constantly trying to minimize it? Do you try substituting something "better"? Let's consider how the size and quality of your ego automatically impacts your ability to Magnetize Money.

HEALTHY EGO VERSUS SELFISHNESS

First we had better define that slippery thing called "**ego**." Which of these does it mean to you?

1. In action, putting yourself ahead of everyone else.

2. Starting most sentences with the word "I." (In Iacocca's short paragraph at the start of this chapter, he managed to use that word five times. Thrice he used the word "my.")

3. Competing more than necessary — and feeling that you always must win — and that "win" means "I win, you lose," never "Both of us win."

4. Being a narcissist or an energy vampire.

5. Having and using a strong sense of self.

However you have defined having an ego, you can be sure this belief has had an enormous impact on your financial flow. So let's investigate further.

WHO'S ON FIRST?

Putting yourself ahead of others, does that have to be bad? I'm going to use Elizabeth as an example of what I have found using energetic literacy on many first-time clients with money problems.

Poor Elizabeth is practically allergic to anyone like Lee Iacocca. She abhors any big-ego person who clearly and unapologetically puts himself first.

A tasteful choice, sure. Except it brings consequences. What shows up in Elizabeth's own Root Chakra databank about **The Presence She Brings to a Room**? Behold one sad inch.

Between the personal conflicts due to STUFF and some misguided habits of ignoring her strengths as a person, Elizabeth has carved out a nice little niche for herself in life, akin to an ostrich with head in the sand. Except, ironically, Elizabeth has been trying to Magnetize Money. Is she kidding?

Does she really believe she can Magnetize Money just by adding a few success tips from an expert like Brian Tracy? As for LOA practices, will they contain anything that could improve her auric modeling around personal ego? Not really.

At present, Elizabeth projects a very clear message energetically: "I'm selfless. Don't see me." Alas, she succeeds.

Somehow Elizabeth has never connected the dots. She knows how awful it feels to be ignored, to have her work be ignored. She loathes being underpaid. Justifiably, Elizabeth especially hates when less hardworking co-workers get more credit than she does.

Yet never once (at least before she met me) did Elizabeth think, "So my career is now in the toilet? Hooray! I guess I've been really successful at negating my personal ego."

Beliefs and choices bring consequences. My hope is that by the end of this chapter, you will have made a conscious choice in favor of a strong personal ego.

Or, if you're already unabashedly human, complete with a fine, big ego, you will be inspired to deepen that strong sense of self.

Still, what about the hideous Ego Possibility #2 from our previous survey?

BRAGGING ABOUT I-I-I-I-I AND MY-MY-MY

Enjoying a big, secure ego doesn't necessarily mean that a person brags or boasts.

Neither does genuine ego strength need to correlate with how often a person uses words like "I" and "my." Really there is only one common denominator for those who have a right-sized, healthy, personal ego: It shows in auric modeling.

For instance, what would energetic literacy turn up about your success-related Throat Chakra databanks, such as **Communication at Work**? Someone with a big, secure personal ego shows power and effectiveness as a communicator. Such a person isn't shy about speaking any words, "I" included.

Strength in certain ego-upholding databanks in the Throat Chakra... could be considered energetic requirements to Magnetize Money.

By contrast, constantly talking about "I" and "me" means nothing about auric modeling. Ego-talk could be the desperate striving of someone who's terminally insecure. Only the aura reader knows for sure.

Of course, the aura owner might also have a pretty good idea of what's happening. Know that you deserve to be beautifully secure, not desperate at all. As such a person, you can have a strong personal ego and use lovely manners. Fear not.

Except wait. What about pushiness? Does a big ego automatically cause distasteful behavior, acting like a bully or worse?

DOES "EGO" HAVE TO MEAN "PUSHY"?

Aw, come on. Regardless of the present state of your ego, don't *you* have even one area of life where you're prepared to be pushy?

You must. Otherwise you would live without passion. (And you would also live without much money.)

If you search your soul, surely you will find *something* that you care enough to fight for, if push came to shove. That is so appropriate for a healthy human ego. Healthy pushiness, or its lack, shows in some of your Solar Plexus Chakra databanks.

Although Bill Gates has a sweet smile, only a fool would lightly compete against him in any Microsoft market. Remember when we read his aura before? In some respects, the richest man in the world is a ruthless fighter.

By contrast, consider Earline, one of my clients. She hates pushiness. She especially loathes it in competitive co-workers. Absolutely, she despises pushiness in her arrogant brother-in-law... in anyone, really. Yet the grownups in Earline's life act like toddlers when it comes to pushiness. They test her to learn what they can get away with.

Have you ever been martyred by a pushy boss or co-worker? Maybe it's time to push back.

Pay attention to the objective facts of the situation. Give as much as is reasonable and refuse to give one bit more. If someone like Earline can learn to stick up for herself (which she did), trust me, anyone can.

In *The 7 Habits of Highly Effective People*, Dr. Steven Covey writes that, in most cases, Win-Win works best. Who wouldn't agree, in theory?

It takes a good-sized ego, however, to insist that you and business associates must both gain your fair share. Otherwise, when you look back on negotiations, you may be quite unpleasantly surprised. In retrospect you might realize that you gave away far more than you got, just to claim that hollow Win-Win.

When your Solar Plexus and Throat Chakra databanks are functioning well, however, you can pursue Win-Wins effectively. And if, on occasion, you must implement a Win-Lose, it won't make you cringe.

Workplace conflict calls into question the strength of one's ego. What happens internally while you're trying to negotiate that Win-Win, so beloved of success coaches?

Sometimes a well meaning success seeker pushes aside the healthy reactions that come from a healthy ego. Instead, spiritual or religious beliefs are over-emphasized. A prosperity belief about being perfectly sweet can detract from your ability to Magnetize Money in the real world.

Even worse, over-emphasizing spirituality can make you vulnerable in ways related to how you answer three following questions.

Three Tricky Questions About Conflict

No matter how pure you are, conflict does comes up sometimes at work. Think of the most recent conflict that has impacted you and your money. Could it:

1. Be a sign that you are meant to do different work?
2. Be meant as spiritual test, so you must try harder than ever to stay positive?
3. Or be a warning about secret energy vampires in your workplace?

How you answer these questions can make all the difference in the world — your world. If you really aim to Magnetize Money, just say "No" to all three of these ideas.

Then go ahead and handle your conflict like a mature grownup who has a healthy ego. You have the right to pursue your needs and desires.

> Worry about the signs and tests later, when you're retired on your yacht.
>
> As for energy vampires or narcissists, emotional blackmailers or people who are of The Devil — quit worrying about other people's energy pedigree.
>
> Use your own fine energy pedigree to take the most effective action. Start by shifting your focus to objective human reality. What is happening here and now? Well, deal with it.

Many clients have come to me in crisis, terrified of losing their jobs. I have been able to help them survive and thrive. It takes individualized use of energetic literacy, plus healing STUFF from their auras.

Often, I must help build up my client's ego and survival skills. Some of the concepts that help them might help you, too. Right now. Especially if you hate your current job so much that, whenever you go to work, your survival-smart ego starts screaming, "Let me outta here."

Yes, a consistently unpleasant job is good cause to seek new employment, ideally before you quit or get fired. But maybe that job can be saved. Regardless, you can gain practical wisdom to benefit the rest of your career. So let's take a deeper look at our Three Tricky Questions.

TRICKY QUESTION #1: COULD DISSATISFACTION AT YOUR JOB BE A SIGN "YOU'RE MEANT TO DO DIFFERENT WORK"?

One of the surest signs of a spiritual addiction is that any conflict at work is interpreted as, "I am meant to do something different."

- Do you feel that you would be much, much happier living in a small village, praying and meditating, attracting money due to your glorious spiritual connection?
- Are you convinced that you will get rich doing psychic work, mediumship, Reiki, or E.F.T?
- Is it time to stop everything else and do nothing else but focus on your spiritual work?
- Have you felt increasingly pressured to find that one occupation that will instantly make you rich and famous?

- Would your ideal life be wonderfully spontaneous, where angels inspire you and tell you what to do all day long?

Pay attention to desires like these, but don't necessarily feel you must fulfill them. Consider:

- Until you're independently wealthy, and even then, prayer and meditation will not attract a whole lot of money. Better to get a life and adorn it with 30-60 minutes, tops, of these bliss-bringing ways to spend time.

- Why would a reasonable person expect to get rich doing Reiki or E.F.T? For heaven's sake, take a look at the job market where you are living. How many people can you count who earn a living that way? Deeper into the third millennium, maybe more will. Meanwhile, don't quit your day job. Build up your practice on the side until it becomes lucrative enough to support you.

- Is it time to drop everything else and start acting full-time, get your band together, or write that book? If you're really talented at creative or spiritual work, you will be energized to do it part-time. Then let your success move you into full-time. Otherwise, don't quit that day job.

- Consider that feeling great pressure to be successful as a world server might come, in part, from neglecting your human life. When you have found more balance, adulation from fans won't be needed for you to enjoy being yourself as a person.

- Would it solve all problems for angels to supply inspiration constantly, pushing you around like a piece on a chess board? But wait, you're the human in this angelic dialogue. Spiritual wisdom does not mean constantly begging for guidance, does it?

That last item is so important, it bears repeating: When you are human, spiritual wisdom does not mean constantly begging for guidance. Your angels are here to help *you,* serving at your command.

Ask them to whisper important truths into your ear and subconscious mind, so their ideas will feel like your thoughts. Put yourself back in charge, so your human ego can stand front and center. You'll strengthen your life.

TRICKY QUESTION #2: WHAT ABOUT TRYING EXTRA-HARD TO STAY POSITIVE?

Whenever you try really hard for something in life, yet don't get results, that doesn't necessarily mean "Try harder."

Spirituality works well to support human reality... but makes a lousy replacement for common sense. When there's a problem at work, how about this human workaround: Identify what's wrong and try fixing that.

Energetic literacy can supplement your efforts (provided that you use this resource, too, in moderation). Could there be some very fixable weakness right now in one of your chakra databanks? And how about using full energetic literacy to research the main players in your workplace?

One problem with staying positive is an inaccurate reading of other people in the workplace, e.g., Vibing out folks with Stage 1 Energetic Literacy is not the same as making a detailed assessment.

Another problem is, unintentionally, sugar coating the people in your life. Could you be doing that?

Temporarily put aside your cherished and most positive ideals. Consider: "Who are these folks in my workplace? Are they really as sweet as M&Ms?"

TRICKY QUESTION #3: WHAT IF SOMEBODY IN YOUR WORKPLACE IS ENERGETICALLY TOXIC?

The bogeyman of your childhood has emerged from beneath your bed. These days, he is called "a narcissist" or, perhaps, an "energy vampire."

If ever you were looking for a way to turn off your Magnetize Money circuits, fear that bogeyman. Then make the energy turnoff official by calling that bogeyman a "narcissist" or "energy vampire."

Do you wish to spot narcissists accurately? Then develop full energetic literacy. I think you'll discover that, in reality, very few people meet the requirements of being a narcissist or energy vampire.

To this energetic profiler, at least, a **narcissist** has no emotional awareness of others, zero desire to change, and other chakra problems that form a very specific syndrome of sociopathic tendencies. By contrast, plenty of people with huge, obnoxious egos also have hearts of gold, and might treat you well. (Think of Alec Baldwin's character in the TV show "30 Rock.") Deciding how to best handle big egos will get you farther than adding a bogeyman label.

As for **energy vampires**, they're at least as rare as true narcissists. Granted, it's commonplace that otherwise normal people can drain you, be cruel, or destructive. If you are suffering from this kind of relationship, find a skilled healer who can help you to permanently cut your cord of attachment to that individual. You'll feel better.

What else might help? Consider whether you are among the 1 in 20 people with a lifelong gift as an empath. You might want to research what that means. If you are a born empath, you can develop the fairly simple skill set that turns you into a skilled empath. Otherwise, an unskilled empath does something unfortunate with auric modeling. It's like wearing a sign that reads "Kick me."

For everyone, relationship problems on the job can be serious business. But name calling won't solve much. It's still necessary to use social skills, common sense, and street smarts.

Working with clients, I seldom find energy vampires. Instead I'm more likely to find an unskilled empath or a pretty bad cord of attachment and or specific behavioral problems, all of which can be remedied.

What about **psychic attack,** another common fear today? Helping thousands of clients in personal sessions since 1986, I have found exactly nine cases.

It's easy for an over-subjective, under ego-using, person to feel attacked. Instead of worrying about the remote danger coming from others energetically, handle work conflict by using this Win-Win combination:

- ✦ OBJECTIVE WIN. Take appropriate action to solve real-life problems. On the level of human reality, change what you can, recognize what you cannot change, and develop the wisdom to know the difference. (Hmm, where have you heard that serenity-attracting idea before?)
- ✦ SUBJECTIVE WIN. Take appropriate action to heal problems at the level of your energy field. These underlying

causes can be moved out relatively quickly through Energy Spirituality, Energy Psychology, or Energy Medicine. And meanwhile, try this energetic workaround for handling difficult people.

Dealing with Toxic People

Crisp business manners, like good business dress, can help your work relationships to proceed with dignity. So don't be afraid to be formal. (And, yes, this very same energetic workaround can be used outside business settings, as needed. You could use it even at that risky ritual known as "The Big Family Thanksgiving Dinner.")

It's surprisingly easy to minimize contact with anyone you find personally difficult. Say as little as possible. Appear polite. Avoid paying attention to this person's energy.

Simply go through the motions. Meanwhile, have fun noticing the fascinating wallpaper. And, of course, avoid undermining this approach with terrified self-talk.

DON'T think "Omigod, I must run from this dangerous energy vampire."

DO think, "I'm a strong, confident person, acting appropriately in this situation."

SPIRITUAL HYPOCHONDRIA

"Should I wear pantyhose to the job interview? A healer told me that you lose energy. She wears only organic cotton tights or ones made of silk."

This is a direct quote from one of my clients. Ellen did not mean it as a joke, either.

TV shows like TLC's "What Not to Wear" were made for people like Ellen. If you're going to work, dress for work. Your aura is not so weak and puny that it will be strangled by a pair of pantyhose. (Although you guys might not want to dress that way.)

Useful though energetic literacy can be, never let it overwhelm your sense of reality. I coined the term **"Spiritual Hypochondria"** for over-dependence upon energy perceptions… to the point where effectiveness suffers.

All literacy is meant to support life, not replace it. Once I learned this lesson the hard way while living in a university town. One day, I was walking around with my nose in a book, paying no attention to where I was walking. Hello! I stepped into a big hole in the sidewalk and sprained my ankle.

This brought me a memorable lesson: When you're reading, sit and read. When you're walking, walk.

Overcoming spiritual addiction helps careers because it improves auric modeling. This, in turn, will attract a better quality of human relationship. You'll strengthen your human ego vibrationally.

Spiritual hypochondria can distort life regardless of whether or not there's a spiritual addiction. The hypochondria distorts a person's sense of ego. For example, do you have fears of "selling out" because people in the workplace expect you to dress and act professionally?

No, you're not selling your soul to The Devil just because you agree to wear a tie. And your Throat Chakra won't be strangled, either.

Some lifestyle changes might tweak a person's aura for better or worse. In an ideal world, you could wear cotton tights and no tie, eat only the purest of organic foods, never deal with anybody unpleasant, and need no personal ego at all. There is a place like that, actually. Only it is called "Heaven."

So long as you're living on earth, and human, you might as well cope with this silly, gross world.

Spiritual evolution is stabilized by paying attention to reality and doing the best you can, personal ego included. Sure, do some spiritual practice each day, up to an hour if you like.

Only, afterwards, forget about it. Soon you'll see more money flowing to you, the person who owns that more balanced ego.

A BLIND SPOT THAT EGO CAN'T FIX

Back in the second millennium, most people expected everyone else to be "just like me."

This ego-involvement causes a blind spot. Yet it can be overcome, just like the blind spot resulting from how mirrors are placed on a car.

As a driver, you have learned to overcome that kind of blind spot. Either that or you never dare to change lanes.

So think about the habit you have developed for overcoming your blind spot as a driver:

1. You stop viewing traffic in the regular way.
2. You turn your eyes and attention in a completely different direction, focusing very briefly on what you find there.
3. Quickly you return to normal.

To overcome the ego's blind spot, you can do something similar. Bring in more perspective with a very quick use of energetic literacy.

1. You shift attention from your usual way of interacting with others.
2. Very briefly, you turn attention towards greater insight — whatever will help you to tell what is happening energetically.
3. Quickly you return to normal. You're better informed and, maybe even, safer.

Deep Down, Is Everyone Really "Just Like Me?

When you pay attention at the surface of life, a vague case could be made for that notion of everyone being "Just Like Me." After all, most humans have two eyes, one nose, one mouth.

Floating around in the psychic domain, from the perspective of an entity like Esther Hicks' pal Abraham, all humans might seem more-or-less identical physically.

How about the human perspective on who-you-be? Do you discover something different when using full energetic literacy? (That's a kind of middle ground, deeper than the surface but not as far out as an astral entity like Abraham.) What happens? We can learn about the deepest and most distinctive qualities of anyone, a.k.a. "Gifts of the soul."

Skill sets of energetic literacy include reading body language in depth, face reading (physiognomy, not expression reading), aura reading, or even doing a skilled empath merge. When you know whom you're dealing with at work, it's way easier to Magnetize Money.

Sure, it feels warm and fuzzy to assume that anyone else is "just like me." So what? Truth is, nobody else on this earth exists to be an extension of your human ego.

Warm, fuzzy, and vague expectations about everyone being exactly like you... will keep you stuck at your present income level. By contrast, here are two alternative approaches, either one of which can help you to Magnetize Money:

- Either adopt a service orientation that treats people like individuals
- Or choose to power through. Use charisma, reputation, or your status within a corporation. Or power through by means of an unabashedly strong personal ego.

MINIMIZING THE EGO

Many a prosperity seeker leads a life of quiet compartmentalization. Take Eddie, for example. Sometimes he's dream boarding like crazy, doing all he can to boost income through subjective prosperity teachings. Other times, he amps up the objective success strategies, networking via the Internet until his eyes lose their focus, like a screen cursor run amok. And then, when Eddie goes into serious "spiritual mode," he tries so very hard not to have a big ego.

Have you ever tried to smush out your personal ego? Then, like Eddie, you know that it can't be done without great effort.

Sure, there are spiritual practices to minimize the ego.

Or you can make lifestyle choices based on selflessness.

But unless you're a monk or nun, you need a personal ego. It can't be destroyed, short of a very dysfunctional life.

And it certainly can't be destroyed if you aim to grow rich. Use energetic literacy on any successful person you've personally met. Unless that person happens to be spiritually Enlightened (and maybe even then) there's going to be an enormous personal ego.

What, you want an example? It's coming at the end of this chapter. Yummy Buffet aura samplings will soon be your reward. Before then, I invite you to get this ego ambivalence issue settled once and for all.

Could you be like my client Eddie? He sends the Universe one hideous mashup:

"Bring me great wealth, beloved Highest Power. Only I don't personally want to be here to receive it. Because having a big personal ego would be so spiritually disgusting."

Phooey on that-ey. Choose, once and for all, to embrace your ego. The following energetic workaround can help you to live that way happily (and lucratively) ever after.

For a Stronger Ego

Create a new Agreement with the Universe to reconfigure that ego of yours.

Here's a technique you only need to do once in order to get great results. To prepare, read through all the instructions. (You might even wish to prepare written statements for Steps 1 and 4. Otherwise, improvise on the spot.)

The technique will be done eyes open, so once you've previewed, read through each step and then do it.

To begin this powerful spiritual ceremony, invite your Highest Power to be your witness. Angels and guides, spirits of ancestors — go wild with those invitations.

Be sure to give a specific callout to your subconscious mind by saying out loud, "Subconscious mind, actively pay attention to this ceremony because I am going to end my old pattern around personal ego, then put in place a new pattern."

1. Describe out loud your old pattern, including how it has affected your finances. Begin, *"My old Agreement about Personal Ego went like this."* Then continue with a description, e.g., *"I used to equate my personal ego with being selfish or demanding. I might have sabotaged my career sometimes because of feeling squirmy when there was no need for it. Even though I kept affirming prosperity beliefs, I felt that my human ego was bad, and despised people who seemed too pushy. So I couldn't Magnetize Money the way I deserved."*

2. Announce: "That old pattern is over." Clap your hands.

3. Done! But, for heaven's sake, don't stop this technique now. Whenever you move out the old, you must purposely bring in something better. Otherwise the old will creep back in.

4. Describe out loud your new version of personal ego and how you expect it to support your wealth in life. Begin, "*My new Agreement about Personal Ego goes like this.*" Then continue with a description, e.g., "*I feel comfortable with my personal ego. I accept that this is a safe and even sacred part of being human. I allow myself to feel what I feel, want what I want, and do what I do. It's fun for me, taking reality checks to help this personal ego of mine be effective as I pursue my goals. I have a good-sized, healthy, strong ego at all times, and that's fine with me. Of course, this helps me to Magnetize Money.*"

5. Announce: "This new pattern is now installed." Clap your hands.

6. Announce: "This ceremony is now complete. My new Agreement will stay in place until (or unless) I choose to purposely change it in the future."

Eventually, your personality may refine a strong but healthy ego-expressing way of being you. Welcome this reasonably rowdy, attention-getting presence. It can greatly increase your income, provided that your strength shows appropriately.

Now, here comes a profile of a man who does quite well in the income department. Notice the ego that helped him get that way.

Warren Buffett: Magnetize Money Profile

One of the most respected figures in American finances, the self-made investor is also one of the wealthiest men in the world. Find his picture in our Photo Supplement online.

1. Root Chakra Databank: *Earning Money*
50 miles. Very solid awareness of material life, how things work, where money flows, and how large groups of people choose to spend money.

For Buffet's inner reality, interest in wealth is linked to kindness. If you were competing with him, however, his determination could seem more like ruthlessness.

2. Root Chakra Databank: *Saving Money*

50 miles. Buffett takes money very seriously, like being the master of many prized dogs. He is the owner. He expects obedience. Watchful, he will quickly notice any problem and take action.

3. Root Chakra Databank: *Personality at Work*

50 miles. Exceptionally aware of details, the investor appears more stern than in the two previous databanks. Buffet brings a deeply nononsense approach to practical matters.

4. Root Chakra Databank: *Personality PROJECTED at Work*

50 miles. Warren projects nothing different from who he is the rest of the time, except for slightly emphasizing his emotional warmth.

5. Solar Plexus Chakra Databank: *Self-Confidence at Work*

50 miles. Here is a man who loves business. "I can handle anything and learn from it. And I will come up with a positive outcome."

Note the difference between this positivity versus what people try to give themselves through affirmations and the like.

Mr. Buffett isn't standing in front of some mental dream board, trying with all his might to persuade himself. Great power is in reserve.

Also, he doesn't expect a positive outcome because... his standards are low.

Within his chakra databanks, the mega-investor's sense of inner resourcefulness runs so smoothly, it practically hums. Through his actions and speech, in reality, Buffett displays a lion-like confidence.

6. Solar Plexus Chakra Databank: *Handling Conflict at Work*

50 miles. Warren Buffet can handle major conflict without breaking a sweat. What impresses me most is the social finesse, even delicacy.

Can this man summon up great reserves of power, influence, and money as a way to resolve conflict? Sure.

Does he routinely do the full summoning job? No, the strength is held in reserve for occasions when it's really needed.

Deep down, this man feels wonderfully secure. Rather than over-react to conflict, he will simply deal, then move on.

7. Heart Chakra Databank: *Emotional Intelligence at Work*

50 miles. Although Warren's aura clearly proclaims "No push-over," that includes a remarkably tender heart. As a man who has it made, he can take time to notice and value the people around him.

Warren Buffett hasn't waited for this millennium, or this Mag-netize Money Program, before developing energetic literacy. He has been doing his own version of it for a very long time, right through his heart.

Buffett can feel if a business owner has emotional stability vs. craziness, solid security vs. pretense, feels genuine emotion vs. phony anything.

Between the joy radiating from this man's aura and his ability to learn the truth instantly, I doubt that many people in his presence attempt to lie.

8. Throat Chakra Databank: *Communication at Work*

50 miles. Many chakra databanks in Warren Buffet display a jovial quality. And this good humor might spice up his speaking as well. But the main thing I notice here is the gift for brilliant insight.

Most people wouldn't even try to find a needle in a haystack. We'd be utterly blind to the one tiny flaw in a mega-complex busi-ness plan. Buffett, however, goes there in a flash, traveling via un-canny intuition. And then he can express it.

Explaining is done without showing off, speaking more as if he is sharing a discovery that anybody could have made. Only, on this particular occasion, he just happened to be the guy to figure things out.

9. Third Eye Chakra Databank: *Awareness of his Human Life*

50 miles. Gusto! Appreciation! Warren Buffett could be consid-ered a human thesaurus for living the various nuances of human contentment.

And let's be clear. Buffet doesn't do inner multi-tasking, working on prosperity principles like gratitude. Buffet's version isn't pasted on, forced, or manufactured in any way. It radiates from his aura because of the absence of STUFF.

Warren Buffet's auric modeling is energetically clear, crystal clear. And it includes the habit of noticing his human life, here and now.

10. Third Eye Chakra Databank: *Connection to Spiritual Source*

50 miles. In case you have been keeping track, all of the chakra databanks I have read in this man are balanced, showing the same huge inch-age.

Spiritual seekers take note: Warren isn't exactly a seeker. He's a finder. The spiritual connection is real to him, with the presence of the Divine as familiar as his own nose or feet.

Because this man has been living this way for so long, his personal relationship to Spiritual Source has matured. He has developed more than a solid, huge spiritual connection. When he pays attention to this aspect of life, Warren Buffett is learning ever more about the nuances of his Highest Power, making quiet discoveries one glorious day at a time.

Warren Buffett may be filthy rich but his aura is squeaky clean. It's balanced in that magnificent way that qualifies as Enlightenment.

And this didn't simply happen because he resides in Omaha, Nebraska, the city where you might expect to find the world's largest group of yogis who get together and chant "Om."

Somehow, Warren has learned all by himself how to *be* himself powerfully. He has avoided addictions. He has managed to unclog all significant STUFF from his aura. That healthy human ego lives quite unapologetically.

The mega-billionaire also displays the other indispensible ingredients to Magnetize Money: Integrity of speech and action, plus the ability to follow through in objective reality. To improve your own indispensibles, turn the page.

22. Money Brings Power. Or Is It The Other Way Around?

Why is it that 70 percent of people who win the lottery are flat broke and unhappy within a few short years? Why is it that winning huge sums of money often leads to bankruptcy, divorce, family feuds, and even early death?....
It's because they aren't yet the type of people they need to be to live at the level of financial wealth.
— James Arthur Ray,
Harmonic Wealth: The Secret of Attracting the Life You Want

In our survey of the world's wealthiest, everyone's aura shows power galore. Maybe you're thinking, "Hey, if my net worth exceeded the GNP of some entire nations, I'd be feeling pretty powerful, too."

Sure, but which came first, owning the chicken or owning the egg?

Those round-and-round debates can go on forever, if you're a philosopher. But if you're a philosopher who aims to grow rich, stop going around in circles. Do what you can — right now — to develop the most powerful aura possible. After big personal power flows within you, assess the growth of your financial assets. Philosophize about that.

You can combine wealth and great power in a healthy way, of course, so your auric modeling doesn't make other people cringe.

Hitler had power. Still, would you really want that mustache? Excuse me. Would you really want that aura? On the level of energetic literacy, the technical term for it is "sickening."

By contrast, check out the two success profiles at the end of this chapter. Now those guys' power circuits Magnetize Money beautifully.

Right now, consider:

- Sure, you can increase your inner power. Transform enough and your power will show clearly at the level of your energy field. No power suit, however expensive, has quite the sheen of great auric modeling.
- Along with evolving subjectively, you can use techniques from Part Three of our Magnetize Money Program to carry more power into the objective world, developing skills that do justice to this more powerful version of who-you-be.

But first let's sort out, and heal, confusion regarding power itself.

What's the point of magnetizing all that money anyway?

Assume for a moment that this Magnetize Money Program, and you, have been completely successful.

In this thought experiment, are you are rich now? Hugely. Now that's settled, quickly list 10 things about your life that are different because you have that wealth.

What Changes When I'm Rich

1.
2.
3.
4.
5.
6.
7.
8.
9.
10.

Hey, did you just skip over this part to keep reading? Slow down. Will it waste your time to list some personal, practical specifics?

Not if you really want more money. In. Your. Very. Own. Personal. Life.

What would it really mean if you had so much money that you could use it to light your barbecue? Just for fun, I'll give examples for hypothetical Resourceful Reader Oliver.

What Changes When I'm Rich – Oliver's Version

1. My wife will treat me with more respect.
2. My mother-in-law will treat me with more respect.
3. I can leave my boring job and do my favorite hobbies instead.
4. I'll feel happy because I can buy whatever I want.
5. Wherever I go, people will treat me with respect.
6. I can live in a really nice house in a great neighborhood.
7. It will be easy for me to lose that weight.
8. My clothes will improve.
9. Maybe I'll find a way to reverse that male pattern baldness.
10. I definitely will feel better about myself.

GETTING RICH AND STAYING RICH

James Earl Ray isn't the only one to have noticed that lottery winners can wind up broke. The best explanation I've seen for this comes from one of my heroes, Emmet Fox, who wrote compellingly in *The Ten Commandments* that "Thou shalt not steal" really means "Thou *canst* not steal." You can't keep money for which you don't have the consciousness.

So what would it mean, developing the kind of consciousness where all that money could stick? Emmet Fox wrote as someone with an Enlightened aura. He had tremendous insights and has been enormously influential at helping people.

Still, the practices Fox developed were pure prosperity techniques of the second millennium. Like batteries in an otherwise fine Christmas present, energetic literacy wasn't included. If someone began to use prayer with an imbalanced aura (lacking in strength at the Solar Plexus Chakra, for instance) Fox's approach wouldn't change that.

Actively engaging in our Magnetize Money Program in the third millennium, things can be different now. You can develop the consciousness and auric presence of a rich person.

That's not asking for the moon, or the position of Moon CEO.

Just think how far you have come already. In our Magnetize Money Program, you have already learned how to balance your aura overall, strengthen your Root Chakra presence, improve your effectiveness as a communicator, and strengthen your ego.

Now it's time to grab that indispensible oomph of real power.

Our next step in doing that is to reassess your original list. Go back to your previous assignment, "What Changes When I'm Rich." Rewrite one item at a time, adding why you think having more money could improve things.

Why Will Having More Wealth Improve My Life?

1.
2.
3.
4.
5.
6.
7.
8.
9.
10.

Why Will Having More Wealth Improve My Life?

Here's the example for Oliver:

1. Respect from wife — because she can have more money and status.

2. Respect from mother-in-law — because whenever she starts nagging me, I can buy things to shut her up.

3. Ability to pursue favorite hobbies — because I'll have the time and money to spare.

4. Ability to buy whatever I want — definitely requires more money!

5. Respect from everyone in society — because rich people are respected, and sometimes even groveled to, which sure would be a refreshing change.

6. Buying a nicer house — this is definitely going to require money.

7. Weight loss will be easier because I can afford a personal trainer, a chef, etc. Plus I won't have job stress any more.

8. Better clothes will become available because I can afford to buy whatever I like. This, of course, will increase my prestige.

9. Money will keep me from going bald — because I can buy the very best products and services. (How many male movie stars, for instance, have sad hair like mine?)

10. Self-confidence will develop because, frankly, I'll be able to buy and sell the loyalty of "the little people."

MIXED-UP POWER

Look over what you wrote about "Why Will Having More Wealth Improve My Life?" Take a pen with red ink, or some other contrasting color. Mark up what you wrote, doing edits in the light of common sense.

Is mega-money really the way to accomplish those desires? Often power would work better. Often people mix up money and power. Often their personal power is just plain mixed up.

Let's go back over Oliver's list to test this idea. Because — such a coincidence — his desires for wealth possess some rather universal elements. Since **personal power** is going into enter into this discussion, I had better define it.

- Personal power means solving problems vigorously.
- Objectively, that power requires doing frequent reality checks.
- Subjectively, that power means honoring your own personal ego, complete with thoughts, feelings, and desires.
- Power also requires interacting with other people at the objective level of speech and action.
- For power plays to be most effective, self-confidence is required.

- So is paying attention to feelings like anger and frustration. Emotions like these serve as spurs to action for people who are comfortable with using their power. (While people who don't access power are more likely to squelch feelings like anger.)
- Money can expand personal power, but only for people who have it in the first place. Otherwise extra money will only increase opportunities to feel like a victim.
- Find any self-made rich person and you will find someone with strong power circuits. Successful people take control. They don't outsource it.
- Power shows through voice quality, words, and actions. Power is also, of course, clearly visible through Stage 3 Energetic Literacy.

REALITY CHECK

Let's take another look at Oliver's desires for wealth, shall we?

1. "MONEY SHOULD BRING RESPECT FROM MY WIFE BECAUSE SHE CAN HAVE MORE MONEY AND STATUS."

Unless she's a gold-digger, that disrespecting wife may have other needs that Oliver hasn't noticed. Many a wealth seeker, focused on money, wrongly assumes that other people's priorities are exactly the same.

If Oliver's power circuits are working well within the marriage — neither too big nor too small — he might find his marriage improving until it's just right.

2. "MONEY SHOULD BRING RESPECT FROM MY MOTHER-IN-LAW BECAUSE WHENEVER SHE STARTS NAGGING ME, I CAN BUY THINGS TO SHUT HER UP."

Unless Oliver uses his millions to buy gags for the woman, lavish presents won't solve much. He might just exchange *contempt + whining* for *greed + whining.*

What's a better way to stop the nagging? Forceful, yet appropriate, behavior.

Marriage vows don't require that a bride or groom, or son-in-law, must stick around to be nagged.

Developing basic assertiveness skills is… another book. However, it may be enough to have this simple Aha! Powerful people don't tolerate being disrespected by anyone on a routine basis; powerful people get the message across that behavior like this is unacceptable.

3. "MONEY SHOULD BRING ME THE ABILITY TO PURSUE MY FAVORITE HOBBIES BECAUSE I'LL HAVE TIME AND MONEY TO SPARE."

What are Oliver's favorite hobbies anyway, buying mansions or playing polo? Most hobbies can be started without too much cash.

Finding time, as well as money, requires power. You are the only one who can choose to pay yourself first.

4. "MONEY SHOULD BRING ME THE ABILITY TO BUY WHATEVER I WANT."

It had better. But buying whatevers can grow tiresome.
In life at Earth School we don't buy things only with money. We buy things with time and attention and caring. And we buy them most successfully when we use personal power to follow through.

5. "MONEY SHOULD BRING ME RESPECT FROM EVERYONE IN SOCIETY BECAUSE RICH PEOPLE ARE RESPECTED."

Rich people can also be mocked, feared, and despised. Character lost its cachet in the late 20th century, but expect it to come roaring back in the era of energetic literacy.

Our Magnetize Money approach is designed to help you manifest wealth through strong, balanced auric modeling. While Oliver is in the process of claiming that kind of aura, and wealth, he might as well amp up his personal power for dealing with people.

Acting confidently, paying attention to reality, boldly expressing ideas, taking action with vigor: Any of these power plays will "buy" Oliver more success. Even then, he won't necessarily win respect from everyone, but so what?

One way to know you're truly powerful is when you stop caring whether random people happen to approve of you.

6. "MONEY SHOULD HELP ME BUY A NICER HOUSE."

Now that's true. In this example, power would only do a better job than wealth if Oliver's personal power were accompanied by a gun and Oliver was using both during a holdup. Personal power won't generally get you the deed to anyone's property.

However, what's the fun of living in a nicer house if the servants despise you? Whether Oliver ever has servants or not, he can certainly acquire power. He can gain likeability. That, more than anything, makes a house nice.

7. "MONEY WILL HELP ME LOSE WEIGHT BECAUSE I CAN AFFORD A PERSONAL TRAINER, A CHEF, ETC. PLUS I WON'T HAVE JOB STRESS ANY MORE."

Two words: Oprah Winfrey.

8. "MONEY WILL BRING ME BETTER CLOTHES, WHICH WILL INCREASE MY PRESTIGE."

Clothes make the man. Who's going to argue with an old saying? I will, however, *complete* it. *Clothes make the man dressed*, and whether or not that looks tasteful is another question entirely.

Dressing well is a knack. It can be developed. It can be developed on a modest income. Choosing to dress well, at any price point, is a great exercise in using personal power.

9. "MONEY WILL KEEP ME FROM GOING BALD, SINCE I CAN BUY THE VERY BEST PRODUCTS AND SERVICES."

Hair issues hurt. And I write this as someone who has not only had bad hair days. I have been accused of having "a bad hair *life*."

Although money won't prevent baldness, fine products and services might improve that look. Even rich folk can buy bad toupees, however. And poor folk can make a power statement with the Captain Picard look.

Hair styling is ultimately... another book. Meanwhile Oliver can consider carrying that head with power and style, attached to a spunky aura. What might that look do for him socially?

10. "MONEY BRINGS SELF-CONFIDENCE BECAUSE I'LL BE ABLE TO BUY AND SELL THE LOYALTY OF 'THE LITTLE PEOPLE.'"

Could all the money in the world really buy loyalty? If anything can buy it, consider the purchasing power in real life of power + love + spiritual light.

POWER BEGETS POWER

Once I asked my friend Olympia how she kept her house so clean. "All I do is pay attention," she said. "Mess begets mess, so I clean as I go."

Isn't power similar? When you live with power, and clean as you go, people around you receive a consistent message.

For true success, however, that message can't be applied superficially, like Lemon Pledge. It must go all the way through, strong enough to show through auric modeling.

Here are examples of two success writers whose enormous influence may be related to superb auric modeling about power.

Stephen Covey: Magnetize Money Snapshot

Dr. Stephen R. Covey has sold over 20 million books and been named by Time Magazine as one of the 25 most influential Americans. He writes on families as well as success. Learn more at his official website, www.stephencovey.com.

You're invited to read along with me, Resourceful Reader who has developed energetic literacy. The picture used for this profile is at the "Photo Supplement" online.

1. Root Chakra Databank: *Earning Money*
90 miles. Stephen is resourceful, even crafty. And he's extremely focused on the external measure of success called "making money." For Mr. Covey, the game must be played with integrity and intelligence. Then it becomes fun for him. It is, actually, his favorite game in all the world.

2. Solar Plexus Chakra Databank: *Handling Conflict at Work*
90 miles. Warm and friendly, but mostly clever, Stephen radiates confidence. Conflict doesn't scare him. Instead, he expects an ideal outcome, which he then proceeds to make happen.

3. Third Eye Chakra Databank: *Connection to Spiritual Source*
90 miles. When it comes to religion, Stephen Covey walks his talk. The connection is sweet, humble, loving, and respectful.

Among followers of The Secret, it's supposed to be extremely important to have a happy mood, happy thoughts. Stephen Covey's way of handling conflict provides a refreshing contrast. His "handling conflict" databank shows nothing like a fixed smile.

Nor does his **Handling Conflict at Work** databank suggest a fixed strategy to solve problems. Rather, Covey manifests success through creative use of his assets. Aurically, that includes a fine mind, lifelong learning, sensitivity to other people, and flexibility based on personal power.

Ken Blanchard: *Magnetize Money Snapshot*

As a writer, Ken Blanchard has more than 18 million copies of his books in print worldwide. As an executive for the Ken Blanchard Companies®, his success is equally extraordinary.

Learn more at his official website, www.kenblanchard.com and, of course, find the picture used for this profile at the "Photo Supplement" online.

What fun to give The One Minute Manager a short aura reading — not taking forever but just long enough to assess the power behind his success.

1. Root Chakra Databank: *Earning Money*

50 miles. Ken is an awfully complex man to have given the world the "One Minute" approach. His presence at this chakra databank includes playfulness and a delight in risk taking.

Yowza, what a toddler he must have been!

Blanchard's quality of resolve reminds me of a brick wall. He's a formidable go-getter, decisive and smart; also utterly committed to the pursuit of wealth.

2. Solar Plexus Chakra Databank: *Handling Conflict at Work*

90 feet. Trust me. You don't want to do battle with Ken Blanchard. He has the strategic ability of a grand master at chess.

Although Ken's emotions can become intense during a conflict, he manages to compartmentalize so that the feelings become a kind of extra fuel for his intellect.

Meanwhile, Ken's personality will seem unflappable. In the background, privately, he is constantly calculating and re-calculating his winning strategy.

3. Third Eye Chakra Databank: *Connection to Spiritual Source*

90 miles. The same kind of passion that showed in the previous databank is let loose spiritually. Ken isn't merely connected to his Highest Power. This is a passionate, loving, vital relationship.

It's so real and secure that I would never expect Blanchard to brag about it. He is too busy living it.

One of the joys of energetic literacy, for me, is discovering when a hero of pop culture just wows me. For this aura reader, Ken Blanchard is one of those discoveries.

His energy field could win a beauty contest. His work matches up with who he authentically is. And that combo helps explain why his One-Minute Manager concept works so well.

It's no mere slogan, no gimmick, but a framework for Ken Blanchard to give the world a peek at his who-you-be.

Well, now that you've finished taking a peek at the who-you-be for Ken Blanchard, look at you. Just look at you!

- Your power
- Your healthy human ego
- Your resolve to communicate
- The financial flow created by your emotional give-and-take
- How far you have come already in our Magnetize Money Program

Resourceful Reader, I'm proud of you.

All that tweaking of your who-you-be has really set you up to Magnetize Money beyond anything you have accomplished so far.

Now you're ready to direct your power-packed self toward establishing goals and plans.

Don't delay. You can do it today, and do it in a wonderful way!

23. Goals
That Magnetize Money

If you are bored with life, if you don't get up every morning with a burning desire to do things – you don't have enough goals.
— NCAA Coach Lou Holtz,
Quoted by Jack Canfield, *The Success Principles*

Big bucks don't usually enter a life by accident, not unless they are deer who wander onto a country road. Where they may not last long.

Sure, old codgers like your Uncle Carl may look back over a low-earning, not-bad career and say proudly, "I just wandered along, taking whatever job came along. I haven't done badly."

You, however, aren't likely to imitate that settling way of life. Otherwise, you never would have become interested in our Magnetize Money Program.

Boast to a Ken Blanchard about how flexible you have been, and lucky, and how you never needed to do a thing to get where you are.... Most likely, Ken (or any other success expert profiled in our program) would howl in agony.

It's common sense, really. Uncle Carl could win flexibility points. Definitely, he's had an interesting life. But wandering is not recommended as a way to max out your earning power. (In fact, wandering isn't even recommended for those previously-mentioned deer.)

To Magnetize Money successfully, you need smart goals, followed up by smart plans, persistent actions and the occasional application of elbow grease. Other success programs emphasize this without first preparing your who-you-be.

By contrast, you have learned how to Magnetize Money convincingly at the level of auric modeling. Now you're ready to turn attention to personal goals.

Smart Choices for Your Career

Resourceful Reader, here are seven questions to ask. At least, you must ask and answer them all if you aim to Magnetize Money with effective goals.

1. How would I prefer to make all that money?
2. What evidence leads me to believe I would be good at this work?
3. Which kind of job comes closest to what I have chosen so far?
4. Realistically, how do I rate my financial prospects for earning good money from this work?
5. Which credentials or study or real-life experience will get me there?
6. Am I willing to pay the price to pursue success in this way?
7. How does my aura rate that choice of work? Does that choice thrill my soul?

Answer those questions right away if you like. Or keep reading. You can answer as prompted by our discussion of each question and why it matters.

1. How would I prefer to make all that money?

Start by making a list of all the activities you like to do. Or go straight for job titles.

The longer your list, the better. At this stage of goal setting you're brainstorming, not signing a contract. So let ideas flow.

Making this list can test that strong human ego you've been developing. For pity's sake, don't translate this question into something entirely different, such as:

- Which ways do my heroes make their money?
- How does my father (or spouse) want me to make money?
- What do my guides think? Which life events can I interpret as a sign?

All those different compartments of you, the ones you have been discovering and healing, may bring up different answers to Question #1.

If you're honest with yourself — all of yourself — you might find preferences like these:

- Root Chakra: I want to make money by choosing a career with high status, so I will seem important to others. I'd like to become mayor of this city.
- Belly Chakra: I want to make money by using my creativity. I'd like to paint murals for major buildings in this city.
- Solar Plexus Chakra: I want to make money at a job where I can take on big responsibilities, flexing my power muscles. I'd like to run public transit in this city.
- Heart Chakra: I want to make money in a way that feels good. I'd like to run a homeless shelter.
- Throat Chakra: I want to make money by expressing myself. I'd like to become the main speechwriter for the mayor.
- Third Eye Chakra: I want to make money through uplifting humanity. I'd like to become the mayor's spiritual advisor, become the Billy Graham of Chicago.

So, have you made your **Juicy, All-Inclusive, Big Job List** yet? If not, do it now. You'll need this for what follows.

2. WHAT EVIDENCE LEADS ME TO BELIEVE I WOULD BE GOOD AT THIS WORK?

Boldly proceed with this reality check, our first of several. Before you go back to your Juicy, All-Inclusive, Big Job List, take out a purple pen, or some other contrasting color of ink that you can use to edit your list.

(If you have been writing via something electronic, like a laptop, select a new font color, highlighting, or bolding.)

Now, go back over each item on your List. Add practical details and highlight them, giving yourself a very vivid reality check.

- What do you have by way of experience, education, skills?
- Can you think of a real-life example where you were praised, applauded, received an award, or otherwise were told that you showed talent?
- How does that praise connect to the occupation you have in mind?

Maybe you'll go through a good news-bad news sequence. For goal setting, that's okay. What matters is that your career choice must have some passion, some juice... and enough good news to encourage you. For instance, about becoming a professional speechwriter:

- Good news: I ran for president of the junior class in high school.
- Good news: I loved making my big speech at the auditorium.
- Bad news: However, I did come in last in that election.
- Good news: Still, that got me interested in writing speeches. Since then I have followed political campaigns and critiqued the speeches I've heard.

At this step of inquiry, you may need to eliminate certain choices. Sometimes, after you start thinking realistically, you can tell that a particular career won't really work for you. For instance, about becoming the mayor's spiritual advisor, like the Billy Graham of Chicago.

- Bad news: I have never done any professional teaching or advising.
- Bad news: I have never found a religion I really wanted to belong to.
- Bad news: Come to think of it, whenever I try advising my friends they develop fidgets and find urgent things to do elsewhere.

Many of my clients have never planned as far as this Goal Setting Question #2. For instance, Law of Attraction followers have equated "something that makes me happy" with "what is meant to be" and "what will make me rich."

It will be a long time before I forget talking with my client Coletta. These were her exact words: "I know I am meant to write. Tell me what my first book will be about. Also, what is the title?"

Dreams do matter, but what practical use are dreams without having real skill to back them up? Such dreams are the stuff that hobbies are made of, not the basis for real-life wealth.

If the thought of x-ing out one of your choices seems to break your heart, either copy that item onto a separate list of Important Hobbies or figure out how to get skills that can be listed later.

At some future time you can revisit this chapter, including our Goal Setting Question #2, and have some good news to highlight.

Meanwhile, don't stop doing this exercise in present time. You need goals for NOW, correct?

3. WHICH KIND OF JOB (OR NEXT STEP IN MY PRESENT CAREER) COMES CLOSEST TO WHAT I HAVE CHOSEN SO FAR?

Go back to the remaining items on your Juicy, All-Inclusive, Big Job List. Which job title comes closest to that choice of work you've been writing about, where you can highlight some facts to encourage you?

Who would your customers be? How would you help them? And your payment would come from where, exactly?

In Chicago, or wherever you live (or plan to live), approximately how many people make a full-time living in that occupation?

If the answer is "nobody," that doesn't automatically mean you have found a fabulous ground-floor opportunity.

What do you need most at this stage of planning? Dreams won't cut it. Get concrete information about objective possibilities in the real world:

Do a thorough online search. Consult the research librarian at your nearest public library. Or hire a career counselor to help you spot jobs that you might not think to google for.

Don't skimp on this research. A little short-term help from a professional at career guidance could be one of the smartest investments you ever make.

However you put together the research, incorporate your results into your Juicy, All-Inclusive, Big Job List — which is, by now, starting to turn into a **Street-Smart, Selective, Savvy Job List.**

By now some choices may be looking far better than others. Nonetheless, your questioning process isn't nearly done yet.

4. REALISTICALLY, HOW DO I RATE MY FINANCIAL PROSPECTS FOR EARNING GOOD MONEY FROM THIS KIND OF WORK?

The same sources you just used for career research should help with this question, too. Real information is needed, not some brave hope that you will instantly become the top earner in your field.

Add ballpark numbers to your Street-Smart, Selective, Savvy Job List.

5. WHICH CREDENTIALS OR STUDY OR REAL-LIFE EXPERIENCE WILL GET ME THERE?

In the third millennium, career re-training is common. Certain jobs, like "Brain Surgeon," do require extremely long, arduous years of preparation. This is not optional, ethically or legally.

Yet many skill sets don't require extensive training. Many a millionaire dropped out of college. And some official-sounding certifications are worth very little, such as proudly earning an official Certificate of Completion from the Acme Academy of Office Receptionists.

Once you master a skill and can prove it, depending on your chosen field, that can be all you need. So answer Goal Setting Question #5 accordingly.

6. AM I WILLING TO PAY THE PRICE TO PURSUE SUCCESS IN THIS WAY?

This question isn't only about the cost of college credits (or equivalent training). Every job comes with a price. Once I had a client with the glamour job of TV producer. William had held this enviable job for five years.

Did that make him happy? For William, the price of his job included making a teensy salary, working long hours, and being available 24/7 to receive calls from a crazy-demanding boss.

All the jobs that remain on your list can have hidden costs, too. Write them down.

That's not being negative but realistic. Constantly being on call might seem delightful, inconvenient, or a definite deal breaker.

In *Outliers,* Malcolm Gladwell introduces the concept of 10,000 hours of work being needed to develop real mastery in a field.

Personally, before making serious money, I did have to invest that much time in my specialty (energetic literacy, writing about energetic literacy, and healing clients with energetic literacy).

For decades (three of them, a full 30 years), I would become depressed for weeks after doing my taxes. "What, I worked 60 hours a week, and I would have earned more at McDonald's?"

Every year, the depression would lift when I realized that doing the work mattered more to me than my present income. I chose to keep investing in my career and, eventually, life did pay me back.

How high a price are you prepared to pay?

7. HOW DOES MY AURA RATE THAT CHOICE OF WORK? DOES THAT CHOICE THRILL MY SOUL?

Whatever your present level of energetic literacy, here is a technique that you can use to check out all the choices left on your list.

Introduction to Thrill Your Soul Research

Select one item from your Street-Smart, Selective, Savvy Job List. Talk about it aloud for one full minute, which will automatically morph all your chakra databanks to provide feedback on that particular choice. Then research the consequences:

- *As a complete beginner, or with Stage 1 Energetic Literacy,* notice what happens to your emotions. Then close your eyes and pay attention to how you feel in your physical body. Do you feel strong or weak or what?
- *With Stage 2 Energetic Literacy,* check out the energy in different chakras.
- *With Stage 3 Energetic Literacy,* you can do a more sophisticated job to gauge the size and nuance of individual chakra databanks. For instance, check out the 10 databanks in the Magnetize Money Profile.

Repeat this research process with a second career choice from your list, then a third, etc. After talking about each research item, aura-level consequences will be different. This is feedback directly from your who-you-be.

FROM CHOICES TO GOALS

Once you have sorted through different career choices, it's time to commit to one main focus. Pick one **Major Work Choice** that is specific and realistic (and also supercalifragilistic, if you wish to maintain a secret Mary Poppins-like playfulness).

This will become central to your current goal setting.

- If you have followed the sequence so far, your choice will be backed up by a reality check, supplemented by energetic literacy. Excellent!
- Next you're going to bring that choice to life by creating an official **Magnetize Money Goal Sheet.** This process will have the flavor of *prosperity* teachings, since you will emphasize your highest ideals and strongest subjective values.
- Making specific plans to support your Goal Sheet will be covered in our next chapter. That process will have the flavor of *success* teachings, emphasizing objective things you must do to Magnetize Money.

Your Magnetize Money Goal Sheet

In your heart of hearts, what you would like to happen as a result of your making this Major Work Choice?

Make a list. Since this will be private, ask for what you really want. Modesty is for people being observed by others. Here no modesty is required. Just follow these simple steps.

In this example, I'll refer to your splendid Major Work Choice as "XYZ." (You know, to help you keep it private.)

1. Find a place and time where you will be completely uninterrupted. Turn OFF those electronic companions like cell phones. Turn ON any electronic device for recording your goals, such as a laptop. Pen and paper work fine, too. Only don't use a fancy journal, not yet.

2. Heading: "My Goals for XYZ." Now proceed to draft your set of goals.

3. Invite your Highest Power to be part of this process. Include the phrase, "All this or something better, Highest Power."

4.   Optional: Add the names of any other sources of inspiration you fancy, such as angels or ancestors. If you have someone you consider a muse, add that name. (Yes, this is how you get to include someone like Bill Gates in your prosperity team.)

5.   Point by point, list all the specifics that matter to you, e.g., What you want to accomplish, how much money you want it to bring you, when you plan to receive that income, how you want to help people, your ideal clients, etc.

6.   Once you have finished this draft, look it over and tweak it.

7.   Prepare a fancy finished version, which will become your official Magnetize Money Goal Sheet.

How fancy does that Magnetize Money Goal Sheet need to be? Only as elaborate as you desire. Doing this exercise need not add to your monthly bill for stone tablets.

You might copy the words into your nicest journal. Or you might use the following ideas to make the words on your Goal Sheet extra sticky to your subconscious mind:

- If you have created an electronic document, add color and interesting typefaces before you print it out. Voila! Now you have a gorgeous, official Magnetize Money Goal Sheet.
- Or choose standard typefaces and decorate your Magnetize Money Goal Sheet after you print it out, or journal it, using such office supplies as highlighter pens and gold stars.
- Any smell freaks out there besides Rose Rosetree? Use your fingertip to apply just a touch of a favorite fragrance, e.g., a favorite aromatherapy fragrance, your manliest aftershave, a drop of vanilla extract. (The tiny blob may look oily, but the scent will be worth it.)

Just Do It

If a colorful, scent-adorned presentation appeals to you, great. What matters most, however, is that you come up with a written-down Magnetize Money Goal Sheet of some kind.

Go ahead, just do it.

Remember Barry, my client with a spiritual addiction who wanted to drop everything else to become a full-time Reiki healer? Around the same time, Wanda came to me as a client. She, too, had quit her job due to a spiritual addiction. Initially Wanda wanted me to research her fabulously promising career doing Emotional Freedom Technique.

Why was Wanda so good at E.F.T. (she thought)? Was it her extensive training? No, for training she had watched some DVDs shared by a friend. Had Wanda helped many clients? None. But Wanda spent loads of time tapping on herself. Also, she really, really believed.

Our research did turn up a fabulous choice for her. It wasn't E.F.T. but working in the import-export field. Hello! Wanda had been doing this kind of work for 15 years before she soured on her job and quit.

Until our research session, it never occurred to Wanda that she could transfer her skills and experience to working for a different company. (Her spiritual addiction kept her way too busy to consider this.)

Here is the Magnetize Money Goal Sheet that Wanda might have put together to move herself one step closer.

Wanda's Goals for Success

By January 1, 2015, I will have achieved all this or something better with your help, Highest Power.

I am a manager for an established import-export business.

The business has great integrity and attracts clients who also have integrity.

The business is well managed financially, growing at a good pace every year. Our pace of expansion is solid, with work responsibilities keeping me comfortably busy.

I earn $40,000 my first year, with a $3,000 raise every year.

I become indispensible to the company because of my communication skills, my sincere desire to help clients, my listening ability, my intelligence, and fine skills as a negotiator.

This job requires that I travel for no more than three months out of each year. My accommodations are always comfortable, safe, and enjoyable.

I like the corporate culture at my job. I like and respect the owner and other employees. It is mutual.

My work schedule averages 40 hours per week. The job leaves me relaxed and feeling very good about myself, so I can enjoy the rest of my life in a balanced way.

I make at least five good new friends, plus I have an appropriate romantic relationship that is very fulfilling for me.

Every year, I attract at least three wonderful, lucrative surprises.

My growing knowledge of the import-expert field is a valuable asset to management and clients, and that knowledge continues to develop at a comfortable pace, bringing one success after another.

In my spare time, I explore the possibility of going into business for myself, using the next five years to gather contacts, experience and skills that would help me. My long-term goal is to start my own successful import-export business in January 2020.

Through my work now and in the future, I contribute to better understanding of people from different cultures. Clients are able to employ workers who benefit from the economic development. Thus, my work isn't only profitable for me and the rest of my company but represents a true Win-Win, helping to make the world a better place.

A GOAL-FOCUSED DREAM BOARD

What if — unlike Rose but like Wanda –you are very visual? Sure, you can make a dream board to supplement your official Magnetize Money Goal Sheet.

The power of a dream board is well documented. It sends images directly to your subconscious mind, helping you to magnetize those deep goals.

Because of our practical focus, we can make a few important up-grades to the classic concept. For a **Goal-Focused Dream Board,** cut out pictures to symbolize the various components of your edited draft of goals.

If you can't easily locate full-color pictures to symbolize every-thing, search for your pix online, e.g., At google.com, click onto the IMAGE tab, then search.

What if you still can't locate a picture? (Maybe what you desire is too abstract for a photograph.) Cut out a square or circle in a color that symbolizes the underlying *feeling* of your idea.

Printed advertisements often contain background in a solid color; fashion ads, for instance, contain clothing in gorgeous colors. Besides, the chunk of color you need does not have to be huge, only an inch or so. Write the name of what you want on the colorful shape.

Play with arranging the major pictures on your dream board. Then glue them into position. Consider that a symbolic way to commit to your dreams.

Caption each item with specifics.

On regular white paper, write or print out a description of the details that matter to you, e.g., "In my dream job, I travel for no more than three months out of each year. My accommodations are comfortable and every flight is safe and enjoyable." Glue that caption beneath your dream board picture.

Now you have an official Goal-Focused Dream Board.

DEVELOP A MAGNETIZE MONEY STRATEGY

Even if money grew on trees in your back yard, why would that necessarily help you? Even then, you would need a strategy.

Big bills dangling from branches would need to be collected somehow. How often? And in what, thimbles or buckets or little red wagons?

Personally, I like to keep things simple. Okay, money-producing trees plus a few plastic buckets might be rather simple. But I also like to keep strategies in the realm of reality. So forget collecting buckets of money from magical trees. Instead this is what I recommend.

Since you can't do everything simultaneously, strategize. Select a small and manageable number of priorities, your current strategy for success. This will become a basis for making practical plans. Choose just 1-5 most of the most important items from your Magnetize Money Goal Sheet or Goal-Focused Dream Board. For instance:

- Your next step of career development.
- A realistic way to improve your health and fitness.
- One way to boost your social life.

Your current **Magnetize Money Strategy** will come in handy when you make plans. Of course, plans must come next. Because you aim to pocket the kind of money that does not grow on trees.

24. Plans
That Work Your Magnet

Set clearly defined personal, professional and spiritual goals, and then have the courage to act on them.
— Robin S. Sharma, *The Monk Who Sold His Ferrari*

Let's summarize how far you have come so far in our Magnetize Money Program.

Aligning your life from the inside out, you have greatly improved your auric modeling, benefitting from the latest discoveries in energetic literacy.

Resourceful Citizen of the Third Millennium, you're at the leading edge of those who aim to think and act and grow rich. Concepts like auric modeling, chakra databanks, STUFF, and energetic subroutines have given you a sophisticated understanding about how to Magnetize Money.

Now you understand that the Law of Attraction produces results based on a person's full who-you-be.

You have developed new skills for dealing with significant others, especially regarding that who-you-be aspect. In business transactions, you're using new skills along with an energetically literate perspective.

Personal transformation has happened at the innermost level of your own auric modeling. And thanks to energetic workarounds, you have been able to wake up and balance the chakra databanks most directly related to your success in this world.

Definitely, this counts as a great basis for much increased income. But we didn't stop there, because true success requires balancing subjective and objective reality, both.

So you have also looked at your financial prospects objectively, taking the time to develop a Magnetize Money Goal Sheet and/or

Goal-Focused Dream Board. Most recently, you have started thinking about your current Magnetize Money Strategy — what, exactly, you must emphasize first in order to fulfill your ambitions.

Plans are needed now, concrete plans, plus an easy way to quickly upgrade your plans over time as you move toward fulfilling your goals.

A Balanced Journey Toward Wealth

Making plans can be fun. You can combine creativity, imagination, common sense, and your unique flair.

You can also aim for a reasonably *balanced* life. I'd recommend that. The need for balance is one of the most important things I've learned from profiling success and prosperity experts with energetic literacy. Think cylinder, not lollipop or triangle. (See Figure 10.)

To bring you the greatest possible balance, let's do something outrageous. I'm going to ask you to put aside, for right now, all you have done to think in a focused and realistic manner. Like a fine wine,

Figure 10: Addicted, Enlightened, Earthbound

you might need to mellow. Let's mature your personal bouquet. How? You can savor L*I*F*E writ large and combine that with your Magnetize Money Strategy. The following survey of Life Categories can help you do this.

As you read through each of the seven categories that follow, write down your first reaction. Invite your full who-you-be to generate these ideas. Make quick notes as you go. Sloppy and spontaneous scribbles are great for this kind of brainstorming.

1. RELATIONSHIPS

For most of us, family and friendships make life worth living.

Hold on! Family relationships may be great or you may need to supplement them with what I call "**Family of Choice.**" That's where you seek out your own father figure or surrogate mom. You can find sisters and brothers of the heart, locate sons or daughters in spirit.

Don't let the limitations of birth family in this particular lifetime dictate whether you get to enjoy these vital human relationships.

Connections to family of choice might last for a week or a lifetime. However long, your soul will register a sigh of relief. One more desire fulfilled as part of your perfect lifetime!

To activate this potential, simply tell your Highest Power that you are ready to receive the essence of any "family" relationship you choose. Request the equivalent of a loving daughter, big brother, etc.

Sometimes this will even be offered to you before you ask. Now that you understand the concept, notice when you're given some new family of choice.

The Gift of a Daughter

During a workshop in Tokyo, I stood on my makeshift stage (a chair). I was doing my usual outrageous teacher thing. My favorite interpreter, Kaori, stood directly in front of me, translating away.

Suddenly we had one of those little earthquakes that make life in Japan so interesting. Our skyscraper began to shake. Somebody in the group called attention to this particular up-and-down type of earthquake.

(These are different from the earthquakes I had already learned to recognize, where the shockwaves go sideways. Who knew?)

Lights in the building went out. Reaching down, I held Kaori's hand. Or maybe she reached for mine. Balancing on a chair, during an earthquake, in the dark, isn't great fun.

Soon the lights went back on. No worries. We continued the workshop as usual.

Afterwards, I started to thank Kaori-san for holding my hand. It had been so kind, so comforting.

She spoke first. "Rose, thanks so much for holding my hand. It was so comforting."

Of course, I told Kaori my side of the story, too. We shared the special kind of laughter that signals a relationship deepening.

Still later, reflecting on what happened, I felt that this spontaneous hand-holding clinched a kind of deal between Kaori and me. She wasn't just young enough to be my daughter. During that incident, Kaori-san *became* a kind of daughter-figure to me, just as I became a mother-figure to her.

Kaori became my first such daughter, part of my family of choice.

When you aim to Magnetize Money, why spend all that money alone? It's so much more fulfilling to share the wealth and good times.

No matter how much love you have in your marriage or how long you have had your best friend, relationships are like plants. Even the hardiest perennial requires tending.

And all of us need to keep making new friends through the years. It's a life skill, never to late to learn. Search your heart and write down something you could do *now* in pursuit of a more rewarding social life.

2. CAREER

Even if you were independently wealthy, wouldn't you wish to pursue some kind of meaningful work in the world?

Maybe you care most about helping others. Maybe you want to become rich and famous, taking your career ambitions as far as your karma will go. In your heart of hearts, what would bring complete fulfillment?

Depending on your stage in life, your career could be "full-time student." Or "giving quality childcare." Or "retirement." Or "volunteer work." Or "part-time business to grow while I keep my day job."

In order to Magnetize Money, you'll need to develop or maintain that career, keeping it ever-fresh and meaningful. So write down some fresh plans now.

3. PERSONAL GROWTH

Only call it "Spirituality" if you like the term. Maybe calling it "Religion" will suit you better. Whatever it's called, aren't you the kind of person who needs a meaningful path of personal growth?

That path may have changed during the years. Mine certainly has. One of the hardest, but best, decisions I ever made involved letting go of a spiritual path that had been my whole life for decades.

What helped in that case was to ask myself, "Is my allegiance to God or to my path to God?"

Whatever your current choices, keep your growth path current. Don't be afraid of change. And do remember to enjoy what you've got.

However you connect up to Highest Power, that can become the core of a balanced life. Although spiritual addiction can be a prosperity wrecker, the opposite extreme (no spiritual connection) might be just as imbalanced for you.

What is one thing you can do every day to keep growing and developing as a person, given the path that you currently consider meaningful? Write down that part of your plan.

4. HEALTH AND APPEARANCE

What fun are those buckets of money if you don't feel well? Besides, feeling good and looking good can contribute to business success.

Exercising, eating intelligently and deliciously, shopping for new clothes — the possibilities can be profitable as well as entertaining.

Physical fitness can be a great way to develop business contacts or make new friends. Your body works for you 24/7, whether you pay attention or not. Honor it now. Write down some fresh plans to improve your health and appearance.

5. Enjoying Material Prosperity

Why bother to Magnetize Money? Right now you have some very specific desires for more financial flow.

What are they? Consciously or subconsciously, you are psyched to save or to spend, to invest, and/or to make specific purchases.

Is now the time to do maintenance on your car? Redecorate your home? Maybe there is one small plant you could buy to brighten up the place.

However much money you magnetize, it is a flow. To keep that flow moving, you need to spend. Do it for the sake of future wealth, even — whatever inspires you to keep in a vibrant state of financial flow.

What occurs to you right now? Write that down.

6. Creativity

Many a major business began as a hobby. But even if they had absolutely no money-making potential, hobbies would still be part of your lifestyle, right?

Recreation makes life bigger. Creativity is no mere frill. It's a need.

And one of the best things about hobbies is the total lack of pressure. You never have to turn pro. Do that singing in your shower. Dance where the lights are low. Cook something new, whether it tastes great or not. Buy a coloring book and squiggle outside of the lines.

A day without creativity would be such a terrible waste. And why would you ever need to do that to yourself?

When you write down some ideas in the creativity category, you don't have to take this part of your life seriously or turn it into some grim chore.

Playing, creating, exploring, being silly as only you can… surely you can find a way to do that for 10 minutes or longer every single day.

7. Community

Who are your people right now? How do you connect to your neighborhood? Are there peers in your profession who form your primary community? Of course you can become socially connected in multiple ways that bring meaning and scope to your life.

Do you have political passions? What can you do about them? Gossip and grumbling are the refuge of the powerless, after all.

If you could choose one group of any kind to volunteer for, what would that be? A small monthly commitment with the group of your choice might be no big deal to you, yet become a "big deal blessing" to others.

Any of the life areas we have explored so far can be linked to community of sorts.

That matters. It is human to need community.

Even for the sake of gaining more wealth, it would be smart to join in, sign up, have a heart that you share with others. When you leave home to network in person, you strengthen connection to some segment of society.

How could you reach out to community? Given all that you do in this world, you must have some groups in mind. Or maybe there is some kind of new community that you would prefer to explore. At Earth School, so much of our evolution happens through relationships.

Energetic literacy does bring this suggestion, however. Community through technology is immensely popular now, but make no mistake. Aurically this has big limitations.

When you talk with someone in real time, in person or by phone, an **energetic hologram** of that person's energy presence is stored in your aura, enriching you. And vice versa. (How do I know? I read them for clients.) By contrast, you will give and receive no such imprint from social networking, texting, or emailing.

Sure, technology is a way of life, and fun. Just consider this. Our grand social technologies succeed at bringing up-to-date information. But, energetically, they can deliver only a false and hollow sense of community.

You could do social networking until you are Bluetoothed in the face, but for all the enrichment to your auric field, you might as well sit in the dark, listening to old radio broadcasts of yesteryear. You might as well play couch potato, watching mind-numbing amounts of TV.

So when it comes to community, dare to be counter-culture. Keep a sense of proportion about the enticements of so-called "connection" through technology. Supplement "friending" with real-time face time.

Okay, write down something now, an idea to strengthen your sense of connection.

Your Plan, Just for Now

Now for the grand finale! You need a practical, personal plan, not for all time but for this particular here and now. For reference, find each of the following and place them within reach:
- Notes you just made about Life Categories
- Your Magnetize Money Strategy.
- Your Magnetize Money Goal Sheet or Goal-Focused Dream Board.

Refer to them as needed while you follow the instructions below. And yes, while you write this, I still recommend that you be sloppy. This is to be your almost final draft, not a finished product.

Your Official Magnetize Money Plan

I, [spell out your full name here] aim to accomplish the following by [write a date one month from today]. I request help from my Highest Power. All this or something better!

1. Relationships
2. Career
3. Personal Growth
4. Health and Appearance
5. Enjoying Material Prosperity
6. Creativity
7. Community

Ridiculously Small Action Steps

Now it's time to edit your Magnetize Money Plan. For best results, break each task into a **ridiculously small action step.**

Yes, that small part is really important. Make sure that each action step is ridiculously easy, teensy-sized. If not, downsize further. For instance, if you aim to research college courses:

1. DON'T choose the action step of "Research all possible college courses in my area with my desired major."
2. Instead, DO choose the action step of "Go online for five minutes each day, researching college courses."
3. Now you have a manageable, teensy action step for your Magnetize Money Plan.

Any given day, while you do that small action step, what if it turns out you're in the mood to do extra? Nobody is going to stop you, right?

So keep each action step small. You're more likely to follow through. Let success builds on success.

Go Official

Now write or type or electronically save this edited version, your official Magnetize Money Plan. Well done!

Keep it Fresh

Choose one day per month to review your Magnetize Money Plan. Personally, my routine aims for the first day each month. Besides being easy to remember, I find that Day One of any new month brims over with start-up energy.

Every day, every month, every January 1, every birthday represents an exciting new beginning here at Earth School. Yo, Surfer! Catch the wave.

Of course, Magnetize Money Plans can be made from dry land. On any day that delights you. What matters is planning consistently.

Avoid skipping any month entirely. Spend the half hour or less that you'll need to give practical direction to your days.

Consider using a word processor or other electronic aid to store your Magnetize Money Plan. That way you can easily cut-and-paste your newest plan based on what you did the previous month.

Electronic edits are easy. (Personally, I usually get the job done in 10 minutes or less. Current plans, check. Now on to fulfilling them!) Here are my favorite tips for a Magnetize Money Plan:

- Print out your current Plan. Keep it somewhere you can see it easily. For privacy at your desk, you can keep it folded up under a paperweight, just one meaningful edge sticking out. Night tables are great for this purpose, too. Also handbags, glove compartments of cars, or a back pocket of your favorite blue jeans. Sit on your Plan all day long, why not?

- Last thing at night, read through your Magnetize Money Plan. Or dunk your subconscious mind in it the very first thing every morning.

- While recharging during sleep, encourage your subconscious mind. Use your current Magnetize Money Plan plus your Magnetize Money Goal Sheet. Tuck one copy of each into your pillowcase so you can dream on those goals. (Once upon a time, you may have kept a much-loved, rumpled-looking stuffed animal near your pillow, too. Now, these very adult, folded documents will look less obvious, just a slightly wrinkled rectangle in your pillow case. More useful than even a lovey, and far more private!)

- Starting next month, turn each present month's Magnetize Money Plan into a monthly **Magnetize Money WIN Sheet.** To create this, find the electronic or printed-out version of last month's Magnetize Money Plan. Check what you have accomplished and add words of praise and encouragement, highlighting, gold stars, etc. It's very fulfilling to your conscious and subconscious minds to see these wins.

- Make each month's WIN Sheet right before creating your new monthly Magnetize Money Plan. That way, you can track the progress as you fulfill your life's goals.

A FANCY FLOW CHART

This variation on Magnetize Money Plans is especially for you Resourceful Readers who are visually oriented. You can create a Fancy Flow Chart of your Magnetize Money Plan. (Note: Some people prefer to do this with their Magnetize Money Goals instead. Your choice! But here I'll refer to making the **Fancy Flow Chart** of your Plan.)

Start with your most current Magnetize Money Plan. Then sketch a diagram, a flow chart, to represent how your various plan components might fit together.

It's possible to work at many parts of your success at the same time. By making a flow chart, you'll appreciate *intellectually* how the various parts could fit together; you'll also encourage yourself to play with the *emotional* impact of your proposed plan sequences.

Are you willing to take half an hour to beautifully upgrade your plans in this way? Then add extra power to your words by helping your plan literally to take shape. Or shapes.

Shapes like circles, triangles, and rectangles can be used to add visual power to your Magnetize Money Plan. Each shape also has symbolic significance that can speak to your subconscious mind.

- **Circles** represent a state of wholeness, peace, feminine energy, balance. Most people respond emotionally to rounded shapes.
- **Triangles** bring extra-dynamic energy. Granted, it may be hard to fit a lot of words into triangles, compared to other shapes. Still, you might want to include at least one for oomph.

  Why a triangle? If one geometric shape best symbolizes ambition and masculine energy, that would be the noble triangle. (You can create a similar dynamism by including diamonds, stars, and other complex shapes that contain points.)
- **Rectangles** emphasize logic, order, security, the sense of enduring financial stablity. Squares are an especially potent version of that symbolic energy.

Fancy Looking, Realistic Plans

Here are step-by-step instructions for constructing a Fancy Flow Chart.

1. Use separate bits of colored paper containing shapes as frames for the background. Also print words on plain paper with the content of each item.

2. Paste or tape each plain text item onto its shapely frame. Thus, each shape will contain the words of one plan item.

306 MAGNETIZE MONEY WITH ENERGETIC LITERACY

3.   Arrange the shapes in a sequence that feels right to you —
not just logical but feeling right, like something you really get
excited about doing.
4.   Change words as needed. Add new chunks of shape plus
words. Take away what doesn't work for you. Tweaking can be
the most important part of your planning, because it emphasizes the YOU in YOUR Fancy Flow Chart. (Is this "Just
more work" or "Being artistic"? You decide.)
5.   When you're satisfied, paste the shapes onto a large piece
of paper or poster board. Connect the shapes with lines. Ta da!

See the Online Supplement for samples of a Magnetize Money Goal
Sheet, Magnetize Money Plan, and Fancy Flow Chart.

Honor Your Flow

When it comes to fulfilling your plan, there are two kinds of people.
Shocking, right?

Some of us need focus in order to become big achievers. We need
to write things down, make dream boards or flow charts. For us, the
more thorough and visually appealing the documentation, the better
we'll do.

Others of us prefer a no-frills approach. Our notes-to-self can be
electronic or written or mental— whatever is easier. It's as though we
don't want to waste our precious action time by making a big visual
display. Once we clarify inwardly what we intend to do, we know we
will follow through. That simple.

Whichever style of achiever you are, go with your flow. What
matters in the end is not how stylish your visuals may be but what you
accomplish. That's why we call this program "Magnetize Money" rather
than "Magnetize Artwork."

Going with your flow is a way to demonstrate to yourself that
you like yourself. Plans will only magnetize serious money if you figure out the action steps to go with them, make the plans, and do the
work. Goodbye, lollipop. Hello, power-packed, fully-dimensional life,
moving purposefully towards an ever-greater success.

25. The Simplest Technique

Do not let other people decide what you are to be.
— Wallace D. Wattles, *The Science of Being Great,*

You're so close to completing our Magnetize Money Program. Here's a gift to help you celebrate.

I am delighted to present this technique with grateful acknowledgment to the man who originally developed it. Simeon Hein, Ph.D., is the author of *Planetary Intelligence,* creator of an online course called "Resonant Viewing." He generously consented to my sharing this technique with you here.

The Simplest Way to Magnetize Money

To start this wealth snowball rolling, you will need pen and paper, plus about five minutes of your precious time.

1. Draw one box on the left side of the paper. Inside this Box #1, write "Wanda Smith in the present."
At least, write "Wanda Smith" if that is your name. Your own name is the one to use here.

2. Draw a second box on the right side of the paper. Inside this Box #2, write in detail what you wish to magnetize into your life, including a date. Also include these words: "All this or something better, Highest Power."
Of course, substitute the name for Highest Power that works best for you.

3. In this technique, you will be opening up pathways to magnetize, or attract, whatever you desire. Manifesting is a two-way street. Therefore, you will be drawing *pairs* of lines to go back and forth between the two boxes. Start with a line from Box #1 (symbolizing you in the present) to Box #2 (symbolizing you in the future).

The line symbolizes something, too. You are connecting your present self to a desired version of self in the future.

4. Immediately afterwards, draw a second line from Box #2 back to Box #1. This symbolic line pulls that desired future state into your present.

5. Draw 1-3 pairs of lines daily, using the same diagram. Every pair of lines is a call and response, request and attraction.

6. After using up one sheet of paper (because it is so very full of lines) make a new sheet. Same two boxes, great new lines.

Wanda
Smith
in
the present

By January 1, 2020
I am spiritually Enlightened.
I'm a millionaire with my own import-export business.
I am in a fulfilling marriage.
I have wonderful friendships with balanced give-and-take.
I'm active and respected in my three favorite communities.
I am healthy and look attractive, with a weight of 125 pounds.
I wake up happy every day.
All this or something better, Highest Power.

FIGURE 11. SAMPLE BOXES

Figure 11 shows an example of The Simplest Technique, drawn for Wanda. Remember her? She's the one who decided to go into the import-export business. For her, or you, look at all the preparation done so far to make this technique powerful:

YES, YOU HAVE BEEN STRENGTHENING YOUR AURA

Who-you-be is a vital requirement for success. When you truly like yourself, that shows clearly in your aura. Our Magnetize Money Program has been designed to help you get to know your human self better and like it more than ever before.

Our many energy workarounds have helped to bring greater strength to your energy field, even helping you to get rid of unproductive energetic sub-routines.

If you had a spiritual addiction at the start of our Magnetize Money Program, you have begun to change that. Excellent!

YES, YOU HAVE GAINED NEW RESPECT FOR REALITY

You have begun to augment prosperity and success techniques by positioning yourself squarely in reality.

You know better than to aim for pie in the sky, not if you want food with real-life taste and nourishment.

You're motivated, having read energetic literacy profiles. There's no substitute for a strong Root Chakra presence. Or for engaging in human reality as though you really believed in it.

YES, SUCCESS SKILLS CAN SUPPLEMENT WHO-YOU-BE

Based in strong auric modeling, success teachings and skills can become more productive than ever before.

If STUFF is blocking your progress, be willing to seek help from professional healers who can facilitate permanent healing at the level of your aura. But otherwise energetic workarounds can do the job. Success techniques plus strong auric modeling really do Magnetize Money.

All this has prepared you to get the best results from The Simplest Way to Magnetize Money. Don't try to shortcut your way to riches by going through the motions of this technique without all our pre-requisites.

In the third millennium, humanity is too evolved to go that slow route of only including surface reality. With your high-vibe third-millennium consciousness, you know to bring along the clearest possible version of who-you-be, the magnetizer of all your prosperity.

PRACTICAL TIPS

Here are some extra DO and DON'Ts to help you gain the most from our Simplest Technique to Magnetize Money.

- In Box #1, DON'T just give your first name. I know we live in a first-name culture, but you don't want to magnetize results to go to any generic person with your first name.
- Unless you have an unusual stage name that consumes your entire identity, like Lady Gaga or Madonna, DO write your full name, which includes a last name and maybe even a middle name.

- In Box #2, DON'T include others, only yourself. When I started doing this technique, I included my husband, Mitch, whom I adore. But you know what? He is free to draw his own boxes.
- DO remember to include yourself only whenever you set goals (not just when you use The Simplest Technique to Magnetize Money). Planning for others can cause a form of astral-level STUFF called "Psychic Coercion" — bad karma for you and the other person as well.

- In Box #2, DON'T write anything too big to believe. Dream big, not impossible.
- DO feel free to revise Box #2 over the years.

- In Box #2, DON'T go all passive and meant-to-be. DON'T write something sweetly submissive, like "I discover my purpose and I live it."
- DO choose a purpose for yourself.

- DON'T discard common sense when writing Box #2. *Astronaut* may not be a viable career path for you. Get real.
- DO tell Highest Power what you want and then trust in your help. That Highest Power isn't passive. If you're asking for something inappropriate, Highest Power will substitute something as good or even better.

FOR EXTRA-QUICK MANIFESTATION

When Dr. Hein gave permission to include his technique in this Magnetize Money Program, he added these words of advice:

Whenever you draw your pairs of lines, be detached from the outcome, trusting that the universe will deliver to you everything you have visualized, in the best way possible.

Tension, stress, and trying to make things happen exactly as you visualized them, can take away from the natural abundant flow of the universe and its ability to deliver all good things to you.

However, having said that, in Step #2, it's good to have as much detail as you can imagine in your second box. This seems to help connect you to that reality where your wishes have already been manifested.

I would add a reminder that you use this technique sparingly. Draw just 1-3 pairs of lines once a day. This is our simplest technique in the Magnetize Money Program, not our *only* technique.

THE WHY BEHIND THE HOW-TO'S

Why does this technique work? Let's delve into the mechanics a bit. (This is, of course, my explanation rather than Dr. Hein's.)

What is your energy field in the first place? You have a set of energy bodies around your physical body. Together they constitute your aura.

These various bodies include ones about your emotions, your health, even your connection to what is technically known as The Causal Plane. This plane is all about what makes life work, on earth and elsewhere.

Causal Plane information is designed in a kind of cosmic binary code: Yes or no, stop or start, create this or that.

This simple toggle of yes or no doesn't means "simplistic. " Far from it. Today's computer programmers use binary code in some rather elegant ways. A different type of programming today is source code. This, too, is built into how life works on The Causal Plane.

In our Magnetize Money Program, you have learned that the deeper you go, the more amazing — and powerful — human life becomes. As part of the hidden fun, your human body contains layers of aura corresponding to various psychic-level planes and also to spiritual planes. For example, your aura includes both astral-level STUFF and akasha-level gifts of your soul.

Given this perspective, let's consider what it means to physically draw these boxes and make the connecting lines.

The deepest levels within you are activated by doing the technique.

Then, the technique's simple motions of drawing and seeing set up a cascade effect all the way through to the causal level.

Of course, having an auric field that is relatively free from STUFF will help, too. The cleaner your who-you-be, the faster you can shape your destiny, pulling your future into your present. And the clearer you are, more STUFF-free, the more fully you activate those inner levels in a *congruent* way, broadcasting a powerful signal through space and time.

SURE, YOU CAN SHAPE YOUR FUTURE

Free will matters way more in the third millennium than in past eras. Remember, ours is the age where energetic literacy is becoming available to all who want it. This can dramatically shift your own expectations about free will vs. determinism. Certainly this has happened to me and many of my clients.

Before most people had Stage 3 Energetic Literacy, how could we explain the difference between success in life versus failure? Often people used the concept of **willpower.**

According to this traditional kind of belief, God would shape your fate. You had a purpose. Using your will, you could work hard to fulfill your set purpose.

If your life turned out badly, that meant you weren't trying hard enough. Maybe your fate was just bad. Otherwise you were a slacker.

Certainly, it's better to use your willpower than settle for being a slacker. Yet how many times has it happened that you tried your very, very best and it simply wasn't enough?

Think of all those hardworking LOA teachers I researched for you. They were using willpower aplenty... inadvertently bringing on spiritual addiction.

Pouring work and hope and tears in the direction of an existing imbalance is a terrible use of free will. Results are bound to be terrible, too. Ironically, this sets up a vicious cycle where one's only alternative to willpower may appear to be surrender to "meant-to-be."

Except now there's a third choice. In this third millennium, Stage 3 Energetic Literacy can help anyone to evaluate how well you are doing as you use willpower to Magnetize Money. Reading the details about impact on chakra databanks can be wonderfully informative.

Furthermore, consider how much better we can get un-stuck from difficulties, being able to tell which STUFF is blocking us. With a stuck and puny Root Chakra databank about **Earning Money,** no amount of willpower or forcing is going to make much of a difference.

With the ability to use energetic workarounds, or otherwise remove STUFF, that dreadful old dependency on willpower can end.

Forcing, pushing, denying one's feelings in the pursuit of a grand plan, using no self-authority — how very second millennium!

Life Purpose is a beautiful concept. In my experience as a healer, however, learning about Life Purpose can improve one's mood, not much else. Not surprisingly, many a first-time client, whose auric field is horribly clogged up with STUFF, answers my question, "How do you want your life to get better" by begging, "Tell me my Purpose."

It's as though life has become so tremendously frustrating, my client is resigned to feeling miserable until his very last breath. If, at least, he could know the future, maybe he could find it easier to wait out his life sentence.

But a reading is not a healing. However inspiring, a reading is merely informative. It leaves STUFF stuck in a person's energy field.

Similarly, techniques not based in full energetic literacy can leave STUFF right where it is. Or even create new STUFF. For instance, recently I did a blog post about "Living From Your Heart Chakra."

This sounds lovely in theory, doesn't it? In practice, it means emotional addiction, less effectiveness in life, horrible auric modeling. By now you can well appreciate this.

Responding to that post, Francesca sent in a comment. She is one of those Resourceful Winners who has been my client for years. In fact, she is one of those clients with an interesting story about keeping a very prestigious job in a toxic work environment.

For a while, her future at that job looked questionable. The problem wasn't Francesca's fate but simply job-related STUFF that had accumulated in her auric field. In session, we moved it out. Since then, her career has been moving full-speed ahead. (No big amounts of willpower needed for this, either.)

Francesca wrote to thank me for the ideas about not choosing to live from the heart chakra, or any one chakra. She was especially struck by a statement in the blog about what we, here, call "auric modeling":

Maybe you have noticed that, eventually, the way you treat yourself will outpicture as how others treat you. I fear that Gladys has, inadvertently, called in some rather dramatic experiences of having other people show her extreme disrespect, because that's what she does to herself.

Truth is, you can't disrespect yourself deep down and then turn around and Magnetize Money. The Simplest Technique works as part of a balanced life, balanced inside and outside.

So What About You?

Congratulations. You have now learned our last goal-and-plan related technique, Lucky #11, The Simplest Technique.

You're nearly a graduate, now, of the Magnetize Money Program. Mostly you spend your time being yourself fully in the here and now, enjoying life as a full-bodied, practical human person. That gusto can balance your service to the world and spiritual aspirations, both.

When you live this way down to the who-you-be, your auric modeling becomes superb. Plus you have your choice of many energetic workarounds to keep you moving towards full success and prosperity. (That's success as *you* would define it).

Part Three of this program has given you practical ways to focus attention on getting exactly what you want, creating goals and plans from many angles.

Many of you Resourceful Readers were highly sophisticated before you even began to explore this Magnetize Money Program. Who knew you could become even more sophisticated?

Just look at all the practical ways you can refine moving forward on your chosen path:

1. A Juicy, All-Inclusive, Big Job List
2. A Street-Smart, Selective, Savvy Job List
3. One Major Work Choice
4. A Magnetize Money Goal Sheet
5. Optional: A Goal-Focused Dream Board
6. A Magnetize Money Strategy
7. An Official Magnetize Money Plan
8. Ridiculously Small Action Steps
9. Magnetize Money WIN Sheets
10. A Fancy Flow Chart
11. The Simplest Technique

Mix-and-matching these resources can be simple. Turn the page for a summary of how to use the Magnetize Money Program in daily life.

Magnetize Money Program
What to Do When

DAILY

1. Do The Simplest Technique. Pull your desired future into your present. Simultaneously you will be preparing yourself to receive that future.

2. Today, use your current Magnetize Money Plan. Refer to it throughout your day, doing as many of the actions as you reasonably can. Check things off when they're done.
What you don't finish today can go onto your Plan for tomorrow. Giving yourself a hard time is never part of this Program.

3. At the start or end of your day, take a few minutes to write down your new Magnetize Money Plan for tomorrow. Add to it as appropriate.

4. Keep your aura in balance by doing no more than 30-60 minutes per day, tops, of spiritual and/or religious activities. That Third Eye Time includes prayer, scripture reading, meditation, yoga, aura reading, energy healing techniques, etc.
(For most of you Resourceful Readers, 30-60 minutes daily is the upper amount of Third Eye Time for a balanced day, helping you to avoid spiritual addiction and develop a balanced who-you-be.)

5. Optional: Actively improve your auric modeling.
Use a technique of energetic workaround from this program or any method you trust for permanently removing STUFF. Of course, any such activity would count for part of your day's Third Eye Time

MONTHLY
(At the end of a month or the start of a month, your choice.)

6. Review your Magnetize Money Goal Sheet and/or Fancy Flow Chart. Congratulate yourself on your WINS and write them down.

7. Update your Magnetize Money Goal Sheet and/or Fancy Flow Chart. Any changes? Record them.
As the months go by, wow!
- You're evolving spiritually.
- You're making progress toward your objective goals in life.
- You have less STUFF in your energy field.
- Your energetic literacy is improving until you read fluently, whenever you like (At least this can happen if you choose to make it happen and take action accordingly.)

8. For any and all of these reasons, your desires may change. As you accomplish more of your goals, you may be ready for bigger — or smaller — and better.
Don't just keep goals in your head. Write them down. Include them on your latest Magnetize Money Goal Sheet or modify your Fancy Flow Chart.

YEARLY
(On your birthday, New Year's Eve, or some other important time.)

9. Take a depth look at your Magnetize Money Goal Sheet and/or Fancy Flow Chart. Revise as appropriate. Congratulate yourself.

JUST FOR FUN

Here's a secret (or former secret) about this Magnetize Money Program. When designing it, my intention was to help YOU bring in

$10,000 more per year until you reach your personal goal for financial success.

Well, just for fun, why not keep track?

You already have at least one day per year when you add up all your savings, assets, and investments, right? Because you already save for retirement and do financial planning, right?

Then let's be bold. I'm going to suggest that, while doing these calculations of your net worth and income, you compare the figures for each full year. Start with the first full year that you have completed the Magnetize Money Program and have been using it regularly. Chart your progress.

But don't stop there. Just for fun, send a comment to my blog. Did you really earn $10,000 extra that year? Or less? Or more?

What personal Aha!s have you had during that time?

You're invited to share any insights or experiences related to your journey into greater worldly effectiveness. My blog, "Deeper Perception Made Practical," has a place reserved just for you to participate in this ongoing conversation.

GO TO WWW.ROSE-ROSETREE.COM/BLOG.
SEARCH ON "MAGNETIZE MONEY PROGRAM RESULTS."

To comment, you won't have to sign in, friend me, or otherwise make a big deal commitment. Your comment can even be anonymous.

You see, every comment must be approved. (That doesn't mean screening responses, except for my usual policy of disallowing spam.)

Having the blogmaster approve all posts means that you can write in your first line of comment something like this, "Make me anonymous here." Easy as smiling at you!

For additional follow-up to this book, you're also invited to participate in my Magnetize Money Workshop and personal sessions. Information about all this and more can be found at the official Rose Rosetree website, www.rose-rosetree.com.

26. Spirituality Made Accountable

In Japan, spirituality has traditionally been at the core of daily life, even in business. Gradually, however, the emphasis has shifted. Rather than simply honoring an abstract, metaphysical dimension, people are demanding results. Spirituality has become accountable.
— Masumi Hori, Foreword
Let Today Be a Holiday: 365 Ways to Co-Create with God, Rose Rosetree

Hasn't liking yourself always been important for the pursuit of wealth?

Desire for self-improvement runs like a golden thread throughout *prosperity* teachings of the first two millennia. Spiritually loving yourself, however, didn't necessarily mean liking yourself as a human.

Also, subjective striving was often over-emphasized, compared to actively earning riches. The striving could even turn frantic.

Meanwhile *success* literature promoted a public likability, as with Dale Carnegie's techniques to influence people by cleverly tricking them into liking you. That was different from winning friendship with others or yourself, very different from changing in ways so that you would like yourself more.

Unfortunately success teachings sometimes encouraged greed as much as likeability. Captains of industry would follow their not especially pure acts of financial acquisition by doing a very public balancing act called "philanthropy."

Perhaps public good deeds might also promote self-liking and, as needed, ease one's conscience. For instance, Rhodes Scholarships bear the name of a European man whose money came from the dirty business of mining African diamonds.

Cecil Rhodes wrote to a friend, "I contend that we are the first race in the world, and that the more of the world we inhabit the better it is for the human race."

Today's school children in America don't remember the era of apartheid ushered in by men like Cecil Rhodes. Yet this is his horrific legacy, not just the generosity of his famous scholarships.

Unlike Rhodes, you have access to powerful ways to get rich while keeping your goodness 100% intact. Living in this third millennium, spiritual vibrations are higher than at earlier times in history. People, on average, are more spiritually evolved.

Greedy managers of ages past, and their exploited employees — they could have been you and me in previous lifetimes. Victimization over wealth is one of the longest running soap operas on earth. Bullying others and being bullied, in turn, are both distasteful to the discerning spirit.

Fortunately, each lifetime brings cumulative learning. Eventually an old soul says, "Enough, already. On to new ways of doing business."

Yet many people who are wiser than average, smarter and more capable than average, still aren't achieving their financial potential. And I don't just mean citizens of Garrison Keillor's Lake Wobegon.

Millions have trustingly applied the Law of Attraction and The Secret, which caused them to favor idealized, over-subjective versions of reality. Meanwhile, human components of self were disliked or denied. Consequently, success remained elusive.

Millions worked with other prosperity teachings, such as affirmations and seed money. These wealth seekers used sweet words and generous actions idealistically. Yet this prosperity work could cover up stuck power circuits or conceal shame over personal ego.

For these prosperity seekers, too, success remained elusive.

Millions have sought success in more objective ways, working long hours without the rewards they were promised. Money and status were liked, but the wage earner? Maybe not so much!

Yet all these success and prosperity seekers were motivated by an inner wisdom. They were yea-sayers, not naysayers, to full effectiveness in life. Instinctively they knew to keep striving. They kept asking, "What more can I do to make a difference?"

Isn't it time for the world's wisest people to become truly effective? So much disappointment has been caused when success and prosperity teachings weren't supported energetically.

Sure, energy has been expended, in the form of correct actions taken. But every ambitious wealth seeker *has* energy too, electromagnetic energy in the form of chakra databanks. At that level, if you don't like yourself, it shows. If you're stuck, it shows. Following the example of a Brian Tracy won't magically give you his chakra databank mojo.

Now that you know about auric modeling, you can attract success and prosperity as never before. You can show the world a set of chakra databanks that effectively Magnetize Money.

By contrast, only limited results can come from all those smart ideas from the last millennium with their emphasis on clever words, vigorous actions; emails and faxes and business cards swapped; hours spent on "building your brand."

Your brand was, and always will be, your auric modeling.

Our program's third millennium skills of using energetic literacy, complete with healing practices and energetic workarounds, have shown you how to give the world a dazzling, effective version of yourself, complete with congruent auric modeling.

Thanks to our Magnetize Money Program, no longer will you be sending the world a mixed message. Whatever success and prosperity practices you choose from now on, they can be based on a more powerful version of who-you-be.

Liking yourself all the way down to your chakra databanks — now that can bring oomph to your pursuit of success. You deserve to live your highest ideals, with an authentic kind of auric modeling that translates into full worldly effectiveness. Like Masumi Hori, an astute and mega-successful businessman quoted at the start of this chapter, I believe it's high time for spirituality to be made *accountable.*

Having correct beliefs, being passionate about them, caring so much about being a good person: Don't let all this virtue be its own reward. The best things in life may be free, but they can be perfectly compatible with having financial abundance.

The trick is to live fully, with gusto and a strong sense of reality. Top business executives today make appointments in 10-minute increments. You can develop a similar sense of time, cramming your day with productive and varied activities.

When you really like your own who-you-be, living vigorously as a human being, it's easy to find varied, productive activities. You may

connect with people more joyfully, too. No longer are you mainly kill-
ing time while waiting to be escorted into heaven.

Making real-life money may never be easy compared to bringing
out the old Monopoly set and dealing yourself a fortune. However,
Magnetize Money isn't rocket science either (unless being a rocket
scientist happens to be your day job). Whatever that day job may be,
you can grow financially by doing work that fulfills who-you-be, attracting maximum success because your aura is alive to the maximum.

As we have been exploring together in this Magnetize Money
Program, ideals about prosperity tend to strengthen the subjective
side of life, mostly expanding your chakra databanks from the head up.
This alone can't make riches land in your pocket.

Where does your clothing have the most pockets, anyway? Are
they usually found flapping above your neck?

For objective success, you'll need to use your full self, like that
personal self, and wake up chakra databanks all over your body. As that
happens more and more, your wealth will grow accordingly. So, too,
will you find new reasons to fall in like with yourself, with your friends,
with your God.

10 Secrets for Success and Happiness In the Third Millennium

1. If you want to make big money, make earth your primary
residence.
2. Before you follow anyone's advice, use energetic literacy to
consider the source.
3. To network better, open your heart and your throat.
4. When you make plans to Magnetize Money, get all your
chakras on board, not just one or two.
5. Fear of success is real, at the level of STUFF. If you sabotage
yourself, or consistently can't get ahead, find a way to effectively heal that very personal kind of STUFF.
6. When stuck in your career, try something *different,* don't
simply try *harder.* Take action both objectively and subjectively (e.g., Objectively, position yourself differently in the
marketplace. Subjectively, move out underlying STUFF.)

7. Set clear goals. Make concrete plans. Follow up on them daily.

8. Use your free will to become successful. Take focused action, not waiting around to be told what is "meant to be."

9. Balance your objective and subjective reality. Do this so thoroughly that it shows with Stage 3 Energetic Literacy.

10. Don't be vague about your sources of inspiration. Find human mentors when you can and, daily, call in help from your current choice of Highest Power.

HOW CAN I DO MY SPIRITUAL WORK?

One great longing shows consistently among my clients worldwide. And it isn't a longing for wealth. We want to do meaningful spiritual work, whether that be to heal or to teach, to write or to create a beautiful spiritual community.

Magnetize Money? For millions of us, this is a means to an end.

Guess what happens when clients hire me to help them research life choices, using energetic literacy? These mainly spiritual occupations seldom inspire anyone's full set of chakra databanks.

Sure, some Heart Chakra and Third Eye Chakra databanks adore goals like full-time Reiki healer, spiritual counselor, or workshop presenter. Meanwhile, hundreds of other chakra databanks are screaming, "Noooooooooooo. That's so not the life for me. Please, not that full time, not in the world as it is right now."

In the choir of human life, many of us are glorious altos, basses, and baritones, not the glitzy soprano soloist.

It can seem unfair when you're researching away, full of plans to change the world, and what thrills your energy field is that seemingly insignificant job as a car mechanic, a schoolteacher, or a nurse at your neighborhood hospital. "So many lifetimes on earth and all I have to show for it is this lousy job as a librarian?"

Yet jobs that deal with everyday human problems can bring the biggest spiritual evolution. Energetic literacy shows all the juicy details, so take a look at what really thrills your soul. Or hire an expert who can help you to do that very vital kind of aura reading research.

Inspiration Minus a Sense of Proportion

Zelda was a believer in affirmations. She wrote them on index cards, taping them onto the long hallway by her front door. This long hallway had a mirror where Zelda added one card at a time.

She considered this mirror her shrine. Every day she would read her collection aloud.

Over the years, Zelda's practice continued until her Mirror of Inspiration was covered with cards. How long did Zelda spend daily, reading aloud her wonderful affirmations? 90 minutes.

Zelda hasn't yet thought to affirm, "I make my spirituality accountable now" or "Every day, I take effective action toward my material goals." If she did, I'm afraid that poor Zelda might just add more cards to her wall, extra words for her to read daily.

INCREASING YOUR ENERGETIC LITERACY

In this third millennium, millions of people have become really skilled at energetic literacy. What if you haven't yet joined the crowd?

Anyone can gain this skill set. But it won't be as easy as learning to burp. You need a teacher.

That can be a personal teacher or a book you respect. It can be a friend who already reads auras well and is willing to teach you (and who also happens to be a good teacher).

Here are 10 Consumer Tips for developing energetic literacy, meant to save you time and energy. These tips are based on what I have found as a professional in the personal development field over the past 40 years.

1. DON'T SELL YOURSELF SHORT

Aura reading does not require seeing colors. That's a myth. Aura reading means gathering information where you combine the gifts that Highest Power gave you with a technique that is effective for you.

Have you ever tried reading auras but not succeeded? Don't blame yourself. Find a better teacher for you, someone whose system matches up with the gifts that you personally have.

2. Allow Yourself 60 Hours

Developing skill in the discipline of energetic literacy, I have put in more than 10,000 hours (what Malcolm Gladwell, in *Outliers*, suggests is required to get really good at any life skill). I had to. I had a burning desire to work as a professional in this field.

To gain full energetic literacy, you don't need to read auras for five hours daily. In fact I would not recommend that. But you do need to study long enough to get the goods. It's like any major life skill with its own coordination: Driving a car, putting on makeup, playing the guitar, even sex.

Maybe you're so talented, you develop excellent skills instantly. Most people, however, must practice a little.

Please understand, "needing to practice" doesn't mean "lacking talent." A reasonable expectation to gain Stage 3 Energetic Literacy for life would be 20 hours of dedicated study with a good teacher for you. To become really proficient, you would need at least 60 hours.

For perspective, how much time have you spent learning about, or trying, different ways to tweak your diet? Thin may be in, bringing loads of social advantages, but weight loss may not be permanent. By contrast, skills of energetic literacy are lasting and cumulative.

3. Don't Settle

Stage 3 Energetic Literacy doesn't need to be a faraway dream. Unless you're prepared to settle.

In the third millennium, stopping your development at Stage 1 or even Stage 2 does mean settling. Millions of beginners are satisfied with getting an intuitive hit. Then they're onto the next fad.

With some hobbies, it's fine to dabble. Why not take one short class on the latest physical fitness craze? Why not spend half an hour learning to use some new techno-toy? Quick exposure might be perfect for your purposes.

But other worthwhile topics can't be handled that same quick way. If you want to speak Japanese for business, good luck with getting it all in three hours! Compared to Japanese, actually, Stage 3 Energetic Literacy can be learned way faster. Still it takes some time.

Of course, you can always hire an interpreter for speaking another language. By contrast, energetic literacy is a great thing to insist upon doing for yourself. The skill set brings discernment for anything else in life you might do.

Are you the kind of person who likes to choose your own clothing and keep track of your own money? What, you have never been tempted to outsource sex? Then you'll really want to develop the life skill of full energetic literacy.

4. YOU'RE NOT BUYING A BURGER

Don't choose a teacher for energetic literacy based on who lives in your neighborhood. Over the years, I've received numerous phone inquiries from folks who have been spoiled by McDonalds. They expect somebody great to be located just around the corner. Then studying with that teacher is "Meant to be."

I'll bet you know someone like Zinnia, who drives a great distance to get her hair done. Never would she go to a mediocre hair cutting place, however convenient. To learn aura reading, though, Zinnia figures that closer means better, while close + cheap would be best of all. Be willing to spend time and money on what's important in life.

5. DON'T JUST MAKE SOMETHING UP

Having an experienced teacher matters for this particular life skill. Avoid the temptation to improvise — at least until you are well into Stage 2 Energetic Literacy.

This advice isn't meant to squelch your creativity but to keep you safe. Unless you do Stage 3 Energetic Literacy, you're not in a position to know if an improvised method has side effects that could hurt you long-term.

For instance, my friend Zachary is self-taught with energetic literacy. He has explained his technique to me. It involves observing one person at a time and attempting to engage his own energies with that person. Afterwards he notices how his own energies respond.

Works for him. So that's fine, isn't it? Except Zachary doesn't realize that a technical name for his homegrown technique is doing

"Unskilled Empath Merge," and that it results in his taking on STUFF galore. If Zachary were just a bit smarter about things, imagine how much better his life would be. Plus the quality of his aura reading would become more detailed and useful.

6. Talented Without Knowing It?

What if, like Zachary, it is easy for you to feel other people's energies? That means you're a born empath.

An empath has at least one gift for directly experiencing the energies of other people. The gift(s) could be physical, emotional, intellectual, or spiritual. When studying energetic literacy, any born empath will be super-perceptive. Non-empaths explore energetic literacy from the outside while skilled empaths explore it from the inside.

About 1 in 20 people was born as an empath. (So much for the idea that "Everyone is just like me.")

Every empath has huge potential for insightful service to humanity, which can definitely boost your ability to Magnetize Money. But "born as an empath" does not mean "born *skilled*." Just the opposite.

What's so bad about being merely talented as an empath, not yet skilled? You're going to do what Zachary does, habitually pick up STUFF belonging to other people. That STUFF will get stuck in your energy field. Besides being uncomfortable, that extra STUFF leads to unfortunate auric modeling. Other people will think you are messed up in ways that, really, you aren't. Or don't need to be.

If you're an empath, make it a priority to develop the specific skill set for empaths. Do this before studying energetic literacy or Reiki or anything else that would connect you strongly to other people's auras.

While a good teacher of Reiki, etc., will include types of protection, an empath needs something more, dedicated techniques specifically designed for empaths. It's a unique skill set. In short, any born empath will Magnetize Money best as a Skilled Empath.

7. Protection against Energy Vampires.

In Chapter 21, we considered protection against energy vampires. Similar popular terms are "psychic vampires" and "emotional blackmailers."

How much of a threat are they, really? The bigger threat is fear itself, not the so-called "vampires." Avoid spiritual hypochondria of all kinds and you'll have a better life!

What else? Don't use your energetic literacy on people who frighten you. Leave fascination with crazies to tabloid TV. Soon as a person's behavior or energy makes you suspect something wrong, direct your attention to objective reality.

For instance, don't worry that your boss, Zoli, might be an energy vampire. What does he say and do in reality? If you must deal with him at work, deal with that. Don't try to read his aura to better understand what makes him so awful. Instead, use your street smarts. Figure out how to have as little to do with Zoli as possible.

8. Put Websites in Their Place

Websites are great for doing background research on books about auras; same with researching teachers. Just beware trying to actually learn energetic literacy from online sources.

Teachers with skills worth learning care about quality. They don't claim you can learn a complex set of skills instantly. They won't claim you can learn "all you need to know" by reading one quick article. When you study with a real expert, that expert can give personal attention as needed and correct the inevitable mistakes that arise for beginners.

9. Catching Literacy Skills Like a Cold?

Groups can be great for the energetically literate. Online groups and blogs, support groups, meet-up groups — these may provide useful companionship once you have gained some solid technique at energetic literacy.

Support groups are a godsend for 12-Step Programs and certain other types of healing. Any way to tap into collective wisdom, like Wikipedia, can be brilliant for topics about *social sharing*. But energetic literacy is not about consensus of opinion or majority rules. Instead it requires a delicate inward shift to your consciousness, supplemented by validation given by somebody who has developed real skills and will respect your own spiritual self-authority.

What I do with students, for instance, is to offer techniques appropriate to that person's gift set for deeper perception. I also help students break unique habits related to blind spots. It's a deep kind of nurturing, difficult for most people to give themselves.

Once you develop full energetic literacy, online friends can provide loads of fun. Also, you won't risk staying on the surface with people whose knowledge of energetic literacy is confused, at best.

10. SHARE YOUR AMAZING DISCOVERIES

Once you locate an energetic literacy workshop or how-to that you like, find a buddy to share it with. Experiment together, giving each other support. You'll probably have great fun, too.

Ziggy became a fabulous aura reader one fall, meeting weekly with her friend Zara. They went through a book they liked and, together, practiced doing more than 100 techniques. The friends became highly skilled at energetic literacy, plus their relationship deepened.

Energetic literacy can bring you friends for life. Together you can emphasize using your skills to gain more success and prosperity. As aura readers, go back through this Magnetize Money Program and you'll find even bigger results than before.

Today, energetic literacy is at least as useful as computer literacy. Accept no substitute.

MORE SPIRITUAL SERVICE THAN YOU KNOW

Could you be doing more spiritual service than you know? Remember auric modeling. In this way, you have always done spiritual work. That distinctive aura of yours will twinkle and sing to all you encounter:

- Unique gifts of your soul.
- The texture of your particular spiritual connection.
- Every kind and loving impulse stored in your Heart Chakra.

That matters because, essentially, spirituality is caught, not taught.

Remember how auric modeling works? On the level of auras, it's like having everyone in the room jump into one hot tub, everyone completely naked, where all of you busily exchange information about who-you-be.

Who-you-be. That can be such a big deal for serving humanity. Do you live with integrity, truthfulness, kindness? To broadcast that from your auric field, you'll need to develop the genuine article, of course. No gestures made for show can fool anybody, not at the level of auric modeling.

When you develop that third millennium form of literacy, you can consciously read auric modeling whenever you like.

Until then, take it on trust... plus your own common sense. You do touch hundreds of lives every day. Information is constantly being exchanged at the level of auras.

Auric modeling stores a full energetic hologram every time you meet somebody face-to-face or voice-to-voice. So you can change people's lives just by showing up.

(Reminder: Social networking websites won't do it. Nor will emails, texting, or tweets. Those useful technologies don't allow you and the other person to interact directly in real time. Energetically it's as empty as irradiated food.)

Right now, you carry stored-up information about every chakra databank of everyone you have met. These energy presences are some of your biggest teachers, spiritually. For example, some of the people you meet model an authentic "I like myself."

Our Magnetize Money Program was intended to help you become just such a person. Well, go be a teacher to others through your magnificent auric modeling.

Now that you have new resources to Magnetize Money, bring in your full share of wealth. Invest it wisely. Meanwhile, you can help the world enormously just by being yourself without apology or self-neglect.

Don't merely become more successful financially. Like that who-you-be of yours. You can be yourself gloriously. Show the world how.

Index and
You Saw It Here First

A very full index is supplied online as part of our huge Online Supplement at www.rose-rosetree.com. That Index includes many specialized terms that have made their way into print for the first time here.

Especially if you read a lot, you may be used to thinking that different books cover similar topics with a gimmick added here, an interesting turn of phrase there. Not always!

Because my systems are sometimes firsts in their field, I have often originated terms that have (probably) never been used before in any previous book in the English language.

For instance, in *Cut Cords of Attachment* I pioneered the term "Chakra Databanks." When, getting this new book to press, I googled that term and came up with close to 72,000 hits.

Just for fun, here is a list of new terms that aren't well known yet in the context of success and prosperity teachings — or with profiling and aura reading. You can definitely find them, and more, in the Index on the Online Supplement. Follow that phrase!

- Energetic Sub-Routine
- Energetic Workaround
- Spiritual Addiction
- Spiritual Hypochondria
- Stage 3 Energetic Literacy
- Thrill Your Soul Research
- Who-You-Be

Also, "Auric Modeling" was first mentioned briefly in *Empowered by Empathy*. But this is the first book describing it in detail.

Maybe you and I will never ride a starship to "boldly go where man has never gone before." But terms like these allow Resourceful Readers like you to become an explorer and leader in this millennium.

How to Order Rose's Books

It's easy to order these life-changing books
directly from the publisher.
We appreciate your business and will give you quality service.
Within the U.S. and Canada, call tollfree 24/7: 800-345-6665.
For secure ordering online, click on www.Rose-Rosetree.com.

Cut Cords of Attachment:
Heal Yourself and Others with Energy Spirituality

Use this as a how-to and/or a consumer guide for healing imbalances
in your emotional and spiritual life. You know, Resourceful Reader
that means STUFF removal. Learn the only trademarked system in
America for cutting cords of attachment. You can learn to do this effectively, quickly, permanently.

Read People Deeper:
Body Language + Face Reading + Auras

Investigate 50 practical areas of life, including confidence, truthfulness, sexual stamina, loyalty, chemical addictions, intelligence, problem solving ability — what you, Resourceful Reader, now know is
going to impact auric modeling, whether consciously read or not.

Aura Reading Through All Your Senses

Discover the easy-to-learn method of Aura Reading Through All Your
Senses®. This international bestseller honors your personal gift set,
rather than demanding that you be 100% clairvoyant. Trust me, every
person's gift set can become the basis of superb, effortless aura reading.

In this book, doing this has been called developing "Stage 3
Energetic Literacy." You know, literacy usually requires a teacher. If you
let this book teach you, you'll be able to use aura reading to improve
relationships, health, even consumer choices for all that money!

Become the Most Important Person in the Room: Your 30-Day Plan for Empath Empowerment

Most readers enjoy skimming through the book for starters, enjoying the new ideas and the humor. Then, to reap actual results, slow down and do one short chapter a day, including the 10-minute homework assignment. By the end, you can become a fully skilled empath.

Empowered by Empathy

This was the first book for empaths in the English language. It presents a complete system to use consciousness to turn inborn gifts OFF or ON at will. (Later this system would be trademarked as Empath Empowerment®) This contrasts with approaches based on the surface of life, such as "strengthen your boundaries."

(Note: Both Print and Audiobook Editions are available.)

Let Today Be a Holiday: 365 Ways to Co-Create with God

Resourceful Reader, call your Highest Power anything you want, not necessarily "God." This how-to brims over with ways to help you collaborate with That.

Add to your skill sets with over 450 techniques, plus thought-provoking ideas. Now that you are familiar with the term "Spiritual Addiction," you'll appreciate the main goal of this book. It's intended to help people get a human life, especially useful for anyone who has mostly emphasized spiritual life instead.

The Power of Face Reading

Although physiognomy is a 5,000-year-old art, this how-to uses a system developed for the third millennium. Face Reading Secrets® helps you to see the perfection of your physical face data. Read about gifts and STUFF, how they show on the face of anyone over 18.

Sure, use it on business associates as an extra way to Magnetize Money. Once you develop the knack, you can use this illustrated how-to easily. It's like a birdwatcher's guide for people.

ROSE ROSETREE

Rose Rosetree pioneers systems of energetic literacy. She has developed this Magnetize Money Program based on 40 years of service as a teacher and healing practitioner

Her how-to books (including a national bestseller in Germany) and blog, "Deeper Perception Made Practical," are available at www.rose-rosetree.com and 800-345-6665.

This Brandeis graduate has given thousands of personal sessions for individual clients. Corporate clients include Long & Foster, Canyon Ranch, The Food Marketing Institute, George Washington University, The Inner Potential Centre, USA Today, and VOICE.